KASHMIR

KASHMIR: BEHIND THE VALE

KASHMIR
BEHIND THE VALE

M.J. AKBAR

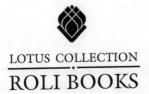

LOTUS COLLECTION
ROLI BOOKS

To
Mukulika and Prayaag

Lotus Collection

This edition first published 2002
The Lotus Collection
An imprint of
Roli Books Pvt Ltd
M-75, G.K. II Market
New Delhi 110 048
Phones: 6442271, 6462782, 6460886
Fax: 6467185
E-mail: roli@vsnl.com; Website: rolibooks.com
Also at
Varanasi, Agra, Jaipur and the Netherlands

ISBN: 81-7436-250-9
Rs 295

Typeset in Times New Roman by Roli Books Pvt Ltd and
printed at Karan Press, Okhla, New Delhi - 110 020

Contents

Author's Note

Every book lives in its own time and place. To throw – I mean that literally – another chapter at the end in order to make it artificially "up to date" works occasionally, but is most often a publishing trick to entice buyers. Neither I, nor my publisher, have any desire to indulge in artifice to push sales. This book is a compact, detailed and I hope engrossing history of Kashmir from Pandit Kalhana and before to 1991. In the decade and more since then, the Jhelum has turned red with blood and that is a related but different story. This book provides the reasons why the most beautiful valley in the world was stained by the mistakes of generations and extracted such a heavy price in young lives. You may recognize the present without the knowledge of the past, but you cannot understand it.

Acknowledgements

The Almighty tends to have a sardonic sense of humour. He creates Paradise, and then lets slip a snake in the apple orchard. The curse of every earthly Paradise is pain. The irony of this pain is that it is self-inflicted, a consequence of free will. Original sin has become a commonplace of history.

When does the modern history of Kashmir begin? With the Dogra dynasty that was gifted the state as reward for services to the British empire in its wars with the Sikhs? Or in the mind of a young graduate of Aligarh Muslim University who, in 1931, wanted a job with the Dogra bureaucracy, and felt discriminated against when he was denied it? Sheikh Mohammad Abdullah dreamed of a Kashmir free from feudalism, free from poverty, and simply free as well.

Sadly, the modern history of Kashmir probably begins on a night in the third week of October 1947 when Pakistan, quite unnecessarily, attempted to seize by force what was still on the negotiating table. The state of Jammu and Kashmir was ruled then by Maharaja Hari Singh. It has not acceded to either India or Pakistan because the Maharaja, like the Nizam of Hyderabad, entertained fantasies of independence. He had signed a Standstill Agreement with both India and Pakistan, a term that meant precisely what it said. But it was obvious that at some point, rather sooner than later, the future of Jammu and Kashmir would be placed on a table at which both India and Pakistan would be seated. But time did not stand still for Pakistan. It sought to win by war what it might conceivably have obtained through peace. That war has not ended. It has mushroomed into a nuclear confrontation. In the summer of 2002 India and Pakistan brought the world as close as it has ever been to the reality of a nuclear war. That of course would have been one solution to the Kashmir problem. No Kashmir, no problem. There would not have been much left of India and Pakistan either. In so many devastated cities, survivors might have preferred the incineration of a moment to years of horrible suffering.

Nothing clears the mind better than the prospect of a hanging. It was with a very clear mind therefore that Pramod Kapoor, the owner of Roli, suggested that a new edition of a book first published in 1991 was required. *Kashmir: Behind the Vale* was my fourth book, the others being *The Siege Within: Challenges to Indian Unity, Nehru: The Making of India,* and *Riot After Riot.* All had earlier been published by Viking/Penguin. I am grateful to Pramod for believing in this book, and ensuring that it reaches a new generation of bookshelves.

I dedicated this book to my children, Mukulika and Prayaag. They were ten years, and a lifetime, younger when it first appeared. They are now at an age when they will fully understand why this book was for them. Kashmir is the hinge on which the future of our subcontinent, and therefore the future of their lives as well, will turn. They cannot protect the future without the knowledge of the past.

September 2002
New Delhi

M.J. Akbar

Introduction

Zahiruddin Babur, a prince of literature and emperor of India, thought he had discovered the meaning of Kashmir. Once you cross the Indus, he wrote in Baburnama, "the land, water, trees, stones, people, tribes, manners, and customs are all of the Hindustani fashion". The first kingdom after the Indus is that of Kashmir, and the "snow never melts on these mountains", which he heard were called the Sivalik Parbat. "Once past Kashmir, there are innumerable peoples, tribes, districts, and provinces in this range. There are people continuously in these mountains all the way to Bengal, even to the ocean. This much has been ascertained and confirmed by the people of Hindustan, but of these groups no one can give any real information. All they say is that the people of the mountains are called Khas. It has occurred to me that since Hindustanis pronounce the sound sh as s, since the principal city in the mountains is Kashmir, which means 'mountains of the Khasis', since *mir* means mountain and the people of this mountain are called Khasia, and since aside from Kashmir no other city has ever been heard of in these mountains, this may be why they call it Kashmir."

Whimsy? Conjecture? More than a thousand miles from Kashmir, on the other side of the Himalayas, in the North East of India, we still call some people of the mountains Khasis. And all across this curving, swerving line of the Himalayas there are tensions between the people of the mountains and the people of the plains.

The latter have never understood the former; the former have never trusted the latter. The syndrome extends far beyond Kashmir: to the tensions between peak and plain in Uttar Pradesh (leading eventually to the creation of a separate state); to the differences between hill and terai in Nepal; to Bengal which has seen a violent struggle between Darjeeling and Kolkata; and then to the troubled North East of India whose diversity is reinforced by diverse violence. In each place, traditional differences have provoked demands for separate political status.

At least part of the tension has to do with distortion and painful caricature. The hill-personality is split into weak and violent; menial and provocative; human, but dangerously so. A domestic servant that has not quite been domesticated. Or a vendor who cannot be trusted. What the plains never see, despite it being plain enough, is that the hill-people are children of nature. We are not talking of a romantic virtue, just fact. They are closer to the elements, and the joys of summer are bought at the harsh price of winter. Their pristine simplicity should never be confused with either lack of intelligence or docility. They are fiercely protective of their identity; they have been repeatedly exploited, and, understandably, they do not want it to persist. They do not prefer violence; you will see more thoughtless cruelty on a single street in an urban sprawl on a single day than you will see in a year in the mountain village. But it is easy to give their search for identity a bad name, in order to hang them. The easiest label is "anti-national", whether in the West or the East of the Himalayas. Sometimes, accusation invites a hostility that did not exist before.

In Kashmir, proximity to Pakistan, the legacy of a confused and even chaotic partition, and the machinations of five decades of bitter politics have turned a smouldering fire into a virtually uncontrollable blaze. But Kashmir is older than Pakistan.

Kashmir, where geography was alchemised into a dream, was often sought, but never truly subjugated. The historian Kalhana (who identified Kashmir's virtues as learning, lofty houses, saffron, icy water and grapes) wrote in *Rajtarangini*: "Kashmir may be conquered by the force of spiritual merit but never by the force of soldiers." Asoka the Great's soldiers brought Kashmir into the Mauryan empire, and he founded the capital, Srinagar; but the spiritual merit of the emperor's Buddhist missionaries had more impact. The Hindu valley, said by antiquity to have been settled by the sage Kashyap, devotee of the Lord Shiva, took to Buddhism. Kanishka, the first Indian emperor of Turkish descent, held the Third Great Council of Buddhism in Kashmir. The land accepted the sword, but bowed to faith. On occasion, though, faith provided inadequate protection, as when the gods did not prevent Mihirakula, the Hun from Sialkot, who looked like Death, and whose approach was known by the vultures flying ahead of his army waiting for the corpses that would inevitably be left behind, from forcing his way to the throne of Srinagar.

The gods were more helpful, using their favourite officer, General Winter, when the unconquerable Mahmud of Ghazni arrived, twice, in 1015 and 1021, and was checked on the southern slopes of Pir Panjal by the snows.

Changez Khan stopped at the door in 1203 but never entered; and under the redoubtable Kublai Khan, Kashmir passed briefly under nominal Chinese rule. When, in 1320, a Mongol tyrant, Dulacha, did choose the right season to enter the valley, seized Srinagar, massacred the people and ravaged the land (Kashmiris emerged, it is said, like mice from holes after he left) General Winter caught him on the way out: a fierce blizzard trapped his army at Banihal. There were no survivors. But the consequences of Dulacha's eight months in Kashmir were far-reaching: the people lost their faith in the ruling family, and the mood was ready for change.

Marco Polo mentions the presence of Saracens in Kashmir. Islam spread in the Valley to any significant degree with the arrival of the venerated and beloved divine, Bulbul Shah, in the first quarter of the fourteenth century. It was what might be called an opportune moment. The collapse of the ruling family left a vacuum that was eventually filled in October 1320 by Rinchin, a Ladhaki, with the help of a Muslim adventurer from Swat, Shah Mir. Buddhism had by now retreated from the valley, and the astute Rinchin, appreciating that a king's faith must not be distant from that of the people, wanted to become a Hindu. That was easier desired than done. The Kashmiri Pandits informed Rinchin, solemnly, that he could not become a Hindu because they could not decide which caste he should join on conversion. Rinchin became a Muslim and a sequence of Muslim dynasties began to rule over Kashmir.

Sixty years after Babur became master of the north by defeating Sultan Ibrahim Lodi at Panipat, his grandson Akbar brought the valley under the political control of Delhi, in 1585.The Mughals seized power from the heirs of perhaps the greatest of Kashmir's kings, Zainal Abedin. The valley's first experience of Delhi's power was benevolent. Although Jahangir sniffed that the Kashmiris never bathed and called them dirty, he was in awe of and in love with Kashmir's beauty. His remark is famous: if there be Paradise, it is this, it is this, it is this. He described a visit to the Guri valley: "How shall I write its praise? As far as the eye could reach flowers of various hue were blooming, and in the midst of the flowers and verdure beautiful streams of water were flowing: one might say it was a page that the painter of destiny had drawn with the pencil of creation. The buds of hearts break into flower from beholding it." (*Tuzuk-I-Jahangiri,* or Memoirs of Jahangir; translated by Alexander Rogers and edited by Henry Beveridge.)

Bernier, who visited Kashmir with Aurangzeb, commented not only on the magnificence of the Kashmiri shawl, just as so many Europeans after him (Josephine was to make this shawl a fashion statement in Europe). He wrote that the people of this "terrestrial Paradise" were "celebrated for wit, and considered much more intelligent and ingenious than the Indians . . . In poetry and sciences they are not inferior to the Persians, and they are also very active and industrious . . . The whole kingdom wears the appearance of a fertile and highly cultivated garden . . . Meadows and vineyards, fields of rice, wheat, hemp, saffron, and many sorts of vegetables, among which are mingled trenches filled with water, rivulets, canals, and several small lakes, vary the enchanting scene."

Such good fortune invites a curse. The curse appeared in the form of Afghans, who seized the province from weak Mughal governors in 1750. Kashmir had rarely experienced such brutal tyranny, and one that was, as the British noted, "unrelieved by honour". Officials were usurers, and that was only the beginning. They killed without thought; oppression was indiscriminate. For seventy years the Afghans destroyed without pity, and stole without mercy.

When Maharaja Ranjit Singh finally defeated the Muslim Afghans, both the Muslims and Hindus of Kashmir were overjoyed. But this joy was short-lived. The physical brutality eased a little, but the economic oppression continued. Moorcroft visited Kashmir in 1824 and was appalled by the extortion and wretchedness. The government took three quarters of the produce from the peasant; everything was taxed at every level. A kotwal had to pay thirty thousand rupees a year (an enormous fortune at that time) as a bribe to a governor for his appointment and then compensate himself through extortion. Moorcroft writes that the government "seemed to look upon Kashmirians as little better than cattle . . . the murder of a native by a Sikh is punished by a fine to the Government of from sixteen to twenty rupees, of which four rupees are paid to the family of the deceased if a Hindu, and two rupees if a Mohammedan". It was not until Raja Gulab Singh fell out with Ranjit Singh's heirs, supported the British in their wars against the Sikhs and was rewarded with the kingdom of Jammu and Kashmir that the people experienced some relief. But poverty and serfdom remained the fate of Kashmiris until the fateful year of 1947.

The modern history of Kashmir begins with the greatest Kashmiri of modern times, Sheikh Mohammad Abdullah. He was born in 1905, two months after his father died. His grandfather was born a Hindu Pandit, whose family converted to Islam in 1766, at a time when there was no material purchase in conversion. In 1931, after a Masters' degree from Aligarh, he tried to join Maharaja Hari Singh's government and applied for a job in civil service. He was rejected. Talk of historic mistakes . . . Within a year he had become influential enough to be arrested. He was named the first president of a new political vehicle, the Muslim Conference.

Within seven years came the defining moment in the Sheikh Abdullah's life, when he made a decision whose consequences stretch to this moment. By 1938, the mood of India had darkened. Paradoxically, it was a general election, India's first taste of real democracy, albeit limited democracy, that released the spectre of communalism into the mass consciousness. The Muslim League, anxious to win the vote of those it claimed to represent, and unable to make much headway, sharpened the rhetoric. Its defeat in the elections of 1936 gave the Congress just a pyrrhic victory; for in power the Congress made the mistakes of inexperience and ego that so often prove fatal in public life. Paradoxically and understandably, the Muslim League grew faster in defeat than it might have in victory. Its leader sought to bring all the important Muslim leaders, and organizations onto the League platform to strengthen the negotiating power of the community in the critical days ahead; and one by one the giants of Bengal and Punjab, who had kept away from Jinnah in 1936 and 1937, edged towards his fold. It was at such a moment of history that Sheikh Abdullah struck out towards a different direction. He raised his voice against the politics that would divide the unity of India.

On 26 March 1938, at its sixth session, the Muslim Conference rejected the philosophy of communal division and renamed itself the National Conference because, in the words of the Sheikh, "We must open our doors to all such Hindus and Sikhs who like ourselves believe in the freedom of their country from the shackles of an irresponsible rule." If the Muslim Conference had remained what it was, there would have been little dispute in 1947 because the Kashmir valley met the Mountbatten criteria for accession with one country or the other: the will of the people, and geographical contiguity. Those who today accuse Sheikh Abdullah of being pro-Pakistani, or subverting India, skim over a nodal question: why did the Sheikh opt for India in 1947. All through the crisis and later, he was Nehru's argument for Kashmir's merger with India. Maharaja Hari Singh signed a document of accession, but the representative of the people's will was Sheikh Abdullah.

Maharaja Hari Singh, as is well known, wanted independence for Kashmir, just as the Nizam of Hyderabad wanted independence for his state. Hari Singh could well become an icon for the Azadi Movement, which seeks independence rather than accession to either India or Pakistan. Kashmir was independent for nine weeks. But Sheikh Abdullah made his preference for India clear long before August, and much before the raiders came across from Pakistan, when he was still languishing in the Maharaja's jail, which is where he was when freedom came. He was released only by the end of September after intense pressure from Jawaharlal Nehru.

Sheikh Abdullah had a rare quality: he was an idealist. Half a century later, a cynic might say that this was his undoing. Sheikh Abdullah was not always right. But his ideals were never wrong. After sixteen months in Hari Singh's jail, Sheikh Abdullah addressed his people at a historic rally in Srinagar on 4 October 1947. Kashmir was still independent; Hari Singh was still Maharaja; the war with Pakistan that would shape the tragedies of the subcontinent was still three weeks away. Sardar Patel had asked the Muslim Nawab of Junagadh, and the Muslim Nizam of Hyderabad, who had not declared for either India or Pakistan to respect the wishes of the majority in their principalities instead of deciding on the basis of their personal wishes. Sheikh Abdullah stressed this in his speech on 4 October. Rajas and Nawabs had no right, he said, to act on behalf of the people; the people must speak for themselves. What then should the Kashmiri people do? The answer was given in public, and reported in the newspapers. Said the Sheikh, "We shall not believe (in) the two-nation theory which has spread so much poison. Kashmir showed the light at this juncture. When brother kills brother in the whole of Hindustan, Kashmir raised its voice of Hindu-Muslim unity. I can assure the Hindu and Sikh minorities that as long as I am alive their life and honour will be quite safe."

On that same day, Mahatma Gandhi told his daily prayer meeting that he wanted to abandon his dream of living up to be 125 so that he could see Ramrajya in India, for life now did not seem worth the effort. The riots had scarred his soul and diminished the freedom of his dreams. In Kashmir there was not a single communal incident during partition, despite the horrors in neighbouring Punjab.

But idealism rarely escapes the cancer of suspicion. The understanding of 1947 between Abdullah and Nehru deteriorated into the misunderstanding of 1953, and thence to the Sheikh's arrest in 1953. It is a long story, and this books tells it in necessary detail. In the past lies the present, and the present seeds the future.

In 1978, Sheikh Abdullah told me in an interview that being sent to jail in 1953 was the "third crisis" in his political life. The first came when he changed the name of his party from Muslim Conference to National Conference despite the opposition of the mullahs; the second came in the shape of the riots of 1947. His colleagues despaired in 1953 and told them that there was nothing now to stop them from declaring for Pakistan. "But the fact is that the ideals we stood for were more important than Pakistan or India. We had joined India because of its ideals - secularism and socialism," Sheikh Abdullah said in that interview.

Socialism, or at least land reform, was vitally important to the Sheikh because that was the only means by which land could be transferred from the old feudal oligarchy to the peasant. Sheikh Abdullah was, justifiably, suspicious of the ruling elite of Pakistan; his fear that it would not change its feudal character was justified.

In 1947, events consumed options. Before any negotiations between the various parties could begin, presumably under the stewardship of Lord Mountbatten, who remained India's Governor General after freedom, on the future of Jammu and Kashmir, Pakistan aborted the chance of a peaceful solution by sending in raiders, mostly Afghan or Pathan tribals, to take by force what had not come by negotiation. The first war of Kashmir between India and Pakistan began on the night of 23 October 1947. Over five decades and more the pattern has not changed. Armed infiltrators, always disowned by the Pakistan government, have crossed the border and tried to seize Kashmir by force. That was always the wrong way to win Kashmir. If there is another war over Kashmir, there will be no more wars. There will be nothing left to fight over.

In the dry and debilitating summer of 2002 the two countries came as close to mutual nuclear devastation as is possible. It was the climax of decades of a confrontation that has become so infused with the illogic of hatred and perversity that there seems to be no space left in for undramatic virtues like humanity and common sense. It often reminds me of Mihirakula, who so enjoyed the shriek of an elephant who fell by accident into the gorge of Pir Panjal that he had a hundred more thrown so that he could enjoy that last death-scream. Water does not flow under the bridge in Paradise; blood does. Since the last edition of this book, terror and response have made that flow a torrent. If there is any qualitative change it is merely this: that what used to be a dread limited to the subcontinent has become a nightmare for the world. It is the prospect of a nuclear war, rather than the prospect of any solution that has placed Kashmir, in the words of the American secretary of state in 2002 Colin Powell, back on the international agenda. A nuclear confrontation is too explosive to remain bilateral.

The sin of every Paradise is original; its curse is lasting. Kashmir is a land of gentle people. The "macho" Punjabi would often taunt the Kashmiri with the tease that the blood of a shaving nick was enough to frighten him. You learn about a people not from the taunt of a neighbour, but from their heroes. The two names that bridge fact and fable in Kashmiri memory are that of Lalitaditya and Zainal Abedin. Lalitaditya reigned for 37 years from 699 and, unusually for a king of the mountains, he went out to conquer his world: Tibet, Central Asia, and south to the bank of the Ganges. These victories would have always made him memorable; but he is revered because he built cities, patronised the arts and valued culture as much as prosperity. Zainal Abedin is more recent, and ruled longer, for fifty years, from 1420. His liberalism, his secular dispensation, his values have made him a part of folklore. There is a third Kashmiri who should have been in such a pantheon, Sheikh Abdullah. But perhaps it will take more time for time to be kind to him.

The Ripples of Falling Empires

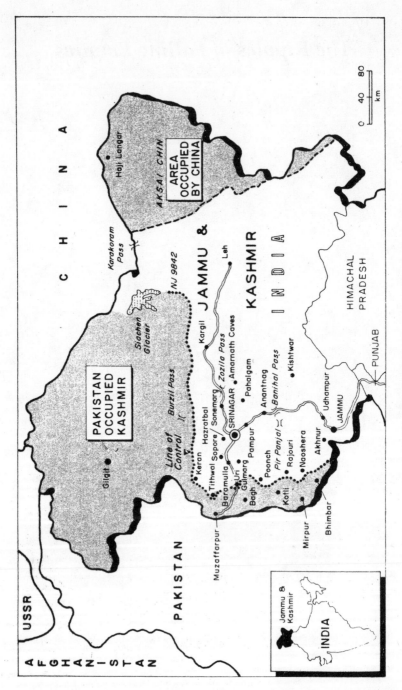

Jammu & Kashmir showing places mentioned in the text.

1

The Rishi and The Raja

History lives in song, in generational memory, in the tale told by a mother plaiting the hair of her young, questioning daughter in the soft afternoon sunlight drifting through speckled apple trees, in the music of a marriage when in the early hours of a grey morning, the singers of the night cluster over a rejuvenated *kangri*, heads bowed towards the glowing embers and spirits abandoned to invisible swirls of floating sound, the energy and rhythm of the last strain even more vigorous, more in harmony with the ideal than the first. The history of a people is so often reduced to the limitations of a page: knowledge is far more than the decaying fragment of a Sanskrit or a Persian chronicle in the library of a Nawab or a Raja himself reduced to an illusion; or in the vaults of a government building imprisoned by an intellectual bureaucracy. History is more real than footnotes in small type which too often sound like an in-house conversation between willing conspirators. The Ibid Syndrome has its place of value and confidence, but our story could profit by dipping into the *Kuttanimatam* of Damodara Gupta, the eighth century poem of the Kuttani (procuress) who teaches the prince how to escape the sexual snares of women, even as we pore over the *Rajatarangini* of Pandit Kalhana, the scholar-poet whose work, written in 1148–49 has been described so picturesquely by the scholar-politician Jawaharlal Nehru in his introduction to his brother-in-law R.S. Pandit's translation, *River of Kings* (Sahitya Akademy, New Delhi, 1968):

> In one long series, as if on a band of gelatine of a cinematograph film, Kalhana brings before our eyes vivid pictures of a bygone age, through episodes which contain the different *rasas* or sentiments of love and heroism, of pathos and marvel.

Had not Kalhana seen in his own lifetime the tragic intervention of greed, frailty, cruelty and murderous incompetence on the course of human affairs? R.S. Pandit notes of Kalhana:

In his history there are no heroes or heroines and the few persons who might be so described are only functionaries of certain groups and have not been too much emphasized; indeed, whether we love them or not for their virtues, it is their vices which make them unforgettable.

But the history of the Kashmiri mind, of its heart and its sentiments, as against the story of mere kings, lies not in chronological narrative, but in the timeless *Vakyas* (Sayings) of Lal Ded, or in the *Nurnama* of Shaikh Nuruddin, whose shrine at Charari Sharif is still burdened each day with the prayers of men and women, both Muslim and Hindu, who believe that the soul of a saint will be at the eternal service of generations of human beings in their incessant search for comfort, for grace, and for aid from the power of the divine.

Time had chipped the name of the ancient city of Puranadhisthana to Pandrenthan by the fourteenth century. It was here, a few miles south-west of Srinagar, that Padmavati was born. Married at the age of twelve, she suffered the typical fate of a woman in her husband's home at Pampur. Mothers-in-law, perhaps seeking a catharsis to match the vicious cruelty that once was their lot, have become symbols of the most perverse oppression in Indian society, and the evidence never stops pouring in, whether it be the fourteenth century or the twentieth. Impaled on the umbilical cord, conditioned by the powerful propaganda of maternal fidelity, the son is almost always a willing conspirator in the cruel subjugation of this outsider seeking to invest and invade something as jealously guarded as the circle of love. If Padmavati had been the normal child-wife, she too would have played out her years of slavery until the cycles of age, death and regeneration created a role reversal.

Padmavati found her release not in revenge but in renunciation. She went into *tapasya* in a forest, found herself and returned to the world as a naked mendicant, oblivious of any material attachment, and with a powerful message to the inner spirit, to the Original Good in every human being layered by the boundless variations of Original Sin. She challenged ritual with a deeper faith. Truth, she said, did not exist in stone, nor in the tyranny of the priest; the stone of the idol in the temple had become a millstone around the neck of the poor, the religion of the age had become an exercise in jugglery and magic to fool the people into subservience and exploitation; she demolished the power of those who made every river and every tree and every simple fact of nature into an object of worship to the unending benefit of the middlemen of religion, the traders in ceremony and cant.

Her spirit of reformation inevitably spread into language; she disdained the priestly Sanskrit and gave the tongue of the people, Kashmiri, a new dimension: thirty per cent of Kashmiri proverbs and idioms are said to owe their origins to Lal Ded's *Vakyas*. Her own life was a splendid example of purity and passion, and the people absorbed this revolt against the intermediaries like priests and intermediates like idols. Her answer was love, service, the unity of man, the discipline of yoga, the intoxication of faith and the rejection of barriers in the name of religion. She sang:

Shiv chuy thali thali rozan;
Mo zan Hindu ta Musalman.
Truk ay chuk pan panun parzanav;
Soy chay Sahibas sati zaniy zan.

(Shiva lives everywhere; do not divide Hindu from Muslim. Use your sense to recognize yourself; that is the true way to find God.)

This synthesis of mystical Shaivism and Islamic Sufism went straight to the hearts of the masses: she became Lalla Arifa for the Muslims and Lalleshwari for the Hindus.

Popular belief can easily establish linkages where formal history might advise caution. In any case, belief plays no less a part in the shaping of a people than clues stuck together into a theory by a disciplined historian. More: belief may reflect a higher truth than arid facts. Who can say with conviction whether Shaikh Nuruddin was in fact suckled in infancy by Lal Ded? And does it really matter that the most beloved of Kashmir's Sufi-saints, Shaikh Nuruddin, was born, according to the Daud Mishkati, in 1356, and no one can offer a specific date for the birth of Lal Ded? The poetic truth of this tradition says far more about the history of the people of Kashmir, about their minds and hearts and needs and passions than barren dates. Nuruddin's philosophy was weaned at the breast of Lal Ded; he drank from her; that is the relevant truth. And he too lived in the hearts of both Muslims and Hindus; the first called him their Shaikh, the second referred to him as Nand Rishi—and in fact his order of the Rishis became a powerful influence in the Valley for many centuries ; traces of it can still be found in the 'Rishi' surname common to Hindu and Muslim alike. Ancient Hindu tradition recognizes seven Rishi Orders: Devarshi, Rajarshi, Kandarshi, Brahmarshi, Parmarshi, Maharshi and Srutarshi. Nuruddin's Rishi Order was moulded by the arrival of Islam, and sought to build bridges between the ancient religion and the fast-expanding new faith. There was enough in common between Vedantism and Sufism—the unity of the Divine, equality, rejection of both the ego and materialism, as well as idolatry—to make this possible. But the social purpose is clear enough too: to promote the harmony between the people through the stress on what was common in philosophy and common to the achievement of inner peace, as well as to challenge the priests whose professional aim was the preservation of the power of their class through the promotion of conflict. Even as these great idealists changed their world for the better, they had the wisdom to reject only elements of the past, not to destroy it completely. They were Indian revolutionaries, not anarchists. The symbols of the soil were integrated into their message: it was a perfect harmony which set the imagination of the people aflame. All over the land of India, in an explosive chain reaction, an astounding spiritual renaissance, which has come to be known as the Bhakti movement, occurred, the vision and genius of one saint seeming to feed another across divisions of time and geography, and a melody of love and devotion was heard in *qawwali* and *bhajan*—an imperishable element of our Indian heritage. At some point they all touch each other, from Khwaja Moinuddin Chishti to Hazrat Nizamuddin Auliya to Ramananda and Kabir and Jayadeva and Nanak and Mira. This brilliant Indian ideology swept past trifling boundaries of kingdoms as surely as it brushed aside the more serious barriers of language and sub-culture. The more sensible kings absorbed its spirit, to their own benefit. When Shaikh Nuruddin passed away, among his pallbearers was a Sultan, Zainul Abidin, whose fifty years of rule is still remembered as a golden age of Kashmir. Even four centuries later, an Afghan governor, Atta Muhammad Khan, thought he could soften the hatred of the Kashmiri for the Afghan by minting coins in Nand Rishi's name. But the Afghan was only misusing the name in a political gambit; Zainul Abidin lived by the message of his contemporary, a message left for us in the memorable verses of the *Rishinama* or the *Nurnama*. The Rishi tells the priest:

> Your rosary is like a snake; you bend it only on seeing your disciples. You have eaten six plates of food, one after the other: if you are the priest, then who are the robbers?

Another verse talks of the hypocrisy of the times:

> During this iron age, I found liars prospering.
> And in the house of the pious I found grief born of poverty.

For true worship of God:

Do not go to the Sheikh or priest or mullah; do not feed the cattle on poisonous leaves. Do not shut yourself up in mosques or forests; enter your own body, control your breath, and commune with God.

He tells the mullah and the pandit:

Having cleansed your face, you have called the believers to prayer. But can I know, O Rishi, what you feel in your heart, or why you are bowing your head? You have lived your life without seeing God; tell me, who did you pray to?

This message of harmony created a reservoir of humanism which became the ideological fountainhead of the modern Kashmiri mind, gave a unique quality to the Kashmiri identity, provided a conviction which long preserved Kashmir from the unspeakable and unbelievable bloodshed which Indians have inflicted upon each other in this century in the name of religion. It can only be described as the faith of Kashmir, a faith which has been witnessed by anyone who has visited the Valley and had the good sense to see beyond the extraordinary beauty of mountain, lake, forest and glade into something far greater, far more luminous, far more enchanting: the beauty of the Kashmiri heart, the Kashmiri soul. When that spirit has prevailed, there has been peace. When that spirit has been under siege, from within or without, there has been the wailing of a mother beside the most painful coffin in human experience: the coffin of her child. Perhaps it was no accident that Lal Ded gave suck to Shaikh Nuruddin and Nand Rishi was a contemporary of Zainul Abidin. Kashmir has always flourished best when the Rishi has influenced the Raja. Sadly, that has not always been its fate.

2

Of Human, and Inhuman, Bondage

The poet did not quibble:

Agar firdaus bar ru-e zamin ast
Hami ast o-hami ast o-hami ast.

If there is a Paradise on earth, he said after seeing Kashmir, it is this, it is this, it is this. One problem, however, with any Paradise is the envy it tends to arouse. Kashmir has been coveted by a succession of armies, at least from the time of the Aryans. Many came to conquer, but only a few were able to stay: Kashmir absorbed those few who broke the forbidding defensive wall of the Himalayas. The *rawaj* of Kashmir, its culture, enveloped the outsider instead of the reverse. The Kashmiri identity was always the dominant reality, making the Emperor Jahangir remark that he could not distinguish a Kashmiri Muslim from a Hindu. But he could distinguish the Kashmiri from the Mughal.

Geography certainly played a significant part in the preservation of this distinct identity. In fact, Kashmir's geography has often compensated for the naïveté or the ineptitude of its rulers. Its main passes—Zojila and Burzil in the north-east; the Tosamaidan at Pir Panjal; Banihal; or the route through Uri in the Jhelum valley—had the useful merit of being easily guarded, if not always by the valour of the Srinagar infantry then at least by the snows of our familiar interventionist in history, General Winter. Mahmud of Ghazni might demolish and loot where he wanted on the plains of India, but his armies were incapable of defeating Kashmir's mountains and its weather. Jahangir, son of the man who finally brought Kashmir into the ambit of Delhi's politics, put it succinctly in his memoirs:

Kashmir is a garden of eternal spring or an iron fort to a palace of kings—a delightful flower bed, and a heart-expanding heritage for dervishes.

Perhaps nature had to place a purdah around something so beautiful. Pandit Kalhana, the first great historian of Kashmir, adds another dimension to the concept:

> The country may be conquered by the force of spiritual merit, but not by the force of soldiers. The inhabitants are afraid only of the world beyond.

True. Kashmir succumbed far more easily to Buddhism or Islam than to weapons. Kalhana mentions the legend recorded in the *Nilamat Purana* about the origins of this lovely land. At the beginning of Kalpa, or Creation, the Valley was a lake hundreds of feet deep, called the Sati Saras, or the Lake of Sati, consort of Kashmir's preferred Lord, Shiva. In this lake lived the demon Jalodbhav or the One Born in Water, who terrorized the Nagas, snakes who guarded the waters (the word is still used in place names, as in Anantnag). To the human eye, the Nagas either took a plain form, or sometimes appeared as clouds or hailstorms. In the age of the seventh Manu, the Sage Kashyapa, father of the Nagas, learnt about the brutal oppression of his progeny while on a pilgrimage to the Himalayas. An angry Kashyapa appealed to Brahma the Supreme as well as to other gods. It was not a request which the gods could ignore and they took up position on the mountain peaks surrounding Sati Saras. But the demon had one infinite advantage—he was invincible as long as he remained in the womb of water. He simply refused to emerge. The Lord Vishnu then called upon his brother Balabhadra to end the stalemate; he took up his ploughshare and pierced the closed ring of mountains at Baramulla. The waters drained from Sati Saras; Vishnu engaged the demon and slew him with his disc. The pleased sage settled in the dry Valley, and Kashmir was named after him. But when the gods and goddesses saw the Valley they were so enchanted by its beauty that they too refused to leave. And so the gods settled in the mountains of Kashmir, while the goddesses took the shape of the sparkling, abundant, fertile rivers.

Geologists rather spoil the legend by confirming it: by looking at the lacustrine deposits and pronouncing that yes, indeed, a great lake once did exist, a post Ice Age earthquake did shatter the mountains and dry the Valley. There are times when science should surrender to poetry.

The gods had opened a gate to Paradise. Inevitably, much more came in through the gate than went out. A chink had been struck in the lofty and exquisite armour protecting Kashmir.

It is reasonably certain that a branch of the Indo-Aryans who took the course of the Oxus and the Jaxertes separated from the main body of migrants and eventually settled down in the Kashmir Valley. Pandit Kalhana begins his history, however, with Gonanda the First, a contemporary—and antagonist—of Lord Krishna. Gonanda lost his life in battle with the Lord, as did his son Damodara. Krishna himself determined the succession, and made Damodara's pregnant wife Yasovati the Queen Regent. When the nobles protested against a woman being given power, Krishna admonished them by reciting a verse from the *Nilamat Purana*:

Kashmir is Parvati; know that its ruler is a part of Shiva.

Popular belief insists that after the three Gonanda rulers, twenty-three generations of Pandavas (who eventually triumphed in *Mahabharata*, the War of the Cousins on the fields of Kurukshetra) ruled Kashmir, the dynasty being founded by Haranadev, a great-grandson of Arjuna. The ancient temple on the hill of the Shankaracharya in Srinagar is said to date from the Pandava era. However, romantics might feel a trifle disillusioned over the manner in which the scion of the Pandavas seized the throne. He entered the service of Gonanda the Second, rose to high office, and then bribed treacherous courtiers to murder the king.

History shifts to firmer ground by the time we reach Ashoka (273–232 BC) the first of the great monarchs to rule all or most of this vast subcontinent stretching from Burma to Central Asia. The fault for the gap in the record is not Kashmir's; the manuscripts have perished. Kalhana has noted the sustenance he took from at least eleven previous historians. And scholarship comes at the top of his list of Kashmiri virtues; in order:

Learning, lofty houses, saffron, icy water and grapes.

However, though the Persians and the Greeks certainly knew of Kashmir, even as well documented an event as Alexander's campaign (327 BC) does not mention its existence. A new power rose in India in the ebb of Alexander's invasion. One of the princes studying in the world-famous university of Taxila during the Greek advance was Chandragupta of Magadh (322–298 BC.). A brilliant leader himself, and doubly fortunate in having one of the truly gifted minds of Indian history, Kautilya, as first his tutor and then his mentor, Chandragupta slowly expanded the frontiers of his rule till he had pushed the Greek viceroys beyond Gandhara. Taxila revolted during his heir Bindusara's reign, and Susima, the king's elder son, was sent to quell the uprising. When he failed, his younger brother Ashoka was shifted from Ujjain to Taxila. He not only crushed the rebels, but also brought the Valley of Kashmir into the ambit of the Mauryan empire. Kalhana says that it was Ashoka who founded the capital of Kashmir, Srinagar, which quickly evolved into a flourishing city with "ninety six thousand dwellings resplendent with prosperity." Still a devout Hindu, Ashoka constructed a string of famous temples, and a son, Jaluka, was born to him after prayers to the Lord Shiva at the shrine of Harmuktaganga.

When, satiated by military conquest after the corpse-strewn victory at Kalinga in Orissa in 261 BC, the emperor turned a Buddhist evangelic, Ashoka made Kashmir the northern crucible of his mission. The Buddhist Council held at Pataliputra sent Majjhantika at the head of 5,000 monks to the Valley and Gandhara. But while Gandhara became the conduit for the flow of Buddhism into Afghanistan and Central Asia, Hinduism proved more durable in Kashmir. Jaluka, the child born through Shiva's favours, broke away from the parent empire and established an independent state which, with obvious determination, promoted the worship of Hindu deities, the chief inspiration and example being Jaluka himself.

It took another two centuries for Buddhism to return to Kashmir at a significant level. A nomad people, the Yu-echi, pushed out from their homelands on the borders of China by the Huns, had managed to settle in the valley of Kabul. Around AD 15, the chief of one of the clans of this tribe, the Kushan, Kadphises, emerged as the kind of leader who could unite his own people and conquer others. He brought the whole of Afghanistan under his control and established the base of a great empire. His son, Kadphises the Second, was a brilliant warrior who stretched his domain up to Varanasi in the east along the fertile and rich Gangetic plain. And his son, Kanishka, was to become the most famous of the Kushan kings, ruling from Bengal to the Oxus.

Like Ashoka, Kanishka too was a convert to Buddhism; and of course there is no zeal greater than that of a new servant of any faith. It was entirely predictable that he wanted to eclipse the impact of Ashoka with an even greater contribution—and while comparisons are always inexact, the spread of Mahayana Buddhism can be dated from the Council organized by Kanishka at the Kundalvan monastery near Srinagar. If Buddhism went south to Sri Lanka, Burma, Indo-China and Indonesia from Ashoka's Pataliputra, then it moved swiftly into Central Asia, Tibet, and from there to China and eventually to Korea by AD 372 and Japan by AD 552 from Kanishka's Kashmir. It is interesting that the Buddha himself had praised Kashmir as the ideal focal point for the spread of his message; the environment, he said, was made for meditation and for the practice of a religious life. Ananda, the Buddha's constant companion had a disciple called Madhandina who, said the Buddha, would take Buddhism to the land of the blue forests, subdue the malevolent Husuta Nagas and sit cross-legged, miraculously covering the whole of Kashmir and making its 60,000 villages a haven of peace. As Ashoka had done, Kanishka also gave Kashmir to the Buddhist church. Buddhism did eventually reign over these villages, its essential simplicity a powerful attraction for the ritual-burdened masses. But just as an oppressive priesthood had caused the degeneration of Hinduism, so did the excessive zeal of Buddhist monks create the conditions for the restoration of Shaivism. The vagaries of power also play their role in nudging public opinion in one direction or another, and the decline of the Kushans had its parallel impact on the state religion.

The Kashmir from which emerged Buddhist missionaries like Kumarajiva, Yasa, Vimalaksha and Sanghabuti, who reached northern China in AD 381; Gautamasangha, who followed in AD 384; Dharmayasa, Buddhayasa, Vimalaksha, Buddhajiva, all of whom spent years propagating the faith in China; Gunavarman, who took the message first to Java and from there, on royal request to Nanking; whose scholars converted Tibet and the vast plains of the centre of Asia, was itself destined to return firmly to the fold of Shaivism by the start of the sixth century. It is another matter that the king whose name is synonymous with the restoration is also a symbol of terror: Mihirakula, the Hun.

The white Huns who had dislodged the Yu-echi Kushans from north-west China did not end their migration there. One branch went towards Europe where its name was soon to strike dread as the tribe of Attila who ravaged both tribal and civilized Europe. Another branch turned south from the Oxus. By the last two decades of the fifth century the white Huns had eaten away huge chunks of the western parts of the Gupta empire. Mihirakula's capital was at Sakala, now Sialkot in Pakistan. He made a name for himself with a string of victories but his expansionist ambitions were punctured by two defeats which destroyed not just him but also ended the Hun threat in the subcontinent: the first by the ruler of Malwa, Yashodhavarman, and the second by Baladitya, the king of Magadh. Driven out of his land, he sought refuge in Kashmir, where, like the proverbial cat who went on Haj pilgrimage after eating 900 mice, he set himself up as a champion of Lord Shiva. Whatever his other faults, and they were clearly many, Mihirakula was a good judge of social conditions. It was the right cause to take up at the right moment. And such is the power of religion that by the time of his death he had even begun to be respected for his devotion to Shiva. This was the man who had arbitrarily ordered the massacre of thousands of families on a whim that there was not a woman chaste enough for him among them. This was the man after whom that dangerous precipice on the Pir Panjal Pass, Hastivanj (the destroyer of elephants) is named. (He was crossing the pass when one of the elephants in his train slipped and fell. The shrieks of the terrified elephant so amused Mihirakula that he ordered a hundred more elephants to be thrown down—all so that he could enjoy those shrieks of terror.) It says something about the ability of tyrants that even such a man, who came only as a refugee to Srinagar, was able to manipulate his way to the throne of Kashmir.

Kings best forgotten followed Mihirakula until we come to the Karkota dynasty, beginning with Durlabhavardhana in AD 625. The greatest of this line is Lalitaditya, whose rule of thirty-seven years saw an unprecedented expansion of Kashmiri power to Tibet in the east, Badakhan in the west and Punjab and Kanauj in the south. Pandit Kalhana describes Lalitaditya's ambition:

> For rivers which have set out from their own region the
> ocean is the limit but nowhere is there a limit for those who
> are frankly aspiring to be conquerors.

But the keenest ambition cannot expand without a secure base, and that security at home was provided by a policy which is as relevant to the twentieth century as it was in the seventh—a policy which has brought peace and then glory to Kashmir when applied, and caused sorrow and poverty when rejected. The first principle was religious tolerance. The king was a Hindu, but the commander-in-chief of Lalitaditya's army was a Buddhist, as were many of his ministers. Inevitably, in that congenial environment, poetry and the other arts flourished, the Martand temple being an outstanding contribution to Kashmir's architecture. But this empire fell apart after Lalitaditya's death during a military expedition to Afghanistan, thanks to self-indulgent successors who quickly squandered Kashmir's brief tryst with imperialism. There was an occasional flicker of hope, in the form of an intelligent dynast, but one decade of good sense is easily swamped by nine of irresponsibility.

The tenth century saw a rotted polity degenerating with each spasm of ambition, as kings became playthings of powerbrokers or officers with enough loyal (read that to mean regularly paid) soldiers at their call, when they were not victims of their own suicidal vices. It is interesting and educative to run through Kashmir's history in the hundred years of the tenth century.

It opened with the rule of Gopalavarman (AD 902–904). He was still a child, and power rested in the hands of his mother Sugandha and her lover Prabhakardeva, a minister in the court of Gopal's father Samkaravarman. In two years, the boy had been killed by his mother and her lover. An alleged son of Samkaravarman was placed on the throne to camouflage the crime. He survived for just ten days. Sugandha seized power for herself. In two years she was deposed by a tribe called the Tantrins, fighting men who had become the latest achievers in this atmosphere of sleaze. They placed their nominee, Partha, on the throne, and for fifteen years the people had to suffer the ravages of these marauders. A severe famine resulted in AD 918, but the Tantrins and nobles only made fortunes selling hoarded grain at exorbitant prices to the starving. In AD 921 Partha was finally removed—by his father, Nirjitavarman. (The topsy-turvy nature of events is already dizzying; worse is to follow.) He lasted just two years. Kings kept changing depending on who bribed whom more successfully until AD 936, when one claimant, Chakravarman, brought in a non-Kashmiri ally, the Damara king, Samgrama, and captured power. For the people nothing changed: the exploitation of the Tantrins was merely replaced by that of the Damaras.

Chakravarman fell in love with two sisters, Hamsi and Nagalata, from the low caste of Dom, and spent his remaining energies on them rather than governing the state. He was killed by his mentors one night in AD 937 while in the arms of Hamsi. His successor, Unmattavanti, specialized in vulgarity and debauchery and quickly became known as the "mad king". Given the fact that his predecessors had not been particularly sane, his excesses must have been something to behold. He starved his imprisoned brothers to death and had his father murdered. Just before he died of consumption in AD 939, he placed on the throne a child his concubines had picked up from the streets and declared him to be his son and heir. Unmattavanti seems straight out of a sadistic black comedy.

Such an heir could hardly last. The army marched on the palace, and its chief laid claim to the throne himself. The problem of course was of legitimacy. He assembled a group of Brahmins to declare him king; in a decision not without its share of humour, they neatly sidestepped the man who had summoned them and chose one of their own, a poor Brahmin youth called Yasaskara who had left Kashmir some years ago but had returned enriched with an education. His nine years of power were an outstanding contrast to all that had gone before: plundering officials were brought under control, and there was such a sense of security that shops could be left open at night; trade and agriculture prospered. But even he could not change the culture of the court. The most powerful woman in his palace was not his wife but his mistress, Lalla, whose favours were not confined to the king. The queen returned the compliment. When Yasaskara lay on his deathbed after a fatal attack of illness, he placed his cousin Varnata on the throne instead of his son Samgramadeva since he was convinced the latter was a product of adultery.

Varnata lasted for about twenty-four hours, short even by the volatile standards of the times. Samgramadeva was remade heir when an angry Yasaskara discovered that Varnata did not have the decency to come to his bedside to thank him after becoming king. But greater indignities were in store for the dying man: his ministers and relatives snatched away the 2,500 gold pieces on his person in front of his helpless eyes as he lay rolling in his final agony.

Samgramadeva did not last even a year; he was dethroned and killed by the usurper Parvagupta, who died of leprosy after a year-and-half of unmitigated oppression. His son Kshemagupta, who lasted for eight years (AD 950–958), was a drunk, a gambler and a debauch. The only memorable thing he really did was to marry Didda, the daughter of the chief of Lohara. Didda was a remarkably amoral woman who was to control the affairs of Kashmir for a long while: first through her useless husband, then through her minor child, and finally directly. Her lusts became famous, whether for the bed or for power. She showed no hesitation whatsoever in killing her young grandsons after her son's death, and ruled directly between AD 981 and 1003 with the comforting help of her lover, a former buffalo herdsman named Tunga. (In spite of all the rigid casteism, it seems that fairy tale social mobility was still possible.) However, Didda did manage to impose some stability in a state riven by misrule; she had that most sublime of virtues in politics, the ability to survive.

But the rather sordid story of these hundred years proves that the Hindu dynasties had rotted to the point of decay, and were it not for those eternal protectors, the mountains, Kashmir would have fallen to the virile kingdoms all around it. The Muslim incursions into the subcontinent had begun by the turn of the century, pioneered by Mahmud of Ghazni, son of Sabuktaqin and one of the great figures of the era. Mahmud headed towards Kashmir twice, once in 1015 and a second time in 1021, both times through the Tosamaidan Pass. On both occasions the formidable Mahmud was checked at the hill fort of Lohkot on the southern slopes of the Pir Panjal range by that well-known strategist and humbler of the mighty, General Winter. Alberuni, who was present during one siege, reports:

After a while, when the snow began to fall and the season became intensely cold, the enemy received reinforcements from Kashmir.

And the sultan returned to Ghazni. After the death of Didda, the succession passed to her side of the family, the Loharas, naturally as a consequence of her design. But though her successors displayed longevity, sense still eluded the kings of Kashmir. Sangramarga ruled till 1028; his heir Hariraja for only twenty-eight days—he was killed by his mother, Srilekha, who modelled herself after Didda. But the nobles prevented another spell of licence, and her younger son Ananta was given the crown. He sat on the throne till 1063, but it cannot be said that he kept his crown on his head all that time. At one point, Ananta, an addict of pan, pawned his crown to a betel merchant, Padmaraja—a most telling illustration of the state of affairs, or, perhaps more accurately, of the affairs of state.

The best of Kashmir's kings in the eleventh century, Harsha (1089–1101) was a Jekyll-and-Hyde character, alternating between wisdom and depravity. Inevitably, the second won the final battle for the control of the king's mind. The strikingly handsome king whose personally composed songs became immensely popular and whose reputation was built around enforcement of justice and encouragement of the arts (he introduced Carnatic music to Kashmir), soon became a victim of his vices. A liberal, he allowed Turko-Afghan influences to fashion not only the behaviour of his court but also introduced their military science into his army by hiring Turk officers. But each innovation escalated into wanton excess. And as the cost of the king's and the nobility's pleasures rose, so did the taxes Kalhana (whose father served Harsha) notes that "even nightsoil became the object of special taxation." Ruinously expensive, politically foolish military expeditions; defeat in battle; reckless looting (including of temples); maladministration; and then flood followed by famine—it was downhill all the way. His personal habits were hardly worth emulating: the import of expensive Turkish slave girls was only a part of the problem. He seemed a trifle indiscriminate in his sleeping habits, including his sisters, aunts and father's concubines in his pleasures. He died in a popular revolt which ended his colourful reign in 1101.

A Kashmir in this condition could hardly have escaped the attention of the Sultans of Delhi in either this century or the next were it not for the armour of rock around the Valley, and the preoccupation of the Sultans with territories to the south of them. Even Alauddin Khilji (1296–1316), whose armies penetrated up to Rameshwaram, left Kashmir alone. But the Mongols were not so generous. Both Changez Khan (1162–1227) and Halaku Khan had slated Kashmir for conquest in their plans. It was however left to another Mongol to take the fury of this particular ill-wind to the Valley. Suddenly, in 1320, Kashmir was routed out of its self-defeating, corrupt complacence by the savagery of 17,000 horse and foot, racing swiftly across the Baramulla Pass under the command of a Mongol whose name still haunts memory, Dulacha. Moreover he chose his weather well: early summer.

Kashmir was ruled at the time by Sahadeva, who in addition to the familiar traits of dissipation and neglect had cowardice as an additional individual hallmark. He first sought to bribe Dulacha, but the Mongol was not interested in tokenism when he had a defenceless Valley at his mercy. Sahadeva simply abandoned his people and escaped to Kishtwar. For eight months the Mongols vandalized the grain, the cattle, the gold, and of course the women. Pandit Jonaraja, whose chronicle takes our knowledge beyond Kalhana's work, describes the land after Dulacha's appetites were finally satiated:

> When Dulacha had left the place, those people of Kashmir
> who had escaped capture issued out of their strongholds,
> as mice do out of their holes. When the violence caused
> by the Rakshasa (Demon) Dulacha ceased, the son found
> not his father, nor did brother meet his brother. Kashmir
> became almost like a region before the creation, a vast
> field with men without food and full of grass.

Kashmir had been forsaken by its kings, but its gods had not forgotten it yet. Dulacha came at the right time; he left his departure a little late; greed delayed him. And he met his nemesis at the Banihal Pass, where a fierce blizzard trapped his whole army leaving no survivors. Kashmir's winter would not be as easily defeated as its kings.

But those eight months of unspeakable savagery were the final blow. The people refused to accept the old order again. They felt crushed and betrayed, and when Sahadeva returned after Dulacha's departure he found a deep and unforgiving anger.

Kashmir awaited a man who could be king.

3

Crosscurrent Affairs: A Dream Come True

For a thousand years the crosscurrents of competing empires have lapped at the borders of Kashmir: Delhi to the south, Kabul to the west, the Turks and the Mongols from the vast plains in the north, China and Tibet to the east. Yet, travelling at a speed much greater than the pace of any cavalry, and with an impact far more lasting than the turn of a battle, were ideas and influences. It was an age of change, and no defence, natural or manmade, has yet been created to block the passages to the human mind. A strange and wondrous combination of events—the arrival of a Musawi Saiyyid disciple of the Sufi divine Shah Niamatullah Farsi of the Suhrawardy order; the presence of an adventurer driven by a dream from his native Swat (now in Pakistan); the death of the great Kublai Khan in distant Beijing, to name but three—created the conditions for the establishment of first Islam and then Muslim rule in the Valley of Kashmir by the fourteenth century.

Mahmud of Ghazni brought the sword of Islam in 1015; the steel clattered against the cold stone of the Himalayas and retreated. Three hundred years later Saiyyid Bilal Shah, immortal in the memory of the people as Bulbul Shah, brought the love and compassion of Islam; and the faith continues to flourish to this day. Some conversions had of course taken place earlier: Marco Polo mentions the presence of Muslims in Kashmir around 1277. It was inevitable that the mercurial rise and consolidation of Islam in Central Asia would seep through the Pamirs, but it was not until Bulbul Shah came in the reign of King Sahadeva that the message took root among the masses. By the time Bulbul Shah passed away in 1327, the king, the king's brother, the commander-in-chief of the army were Muslims, and the first mosque of Kashmir, below the fifth bridge in Srinagar, now called Bulbul Langar, had been constructed: he was buried near the mosque. In an adjoining grave lies the body of his disciple, Mulla Ahmed, who became the first Sheikh-ul-Islam of Kashmir and whose two books, *Fatwa-i-Shihabi* and *Shihab-i-Saqib* are an important contribution to scholarship. Bulbul Shah's most dramatic convert was the king himself. This ruler also happened to be the king Kashmir had been waiting for.

The great Changez Khan never reached Kashmir though he did knock on its door after Tibet fell to him in 1203. It was left to Kublai Khan (1260–1294) to extend the stability of proper Mongol administration to this vast, remote and frozen plateau. On the edge of this Tibetan plateau lay Little and Great Bhanttaland, corresponding to modern Baltistan and Ladakh. Kublai Khan appointed the local Bhantta royal family to administer in his name, and there was peace during the three decades of Kublai Khan's rule. But no sooner did the news of the Khan's death reach this remote edge of the vast domain, than the local passions which had been subdued by the force of empire erupted once again. The tribes launched into a familiar internecine war. The Baltis revolted against Beijing's viceroy, Lha-Chen-Dugos Grub. Lha-Chen lost both the battle and his life, and his handsome young warrior son was forced to flee Ladakh. And that was how the chain reaction beginning from Kublai Khan's death brought the young Rinchin across the Zojila Pass into Kashmir.

The first important village that Rinchin reached after crossing the Sonamarg valley was called Gagangir, distinguished by the castle of Rama Chandra, the commander-in-chief of Sahadeva's army as well as prime minister. Rinchin found shelter and service in Rama Chandra's castle. The minister-general's hospitality must have been encouraged by the sight of several hundred Bhantta fighting men under Rinchin's command. Those were turbulent times; and only a very naïve or a very rash man would have spurned a readily available private army. In fact, another foreigner with a similar body of men was already in service in that castle, awaiting the moment when he and his force would be needed.

Shah Mir's story is out of Ripley's *Believe It or Not.* This young man from the near inaccessible valley of Swat had a dream one night in which a holy man told him to go to Kashmir where he would one day become king. Shah Mir clearly belonged to that rare category of men which insists on making dreams come true. Without wasting any time, without pausing to wonder how or why an unknown wanderer could become king, Shah Mir collected his family and followers and came to Sahadeva's court where he made an immediate impression on Rama Chandra. Understanding each other better perhaps than Rama Chandra understood either of them, Rinchin and Shah Mir became very good friends. Rinchin also fell deeply in love with Kota, Rama Chandra's beautiful daughter who, we shall discover, had a very intelligent attitude towards power. Kota reciprocated this love.

Those eight months of Dulacha, as we have seen, were the hinge on which this story moves. The betrayal of Sahadeva left Rama Chandra holding the fort; and he did that a bit too literally, simply shutting himself up in his castle while the people all around were getting butchered. It was during this brutal crisis that a Buddhist refugee from Ladakh, and a Muslim adventurer from Swat, with no blood or emotional ties to Kashmir, came to the help of the people. Along with Kota, Rinchin and Shah Mir organized what little resistance they could. They might not have been able to do very much, but the people were never to forget those who had been at their side and never to forgive those who had run away.

Rama Chandra assumed the title of king in the vacuum left by Dulacha's departure. Sahadeva, with the help of a Kishtwar tribe which had given him shelter, the Gaddis, attempted to seize Srinagar and was driven back. But Rama Chandra was hardly the hero the people were searching for, either. Sensing the mood, Rinchin struck. Disguised as pedlars, his Ladakhi followers entered the palace, slipped into the king's chambers and killed him. With Shah Mir at his side, and the people behind him, Rinchin became lord of Kashmir on 6 October 1320. Kota quickly put aside what reservations she might have had about her father's murderer and became Rinchin's queen.

He proved an astute ruler. He moved quickly to protect what he had seized, and on every flank, beginning with the people. He ensured their goodwill with an intensive relief and rehabilitation programme, essential after the devastation by Dulacha. His soldiers quelled fresh marauders, like the notorious tribe of Lavanyas (now Lons) and established what Kashmir thirsted for most: peace. Order and justice were the principal achievements of Rinchin's reign, which Pandit Jonaraja calls a "golden age". As for enemies at the top, he eliminated them—not by the sword, but by the far more sensible device of offering them a share of power. And since Rama Chandra's family was an obvious source of danger, he offered his son the posts Rama Chandra had held under Sahadeva. The offer was accepted.

But there was a personal frontier yet to be crossed, a delicate one. Rinchin was a Buddhist, and he was conscious of the fact that a king could not belong to a faith which did not enjoy mass support. Buddhism had virtually disappeared; Hinduism was again the dominant creed while Islam had begun to get a growing number of adherents. Rinchin decided that he had no option but to worship the Lord Shiva, and sent word to Deva Swami, head priest of the Shaiva Hindus.

A solemn conclave was summoned by the pandits, and with great solemnity they informed King Rinchin that conversion to Hinduism was not possible. Why? They could not decide which caste in the hierarchy to place Rinchin in.

The folly of the pandits provided Shah Mir with the opportunity he had been waiting for. He offered Islam as the answer to his friend's confusion. They argued through the night, as Rinchin weighed the personal and political implications. The two friends decided to leave the final decision to the morning.

*

'Allah-u-Akbar!' The first cry that a Muslim hears in the dark shadows that fill the air before dawn is the praise of Allah: God is great! Opens the aazaan. The muezzin tells the faithful: 'Hayya al-as salat! Hayya al-as salat!' Come to pray! Come to pray! The pre-dawn aazaan differs from the four more that will mark the various stages of the day's progress: a special line comes at this point. 'As-salatu khairul mina' n-naum!' Prayer, intones the muezzin from his minaret, is better than sleep.

It was the sound of this call which woke Rinchin that restless morning. He looked out of his window, and saw Bulbul Shah at prayer. He went to Bulbul Shah and poured out the questions of the night to the Sufi divine. Bulbul Shah gave him the comfort and assurance which Deva Swami had denied him. Islam had no caste; it was built on the equality of man and faith in the omnipotence of Allah and His last Messenger, the Prophet Muhammad. To become a Muslim, Rinchin only had to utter the *Qalimah*: 'La-e-laha illallah, Muhammad un-Rasul Allah'—There is no God but Allah and Muhammad is His Messenger. Rinchin became a Muslim that morning, taking the name of Sultan Sadruddin. And thus did Muslim rule reach Kashmir, not by trailing the armies of the night, but in the glow of persuasion at dawn. The mosque which Rinchin built below his hill castle, Bodro Masjid, became a place of veneration for both Ladakh's Buddhists and Kashmir's Muslims; the Ladakhi folk-song of the Bodro Masjid narrates the details of the conversion with far more verve than the Persian manuscripts like *Taarikh-e-Kashmir* by Haidar Malik, the historian-architect who served Jahangir in the Valley, or other texts of the period.

But there were a few hiccoughs to come before stability could be established. The defeat of Sahadeva had not vanquished the family's ambitions. His brother Udayanadeva put forward his claim after Rinchin's death in 1323 from a head wound suffered in battle against rebels. (He was buried in Bulbul Langar.) In the struggle for power that followed Rinchin's premature death, Shah Mir and Kota Rani, astutely finessed Udayanadeva and the nobles loyal to the old order, who had rallied around, by joining them. They invited Udayanadeva to sit on the throne instead of the infant Haidar, Rinchin's son, and Kota secured this alliance by marrying him to remain queen. And then an impatient history chose to repeat itself. The last time it was the Mongol Dulacha; this time it was a Turk, Achala. The last time it was Sahadeva; this time it was Udayanadeva. An invader entered the Valley. The king ran away. The last time it had proved ruinous for the last Kashmiri Hindu ruling family; this time it proved fatal. (Curiously, even in 1947, the Dogras ran away from Kashmir when marauders of the Dulacha-Achala mould, this time sent by Pakistan, reached the Valley.)

The queens of Kashmir have always had a very special vitality, courage and independence of conviction. When her weak, pathetic new husband escaped to Ladakh, Kota Rani stayed back. With her, once again, was her friend Shah Mir. The two proved master tacticians. They sent word to Achala that the throne was his. While Achala relaxed, and complacently sent back a section of his troops, Shah Mir organized both the Kashmiri people and his scanty contingent of troops. When they felt confident enough, they attacked Achala, destroyed his army, captured and publicly beheaded him. Kota and Shah Mir became the most adored leaders of their time: Udayanadeva remained king only in name. The balance of power shifted towards Shah Mir, whose better sense of organization and charitable personality created a growing mystique. When the useless Udayanadeva finally died on the night of Shivaratri in 1338, the inevitable happened: Shah Mir and Kota had to decide who would be the sole ruler. The queen struck first, declaring herself monarch. But when Shah Mir besieged her fort at Indarkot overlooking the Manasbal Lake, she discovered that she could not depend on the loyalty of even some of her ministers. She surrendered. Shah Mir offered her marriage and a queen's comforts. She accepted. But within twenty-four hours of the marriage she was never seen again. Romantics insist that she preferred suicide to marriage but that would be contrary to the track record. Pandit Jonaraja's view seems more credible: Shah Mir simply put out of the way the only person who could now interfere with the promise of that dream long ago.

Which film-script can match such reality?

Shah Mir proclaimed himself Sultan Shamsuddin, and the *khutba* was read in his name from the mosques. The dynasty he established in 1339 would last 222 years, brought down only by the power of the Mughals at the height of their glory. In these two centuries, Islam became the paramount religion of Kashmir, but the key to the success of the Sultanate, despite its share of bigots and tyrants, was the legacy of Shah Mir— identification with the Kashmiri people. As Jonaraja puts it:

> This believer in Allah, calm and active, became the saviour
> of the people and protected the terrified subjects.

The rulers took great care to identify with the sentiments of the people, tailoring their behaviour to measure up to the philosophy of Kashmir as defined by Nand Rishi or Lal Ded or the scores of brilliant men of religion who flourished in this time. The most important of them reached Kashmir thanks to yet another shift in the fortunes of Central Asia.

The memory of Changez and Halaku was still trembling in the stories told to children when another great conqueror rose like a storm: Taimur, the lame warrior who established himself at Samarqand. Balkh fell in 1369; Khurasan and Herat followed as the Mughal swallowed Persia, and ruled on the principle of total fealty from every conquered subject. One group which refused were the Alawi Saiyyids of the Persian city of Hamadan. Seven hundred of them left their native city to escape Taimur and settled in Kashmir, under the leadership of Saiyyid Ali Hamdani, the great scholar and missionary of the Naqshbandi Order of Sufis. Shah Hamdan, as he came to be popularly known, was in the Renaissance mould, author of more than a hundred works, ranging from religion to jurisprudence to politics, physiognomy and philosophical poetry. These Sufis mixed easily into the special religious culture of Kashmir: it was a land, as the Buddha had remarked so long ago, created for meditation and faith. Their lifestyle of self-abnegation, simplicity and rejection of the material world struck an immediate chord in the hearts of a people who had traditionally honoured such values. Abul Fazl describes this culture in *Ain-i-Akbari*:

> The most respected people of Kashmir are the Rishis who,
> although they do not suffer themselves to be fettered by
> traditions, are doubtless true worshippers of God. They do
> not revile any other sect, nor ask anything of anyone. They
> plant the roads with fruit trees to provide the traveller with
> refreshments. They abstain from meat and have no inter-

course with the other sex. There are 2000 of these Rishis in Kashmir.

Whether Hindu or Muslim, their message was the same in essence: that love destroyed hypocrisy, which was at the root of pain, that the purpose of life was worship and peace, not violence.

The dominating reality of Taimur was to have more than one indirect consequence on the life of Kashmir, however.

The Sultanate established by Shah Mir quickly flourished as he introduced the basic elements of sensible statecraft like a standing army and a stable tax system; and Kashmir now awaited the ruler who could convert its growing strength into imperial power. Shah Mir's grandson Shahabuddin sent his army up to Sind in the south and Afghanistan in the west, but these were punitive rather than expansionist expeditions. It was at this point that an unfortunate coincidence set the clock back—and viciously. You can transfer a kingdom to your heirs, but not confidence. Sikandar was sultan when Taimur marched into India in 1398. Taimur's goal was the wealth of Delhi, but Sultan Sikandar shivered nevertheless. He sought to buy his peace with booty, and waited at Bhimbhar for Taimur, on the route of the victorious army's march back home. Such weakness encouraged greed, and he was informed by an envoy that Taimur would be satisfied with nothing less than 30,000 horses and 1,00,000 silver rupees of the Alauddin Khilji mint. Instead of uniting the people, as Shah Mir had done, to defend their country and its wealth, the selfish, shortsighted and frightened Sikandar embarked on a savage campaign to raise this extraordinary ransom. It was inevitable that the communal lobby, particularly among the mullahs, would exploit such a weak man, and they indulged themselves on the pretext of saving the king. While the terrified Sultan stared over his shoulder at the advancing sceptre of Taimur, his officials seized the wealth of Hindu temples, broke idols, imposed the hated *jiziya* tax—and, in this atmosphere of need-inspired greed and communal frenzy—a vicious anti-Hindu policy was unleashed, from forcible conversions to a ban on music and the wearing of the *tika* on the forehead. It was the first display of Islamic fundamentalist power in Kashmir, and it did neither the Valley nor Islam any good. To add to the irony of the situation, it turned out to have been completely unnecessary. When Taimur learnt that an envoy had made such an unrealistic demand, he rushed emissaries to convey that it was unnecessary; simple allegiance was sufficient. That meant some respite to Sikandar but none to the people. The bigots had acquired a momentum of their own, and their hold over the court became so strong that after Sikandar died it grew further rather than ebbed. Ali Shah, the new sultan, was perhaps too young to be able to challenge these forces when he succeeded Sikandar. Five years later, he was not as young, but convincingly proven ineffective. The bigots had reduced the people of Kashmir to emotional and economic tatters. A mood of revolt was building up, and it was left to Ali Shah's younger brother, Shahi Khan, to articulate the mood and lead the revolt. Ali Shah was defeated and killed at the battle of Thanna, near the Pir Panjal Pass, in the summer of 1420.

Tradition says that by this summer, after two decades of repression, there were only eleven Hindu families left in the Kashmir Valley. The memory of that exodus was institutionalized in a typically revealing consequence—the creation of yet another pandit sub-caste. Those eleven families who had survived it all called themselves the Malamasis; those who had deserted Kashmir, if only briefly, were given the slightly inferior status of Banamasis. (Sub-division is a historic pandit disease. Later, when pandits were brought into the bureaucracy, those who learnt Persian to do so became known as the Karkums, while the Persian-pollution-free pandits called themselves Bachi Bhatts: such was the hostility between the pragmatists and the conservatives that, leave aside inter-marriage, the two would not even eat with each other.)

Shahi Khan was only nineteen when he became Sultan of Kashmir, taking the name Zainul Abidin. By the time he died at the age of sixty-nine, he was known among the masses as Bud Shah, or The Great King. How he brought fifty golden years of peace, harmony and prosperity to his beloved land remains an object lesson more than five-and-a-half centuries later.

4

Bud Shah: Days of Flowers

It is simple enough to judge the difference between a good king and a despot or a fool. But at what point in the public perception does 'good' evolve into 'great'? To be known as a good ruler, certain achievements are necessary: the perception of justice, concern and generosity towards the people; peace, and its finest consequence, prosperity; stability; law and order; if possible the expansion of the state through the glory of conquest. In addition, Zainul Abidin displayed a fine sense of statecraft even when he had barely crossed his teens. His management of the unruly tribe of Khukars (famous still in proverb as those who stick to their target with all the adhesive strength of a leech) was an excellent example. He had used them in battle against his brother, but when they began plucking at the fruits of power he guided their leader, Jasrath, towards Jammu and Delhi—thereby retaining both his friendship and his throne, a remarkable feat of diplomacy. Turning his attention eastwards, he extended Kashmiri paramountcy over all of western Tibet. The boundaries secure, reform and reconstruction were possible at home.

Justice soon became synonymous with his name: no one was above the law, friends definitely included. Pandit Jonaraja says in his *Rajatarangini*:

> Though the king was kindhearted, yet for the sake of his people he would not forgive even his son or minister or a friend if he were guilty.

Even a great favourite of the king, Mir Yahya, was not allowed to escape the retribution of the law. He was executed for killing his wife in a drunken fit. Solomon-style stories soon began to circulate around the king. A Brahmin of the Wular Lake area accidentally discovered his stolen cow with a man living in the Maraj district, and the dispute was brought to the king. He threw some water vegetables in front of the cow, now with a calf beside her. The cow ate the vegetables; the calf rejected them. Judgement delivered: the cow had indeed been stolen as the vegetables were from Wular Lake.

Architecture, crafts, trade, the arts—particularly music—flourished. The staging of plays, also banned by the bigots, returned. Zainul Abidin's love and patronage of music became so famous that the Raja of Gwalior sent him books on the subject. The first roads with stone pavings were constructed, as well as the first wooden bridge across the Jhelum in Srinagar, known to this day as the Zainalkadal. Srivara, the court-historian, notes that learning flourished to such an extent that:

> Even women, cooks and porters became poets . . .

Cooks and porters were astonishing enough to Srivara, but women! Clearly the man had not expected to see so much progress in one lifetime. The historian informs us:

> If the king be a sea of learning and partial to merit, the people too become so . . . (he) built extensive lodging houses for students and voices studying logic and grammar arose from these dwellings. The king helped the students by providing teachers, books, houses, food and money and he extended the limits of learning in all branches. . .

Even if we discount the possible excesses of a court-historian, there is a great deal to applaud. The growing legend got a major boost from the simplicity of the king's lifestyle; abnegation is always dear to the Indian heart. He refused to touch the state treasury for his personal needs, his income emanating from a copper mine he owned. It was a character profile sufficient to make Kashmir swoon.

But the transition from good to great, from Zainul Abidin to Bud Shah, was because of decisions of genius, decisions which affected life for generations to come, which changed existing equations and influenced the nature and quality of human life long after the king who took them had passed away. Decisions which were made because they were right, and not because they added to or subtracted from the balance sheet of popularity.

Zainul Abidin began his fifty-year reign on a principle which was to be his consistent guide till he died: he was ruler of Kashmir, not just of Kashmiri Muslims. The state took a firm decision not to interfere with the faith of its citizens. One of the first policies he adopted was to completely reverse the process of state-sponsored proselytization. In fact, in what is probably a unique instance of its kind, there was state-sponsored reconversion. A Brahmin, Pandit Shriya Bhatt, was appointed officer in charge of expansion of Hinduism in the Valley. Emissaries were sent to persuade Hindus in exile to return. To give meaning to the promise, Zainul Abidin abolished *jiziya*, the cremation tax, and banned cow slaughter. The Sultan personally visited Hindu shrines and places of pilgrimages like Kausar Nag, Naubandana Tirath, and the famous Amarnath. For five days a year he donned the robes of a mendicant and fed devotees during the festivals of Nagayatra and Ganachakra.

As is common enough in all cultures, the most important festivals tend to adapt and absorb a new religion; Eastron, by such mutation, becomes Easter. One of the most beautiful festivals of Kashmir was known simply as the Festival of Flowers: those nine days of the month of *Chaitra* (corresponding to March) were aptly named. Anyone who has been to Kashmir in spring, when the hibernating earth shrugs off its blanket of snow and bursts into flower, the colours flaming across the hillsides and gently undulating green, the brooks rippling into soft song as the clear and sparkling water of melting snow begins its journey towards the great rivers of Punjab, will not seek an explanation for this annual celebration: it is a natural burst of joy, a harmony borrowed from nature. It is part of the perverse mentality of bigots that they insist on making joy a very specific target. Perhaps they are terrified of laughter. For twenty years the zealots had killed this celebration of joy. Zainul Abidin resurrected it. And if in *Chaitra* Kashmir bowed before the rose, then in September–October, on the thirteenth day of the bright moon in the month of *Bhadra*, Kashmir paid homage to the river. Small, pretty earthen lamps called *diyas* would be filled with *ghee*, lit and set afloat on the Jhelum as dusk settled over the Valley, and milk and sweetcakes would be offered to the river. This was the day the Vitasta (the Jhelum) was born; the birthday was celebrated by the Festival of the Lamps. Zainul Abidin gave the stamp of royal approval to the return of tradition by his personal participation.

This was not just tokenism. The Sultan understood the meaning of emotional involvement in the state. He supplemented this with more substantial benefits for the Hindus. Pandits were inducted into the bureaucracy, on one condition—they had to learn Persian, the state language. There was no compromise on this, but that was hardly any price. As his rule matured, the encouragement of learning rose to fresh heights. Historians like Jonaraja and Srivara were given state patronage as much as Persian and Arabic scholars like Maulana Kabir (the Sultan's childhood tutor), Mulla Hafiz Baghdadi, Mulla Jamaluddin and Qazi Mir Ali. His library acquired great renown and poets and musicians flocked to his court. Schools were established, and education once again became an investment in Kashmir's future.

Zainul Abidin was not merely just, but determined to be seen as just—particularly in sensitive matters of Hindu-Muslim relations. A story is still recalled of the case the Sultan could not solve. A holy ascetic from Mecca—a Saiyyid, moreover—murdered a sadhu in a fit of jealous anger. It was a delicate matter. The Saiyyid belonged to the Prophet's family; he commanded respect; and the jealousy had been caused by the sadhu's proximity to the Sultan. Zainul Abidin consulted both the maulvis and the pandits, and they agreed that the only legitimate retribution was death. But a politically fine-tuned Sultan hit upon a sensitive solution: instead of killing the man he killed his reputation. He ordered that the Saiyyid be seated on a donkey, facing the tail, his head shaved and his beard soaked in dirt, and paraded through the streets.

Zainul Abidin appreciated the nuance that he could easily lose the trust of the Muslims if he went overboard in the other direction, and was always extremely careful in his walk along the tightrope of equality. He may in fact have gone a trifle too far in restoring Sati, but the point was that the state had no right to interfere in religious practice. The generosity of the treasury was, however, extended to the popular institutions of faith. He built the Khanqah of Sheikh Hamadani and was as liberal in the construction of mosques as he was in the reconstruction of temples. The primary responsibility of the state was justice, equality and economic prosperity. Corruption in revenue collection was strictly curbed; law and order maintained; canals and bridges built; cities constructed; floating islands laid on the Dal Lake (which are still cultivated); while his more magnificent buildings echoed the influence of Taimur's glorious Samarqand, where Zainul Abidin had spent seven years of his childhood as a symbolic hostage of his father's allegiance to the lame conqueror. Music flourished: Mulla Jamil, Mulla Udi, Soma Bhatt and Srivara became famous. Of his three wives, two were daughters of the Hindu Raja of Jammu, and as it happened, all his four sons—Adam Khan, Haji Khan, Vasrath Khan and Behram Khan—had Hindu mothers; but he himself was a devout Muslim, and took pride in the title of Naib-e-Amir-ul-Momineen.

When he "went to Heaven on Friday the twelfth day of the moon in the month of *Jaishtha* (equivalent to 12 May 1470)" after five decades of a peace unknown to Kashmir in many lifetimes, writes Srivara:

> No one cooked his food on the day; no smoke arose from the houses; all were dumb with grief. They lamented and said the king was the greatest among all the sovereigns.

Jonaraja summed up the Sultan's life in memorable words:

> He possessed courage and a will to perform what was
> beyond the power of past kings, and what may be beyond
> the ability of future rulers.

Kashmir was not destined to have another like him. It is not the historian who decides which king is great; the people do that. Zainul Abidin became Bud Shah: The Great King. It was a name which soon acquired mythic proportions: labourers and boatmen began to use it to mark the beat of their labours in the belief that even its evocation would ease the pain of their strained muscles. Bud Shah's life and his rule were the distillation of that spirit called "Kashmiriyat," a culture of synthesis, understanding and humanism; and the history of the next five hundred and more years proved that Kashmir cannot be ruled except by this spirit.

5

Delhi Durbar: The End of Independence

Agar qahat-ur-rijal uftad
Az an seh mihr kamjui
Awwal Kumbu, dujum Afghan, siyum badzat Kashmiri.
Zeh Kumbu hila me ayad
Zeh Afghan kina me ayad
Zeh Kashmiri na me ayad bajuz anduh wa dilgiri.

This was the reputation of the Kashmiri at the barracks-level, and it was not a pretty sight. The song, popularized by the Mughal armies sent by the Emperor Akbar, is caustic. Even if you are suffering, it says, from widespread famine, do not expect any help from three people: the Kumbus, who will cheat you by their cunning; the Afghans, who will only spite you; and the Kashmiris—who will only narrate their own sob stories in response and end up trying to get something out of you rather than giving you anything. The first clash of cultures between Delhi and Kashmir only resulted in the former sneering at the latter, and the Kashmiri wishing nothing more than he be left alone. Very little has changed in five hundred years.

The psyche of the Kashmiris has always been isolationist; they wanted nothing from the rest of the world, and even less did they want to share what little they had. But you cannot protect your poverty-stricken Paradise for ever, and a closed mind is absolutely no defence against imperial ambitions in a changing world. The very geography which had once been isolationist Kashmir's biggest strength now became the enemy of its independence. The politics of an empire emanating from Delhi and spreading towards Afghanistan and Central Asia could hardly permit a little bowl of freedom at the crossroads of its rule. On 16 October 1586, the commander of the Mughal troops, Qasim Shah, finally entered Srinagar, proclaimed Akbar emperor of the land and the khutba was read in the name of the most powerful monarch India had seen since Ashoka.

Kashmir lost its independence that day, and was never to find it again.

But this did not happen without long years of self-destruction: it took more than a century of bad, indifferent or chequered Sultans to ruin the legacy of Bud Shah.

Great kings can do great things, but they cannot guarantee great successors. Unfortunately for Kashmir, Bud Shah's sons were particularly mediocre, and a historic opportunity to consolidate his achievements was frittered away. Even before he passed away, his three surviving sons, Adam, Haji and Behram, had launched their wars of succession. The victor of the decisive round was Haji Khan, thanks to the critical assistance of the treasurer of the state, Hassan Kachi. Sultan Haji quite literally gave himself up to wine, women and song—or, to use the more respectable words of Mahibul Hassan (*Kashmir Under the Sultans*, Iran Society, Calcutta, 1959):

> He spent most of his time in wine cups and in the society
> of women and musicians.

His principal counsellor was a barber, Purna. He died, after a year and ten months in power, when, totally drunk, he fell down the stairs and lost consciousness. His son and successor Hassan Shah proved more durable (1472–1484), but personal decadence seems to have become a family trait within two brief generations of Bud Shah's wise simplicity. Hassan Shah had 1,200 musicians and 1,200 concubines, and, doubtless, if anyone had bothered to count, 1,200 drinking cups too. A pattern of weakness had already formed. The consequences were predictable.

Inability created instability. Instability inspired intrigue. Intrigue led to invitations. Outsiders came ostensibly to help, but soon began to seek power for themselves. The nobles of the court converted their petty squabbles into serious conspiracies; the energy of the state was sapped from the top. Under Hassan Shah the clash between Prime Minister Malik Ahmad Yatu and the Commander-in-Chief Malik Tazi Bhatt became so corrosive that Yatu persuaded the Sultan to recall the Saiyyids, whose bigotry had caused such a serious breakdown in Muslim-Hindu relations, and who had been exiled by Bud Shah. True to form, the Saiyyids immediately rewarded Yatu by killing him and forcing the Sultan to appoint one of their own, Saiyyid Mirak Hasan Baihaqi, Prime Minister. Combined with the fact that the queen, Hayat Khatun, also belonged to the clan, power quickly shifted once again to this brotherhood. Pandit Srivara, who clearly has an interesting turn of phrase, notes in his *Rajatarangini* that during the Saiyyid phase:

Accepting bribes was considered a virtue, oppressing the subjects was regarded wisdom, and addiction to women was reckoned happiness.

It was an age of kingmakers, not kings. For more than half-a-century Kashmir suffered as unscrupulous puppeteers (particularly outsiders like the Saiyyids) trifled with the strings of power. Perhaps the symbol of the era was Muhammad Shah: he became sultan no less than four times in one life, in 1489, 1497, 1499 (marking his long spell; he was in power till 1526, the year Babar established Mughal power in Delhi), and then again between 1529 and 1534. He was seven years old when he was first plumped on to the throne by the Saiyyids to prevent the designated successor, Fateh Khan, a grandson of Bud Shah, from taking over. This could hardly go without challenge: Fateh Khan seized the throne after defeating the Saiyyids with the help of a Kashmiri alliance: they were to alternate again as the balance of power shifted. Muhammad Shah's secret of success lay not in the stars, but in something more banal: he did nothing. In fact he was popularly known as 'Sultan Do-Nothing'. It was a time when there were substantial rewards for doing nothing except keeping a sharp eye out for the main chance. There was a great deal which was rotten in the state of Kashmir. The heirs of Changez Khan and Taimur could hardly resist the temptation to collect such easy pickings.

Descended from the second son of Changez, Chaghtai Khan, and therefore also known as Chaghtais, the Mughals rose to great power under the genius of Taimur. By the time of Babar, their blood had intermingled with the Turks, whose lands they conquered: Babar's grandfather, Abu Said, Sultan of Khorasan between 1452 and 1467, came from Turkestan. Taimur, as we have noted, showed interest in Kashmir but passed on: the conqueror noted in his autobiography that he:

> made enquiries about the country and city of Kashmir from men who were acquainted with it, and from them I learnt that . . . Kashmir is an incomparable country . . .

The wooden buildings of Srinagar, he was told, were strong enough to last six or seven hundred years, and the river through the city was bridged at nearly thirty points. Taimur contented himself with tribute. Babar was not so easily satisfied.

Among those who had invited Babar to take on the Lodis in Delhi was the chief of the most powerful of the numerous Rajput clans, Rana Sangha of Mewar. It is ironic, but entirely in the tradition of Indian feudalism, that though Babar defeated the Lodis at the field of Panipat on 21 April 1526, the birth of the Mughal empire should really be marked at 16 March. 1527. That was the day Babar's hopelessly outnumbered forces tore apart a confederacy led by none other than Rana Sangha in the battle of Kanwaha near Agra. Within two years, Babar received another invitation. From Kashmir.

By 1529, the Magre and the Chak clans were involved in a bitter struggle, and when Abdal Magre asked for help, Babar readily responded. In their first excursion, the Mughals contented themselves with ransom and tribute—though they did record that they were leaving reluctantly. Babar died in 1530, and was succeeded by his eldest son Humayun. His brother Kamran was governor of Punjab, and he sent a punitive expedition to Kashmir in October–November 1531 which preferred to return to Lahore rather than risk winter in a blocked Valley. (The Kashmir army offered no resistance whatsoever, the soldiers simply shutting themselves up in their forts, allowing the Mughal cavalry unimpeded access.) In 1533 another Mughal force, of 4,000 horse, entered the Valley, sent by Sultan Said Khan of Kashgar, once again slicing through non-existent opposition. The importance of this last campaign lay in the fact that it was led successfully by a man who was to play a significant part in the affairs of Kashmir, Mirza Haidar Dughlat Gurgan.

Born in Tashkent at the turn of the century, Mirza Haidar was a first cousin of Babar, their mothers being sisters. By 1540, Mughal fortunes had sunk to ruin in Delhi. The ambitious, and indeed capable, Afghan, Sher Shah Suri, had routed Humayun at Kanauj on 17 May 1540, driving the son of Babar into long and harried exile. Humayun's woes were compounded by the betrayal of both his brothers, Kamran and Askari; with his cousin's stock in desperate straits, Mirza Haidar showed loyalty uncharacteristic of prevalent feudalism. The Mirza even suggested that Humayun make Kashmir his operating base for the recovery of empire. It was excellent advice. Mirza Haidar, who had served Sultan Said Khan before, now entered Kashmir at the head of a Mughal force loyal to Humayun. However, it was a tawdry spectacle: a defeated and betrayed Humayun could provide Mirza Haidar with only 400 troops, including slaves. But the Mirza had something more valuable than troops: information. He knew the truth about the decay in Srinagar. He marched along the Pir Panjal route, up to Naoshera, 122 miles south-west of his goal, Srinagar. Here, more setbacks: his chief commanders, Khwaja Kalan and Sikandar Tupchi left him. But then Mirza Haidar recognized his enemy far better than he knew his friends. Taking the longer Poonch route for the excellent reason that it was unguarded, the Mirza reached Srinagar in October 1540 without having to bother about inflicting even a single serious blow in battle. The wisdom that had brought Mirza Haidar to the court of Kashmir did not desert him with success; he established his control, but he refrained from seizing the crown. He placed Nazuk Shah on the throne and with the help of the Magres, ran the administration for eleven years.

Delhi understood the Mirza's motivations better than Srinagar. Sher Shah despatched a strong force of 5,000 cavalry, along with infantry, under the command of Hussain Khan Sherwani and Adil Khan in support of the defeated claimant to the Kashmir throne, Kachi Chak. Mirza Haidar was completely outnumbered, mustering only 300 horse. It was a fairy-tale confrontation which acquired a fame reflected not just in the deser-vedly-famous history written by the Mirza himself, the *Tarikh-i-Rashidi,* but also in the *Akbarnama.* The Mirza outflanked and surprised the encamped Afghan force at Watanar, and in a furious battle threw them into disarray and flight. Kashmir, therefore, kept the Mughal hope alive for years after it had been demolished in Delhi.

Time, of course, was on the side of this hope. Humayun's fortunes were on the upswing again by 1545, with the recovery of Kabul. But the Mirza's were now in decline, and the fault was his own. The good sense of the early strategy had deserted him; he removed the facade and struck coins and had the *khutba* read in Humayun's name. This was sufficient to turn Kashmiri sentiment against him. Nor, despite his genuine scholarship and cultured tastes (music was a passion), did he prove a good ruler. Abul Fazl even accuses him of being too fond of music for the good of the state. But that was the least of his faults. As the pressures built up he fell into the familiar temptation of bigotry. He equated Islam with the majority Sunni sect, and was as harsh with apostates as idolaters. And he could not have angered Kashmir more than by his vindictiveness towards the much-loved Sufis. The Mirza even desecrated the tomb of Mir Shamsuddin Iraqi at Zadibal.

Mirza Haidar's fatal mistake was to run the state at the expense of "Kashmiriyat". The Kashmiris, so justly famous for their bitter inter-necine quarrels, quickly put their disputes aside and built a common front against the foreign usurpers. Even the Magre and Chak clans cooperated, if only briefly. A revolt by Kashmiri soldiers sparked off a general uprising, and an isolated Mirza Haidar was caught and killed on 19 November 1550. As the *Baharistan-i-Shahi* (the manuscript is in the India Office Library) notes:

What after all did he gain by pursuing a ruthless and oppressive communal policy, except that he accelerated his own downfall?

You could use that sentence in the context of the politics of 1990 and still find it relevant. But the question still needs an answer: if Kashmir is essential to the geopolitics of Delhi, as Mirza Haidar sensed and Akbar believed, then how does Delhi manage the apparent contradiction, of retaining both control of the state and the affection/support of the people? It was left to the great Emperor Akbar to show that this could be done. His legacy was peace and identification with the empire for more than a hundred years: a considerable achievement.

6

The End of Independence

The departure of the Mughal restored not merely Kashmiri rule but just about every Kashmiri vice as well. The Chaks seized control, but power slipped in and out of the hands of weak Sultans with seismic frequency, so that there is a great deal of (purposeless) confusion about who ruled for how long. Did the Sultan Habib Shah rule for one month, as the historian Suka says, or four years, as Firishta reports? There is no point wasting time over the answer. What is both touching and instructive is the inscription on the tomb of Sultan Habib Shah in the Mazar-i-Salatin at Srinagar:

> Dar ziarati rozai ajdadi khud Sultan Habib
> Dida wa guft yin jai shahan tang gardad anqarib;
> Safa o darwaza digar ba pahluyash fazud
> Ta az yin roza na gardad hech Shahi badnaseeb;
> Gahi tameere binat nav shamidam az Sarush
> Sali tarikhash Mazari Sani Sultan Habib.

(It means: Sultan Habib, visiting the graveyard where nis ancestors were buried, cast a sad look and said, 'Soon this place will be too narrow.')

The graveyard will soon be too narrow: that could be the common epitaph of the last Kashmiri kings of Kashmir.

As for the very last one: it is remarkable that when the last Kashmiri dynasty ended, it went neither with a bang nor a whimper, but with a song. It was the stuff of epics; even those who could care not a whit for either the first Kashmiri king or the last are still entranced with the haunting love-story of the prince and the lovely, legendary Zoon.

Yusuf Shah became Sultan at a young age, when his father, Ali Shah, fell off his horse while playing polo and died. By inclination, however, he was a poet rather than a prince, and his songs in Kashmiri and Persian had already become extremely popular. He was at his happiest when wandering alone through the valleys and woods of his exquisite homeland; tradition credits him with the discovery of perhaps the most beautiful valley of them all, Gulmarg, that dazzling carpet of luminous green and heady pine stretching to the skies in summer; a stunning undulation of snow from peak to earth in winter. It was while on a solitary walk one day that Yusuf Shah heard a song in the air, a melody of sadness, of loneliness and grief, a *shikayat* (complaint) against a destiny which had crushed a young life. An entranced Yusuf Shah was drawn irresistibly towards that voice. And met Zoon.

Zoon was the child of peasants, born in a village called Chandrahar, situated amid the saffron fields of Pampur. She had learnt to recite the *Quran*; the family maulvi had also taught her some Persian. The child flowered into a beautiful and talented woman, but the kindness of fortune came to an abrupt end very quickly. The man her parents married her to proved to be an idiot (literally); she divorced him and returned home. If there was anything worse than widowhood for a woman of those times, it was divorce; a woman without a family of her own became rootless, an unnatural burden on her parents, a reject in society. For a talented person like Zoon, the tragedy held a special anguish, which she expressed in the songs she wrote, and in the music she composed for these songs. When Yusuf Shah heard her, he was quite swept off his feet. He made Zoon his queen, and she became known as Habba Khatoon, or the Lady of Love. But of course romance would never be complete without a final tragic twist. Zoon had to lose her prince and her happiness; her fate was separation and loneliness. The fortunes of war carried Yusuf Shah away from her—for ever.

The young Sultan had not inherited the crown after his father's accident without a struggle; his uncle Abdal Chak went to war and only after defeating and killing him in the battle of Nawhatta could Yusuf proclaim himself Sultan Nasiruddin Muhammad Yusuf Badshah Ghazi. However, there remained other ambitions to deal with, and Yusuf Shah's inclinations towards poetry in preference to affairs of state proved to be a costly indulgence. Within months of his accession he was challenged and defeated by Saiyyid Mubarak Baihaqi—the last flicker of a once devastating fire. But if Yusuf Shah was indolent, Baihaqi was incompetent. In a month-and-a-half he had been replaced by Lohar Chak.

Proverb, and observation, credit the spider with issuing an invitation to the fly. History is replete with the opposite. And it was a very large spider indeed who was waiting at the imperial fortress-city of Fatehpur Sikri: the Emperor Akbar.

Yusuf Shah, unable to reconcile himself to defeat, presented himself before the emperor on 3 January 1580. He wanted help. It was a fatal mistake, because he got it. Akbar ordered Raja Man Singh and Mirza Yusuf Khan to march to Kashmir. By the time they reached Lahore, the facts of life had begun to sink into Yusuf Shah. Offered a deal by a frightened Lohar Chak, Yusuf Shah doublecrossed the Mughals and slipped away. The deal was this: Yusuf Shah could return to the throne on condition he came without Mughal troops. Now Yusuf Shah discovered that the facts of life were even more complicated than he had imagined them to be at Lahore. Lohar Chak turned out to be even better at betrayal than him; he was a triplecrosser. Having lured Yusuf Shah away from the Mughals, he gave battle to the person he had just made a deal with. But Yusuf Shah, even minus the Mughals, was superior to Lohar Chak, winning the day on 8 November 1580 at Sopore. Yusuf Shah did not let his artistic temperament interfere with his politics: Lohar Chak's eyes were gouged out, and he was thrown into prison.

Not surprisingly, the Emperor Akbar did not take too kindly to deception. After returning from Kabul in 1581, he turned his attention to Kashmir. He opened with a political mission to the court of Yusuf Shah. Yusuf Shah was by this time a man without illusions: he kissed the emperor's letter, placed it reverently on his turban and acknowledged the paramountcy of the Mughal lord. Many of the Kashmiri nobles, still clinging to their sentiments of independence, did not approve, but they were ignored. Akbar realized, however, that he had been cheated by this display of fealty. By 1585 he had provoked another confrontation; this time, control was the issue, not vague loyalty. A 5,000-strong Mughal force under the command of Raja Bhagwan Das, Mirza Shah Rukh and Shah Quli Mahram left for Kashmir on 20 December 1585, taking the one road generally open in winter, a track called Pakhli in Hazara, via Muzaffarabad. Battle was joined at Kuarmast Pass. That familiar ally, winter, prevented a decisive Mughal victory, but the terms of the truce were heavily loaded against Kashmir: Yusuf Shah had to enter the imperial camp at Buliyasa on 14 February 1586 and was presented before the emperor by Raja Bhagwan Das on 28 March to accept Mughal sovereignty. That day marked the end of Kashmir's independence. In Srinagar, the *khutba* was read and coins issued in Akbar's name, the two great symbols of sovereignty. By the terms of the peace treaty, the departments of mint, hunting and saffron and shawl production became an imperial monopoly, thereby locking political control with an economic key. Yusuf Shah was made a prisoner of Raja Todar Mal, and given his liberty only after Mughal rule had stabilized in Kashmir: he was pensioned off with a modest *jagir* in Bihar with a status of commander of 500 horse, but with an annual income of only 3,600 rupees.

In the meantime, the Mughals set about the task of consolidation with a firm and ruthless hand. Kashmir was much more than a "charming garden" for the Emperor of Hindustan: Akbar was securing his borders, as well as signalling that the fate of Humayun was not going to be repeated. Kashmir provided direct access to Afghanistan, and it was imperative that it come under the subjugation of the Mughal empire. Reasons of state were far more important in this perspective than something so ephemeral as Kashmiri sentiment. The last stubborn fragment of this sentiment rallied around Yusuf Shah's son, Yaqub Khan, and in a burst of enthusiasm announced the repudiation of the treaty of 14 February. Akbar did not need another excuse. On 28 June 1586, Qasim Khan Mir Bahr left with a large army and specific orders to annex Kashmir. He crossed Bhimbar on 1 September; defeated Yaqub Khan at Hastivanj on 10 October, and by 16 October Srinagar had become a Mughal cantonment. No Kashmiri was to rule this "charmed garden" till another October—precisely 361 years later, when Sheikh Mohammad Abdullah took charge of the state after the invasion by Pakistan-supported raiders in October 1947.

Akbar had sent his army to rule, but the guidelines he laid down were significant: "to practise enlightenment, justice, non-sufferance of wickedness, and the accepting of apologies and the chastisement of evil."

However, the first priority of armies is order, not law; and as for practising enlightenment, it generally ends up rather low on the list of priorities. Qasim Khan knew his primary responsibility was to smash all potential for any insurrection in the name of nationalism, and those tribes with a reputation for martial ability paid a price in direct proportion to their fame. In this phase, all Kashmiris were kept out of the administration as the state was taught the full meaning of the power of imperial India. Pacification was not easy, and it was not before the spring of 1887, and the arrival of reinforcements under the command of Mirza Yusuf Khan Rizvi, that Yaqub Khan finally surrendered.

The superiority of arms having been established, Akbar now offered the hand of peace. There was no revenge. Every opponent, every tribal chief, was wooed and won. Yaqub Khan was sent to join his father and given the latter's *jagir* upon Yusuf Shah's death. The deliberate harshness of Qasim Khan was replaced by the equally deliberate benevolence of Mirza Yusuf Khan Rizvi, who remained governor till 1590 and in his three years introduced the enormous benefits of stable and organized Mughal administration: in Sir Jadunath Sarkar's able description, this consisted of:

- The uniform administrative type throughout the Subas;

- One official language;

- One uniform system of coinage;

- An all-India cadre of higher public services, the officers being transferred from province to province every three or four years;

- The frequent march of large armies from province to province;

- Deputation of inspecting officers from the central capital.

Kashmir suddenly became part of a larger world. And the peace of this world of empire would last for more than a century-and-a-half: that was the extraordinary legacy of the Emperor Akbar.

He paid his first visit as soon as Kashmir was calm, in 1589. He left for the Valley on 27 April, reached Bhimbar on 19 May, crossed the Pir Panjal, and entered the palace of his governor Mirza Yusuf Khan at precisely twenty-five minutes past eight on the morning of 5 June. It was clearly a good thing that the emperor travelled, for roads had to precede him. Three thousand stone-cutters, miners for blasting rock and diggers went ahead to smooth the way for such august royalty. But Jalaluddin Akbar was not a monarch lost in the trappings of his own comfort; he also ensured a better life for the people. A standard land revenue rate brought stability and growth to the largely agricultural economy. But the great hallmark of the era was his social legislation and policy. Akbar abolished the hated *jiziya* tax on Hindus, and set about restoring equality to all faiths. The historian Suka says:

> In every house a Brahman who maintained his caste used to pay an annual tribute of 40 panas to the king. The good Brahmans therefore had left the country, those of the middle class became shameless, and the low Brahmans gave up their caste ... Now when Jalaluddin learnt of the condition of the Brahmans, he repealed the practice of levying fines on them ...

Kashmiri nationalism was fine, but could not in the end prevail over what the Mughal empire had to offer: economic growth; sound administration; respect for the minorities. As the *Ain-i-Akbari* concluded, when the historians gathered to pass judgement: "Although Kashmir is populous, and money scarce, yet a thief or a beggar is scarcely known here." Even by the time of Akbar's first visit, the mood of the people had begun to change in favour of the Mughal. Suka, an eyewitness, records:

> Jalaluddin came to see the kingdom of Kashmir, adorned with saffron, walnut, fruits and flowers. The wives of the citizens hastened to see the king. One woman pointed out the king to her beloved female friend, who was anxious to see him; another exclaimed with a flutter that she had seen the leader of the armies; another woman admonished her child who wanted to breastfeed, covered her breast and went to look at the king. After the people of Kashmir had seen the sovereign, continuous festivity was held in every house.

Kashmir may have lost her independence, but, so far, it had been a good bargain.

7

The Politics of Stability

Given the fact that it is still providing mileage four centuries later, perhaps no contribution that the Emperor Akbar made to Kashmir was more lasting than one thought: it was he who suggested that some of the boats plying the Dal Lake could be made residential. Thus was born the houseboat. Of course, tourism was only the pleasure of kings in those days, rather than a source of popular income, but shawl manufacture was a vital industry. During his six weeks in the Valley, the emperor personally ordered that special facilities be given for the production and marketing of this exquisite Kashmiri art. We can already notice the pattern emerging: after the successful application of the stick, a very generous distribution of carrots. And an extremely careful identification with local sentiment.

Akbar's second visit to Kashmir was only half as long as the first, just three weeks, beginning from 7 October 1592. Diwali fell during this time, and the emperor took the lead in the festivities. On his orders, the boats on the Jhelum, the banks of the river, and all the rooftops were illuminated. He also used the visit to further strengthen ties through matrimonial alliances. He himself took the hand of the daughter of his old foe, Shams Chak, while the daughters of Mubarak Khan Chak as well as Husain Chak were married to his son, Salim. The accent during this visit was clearly on a holiday, although nothing that a king does, either in work or in play, is without its significance. Even when he paused on his way to enjoy the saffron blossoms of Pampur, he was also paying homage to a traditional source of local pride. These were gestures addressed to the emotions and they found a welcome response.

Abul Fazl mentions a rather incredible reason for the brevity of this imperial visit to Kashmir: the severe cold and the high price of food. The first is understandable; but, notwithstanding the fact that the quality and quantity of Akbar's kitchen were justly famous, an Emperor of Hindustan complaining about rising prices does seem an exaggeration. On the other hand, if this be true, spare a thought for the common man that winter. But then, the history of that period says that Kashmir was never too far away from famine.

In 1990, the famous economist Dr Amartya Sen, along with co-author Jean Derze, expanded his thesis on the causes of famine into a book, *Hunger and Public Action* (Clarendon Press, London). Famine, they argued, was not a necessary consequence of a fall in food production; it was caused, instead, by imbalances in income levels. Taking the evidence from twentieth century famines, the authors pointed out that the overall food production, whether in Bengal in 1943 or Ethiopia in 1973 or Bangladesh in 1974, was virtually the same as in previous years. Famine occurred either when the income level of a section of the people fell to a point where they could not purchase food, or when food prices shot up thanks to the sudden increase in demand from the privileged sections of the population. Food was actually exported from Wollo in Ethiopia during 1973. The answer, therefore, said the authors, was not just dumping free food, but pumping cash into the starving economy. Dr Amartya Sen and Jean Derze could have used the example of how famine was fought in 1597 in Kashmir.

That was the year of the third and last visit by Akbar to the Valley, and we have more than one account of this visit thanks to the presence, in the emperor's retinue, of Father Jerome Xavier. A Jesuit who served with the Portuguese mission in India, Father Xavier had worked in Bassein, Cochin and Goa before he reached the Mughal court around 1594–95 with no less an ambition than to convert the great emperor himself. He did not manage to inject Christianity into the highest levels of power, but he received a generous welcome and stayed on for twenty-three years as an important member of the Mughal court. He has left a description of this visit.

The timing of Akbar's journey was determined by chance. An accidental fire on the day of Easter in 1597 had destroyed the palace in Lahore, where the court had moved from Fatehpur Sikri. Where better to wait out the reconstruction than in a Kashmir summer? But instead of pleasure Akbar found a severe famine. A letter sent by Father Xavier to Antwerp in 1605 narrates the extent of the misery:

> Many mothers were rendered destitute, and having no means of nourishing their children exposed them for sale in the public places of the city. Moved to compassion by their pitiable sight, the Father bought many of these little ones, who, soon after receiving baptism, yielded up their spirits to their creator.

The governor, Muhammad Quli Khan Turkoman, had proved an effective ruler since his appointment in 1593. Undeterred by either previous defeat or their new relationship with the emperor through marriage, the Chaks had greeted Quli Khan with yet another revolt. It was quickly quelled, and Quli Khan did not allow any undue reverence to prevent him from beheading the emperor's latest father-in-law, Shams Chak. True to established policy, Quli Khan then concentrated on settling popular grievances. One of the major ones was the presence of Mughal troops within the city, and the inevitable harassment. Quli Khan shifted the army permanently to a new, fortified city, Nagar Nagar, on the slopes of the Hari Parbat hill, and made harassment of the citizenry into a cognizable offence.

Emperor Akbar met the challenge of famine in the city, by a set of measures which would have surely met the approval of Dr Amartya Sen. Rather than merely doling out free food, he created work at wages higher than existing rates. He ordered the construction of a massive wall around the Nagar Nagar cantonment, a project which alone provided work for many thousands. The memory of that experience is still part of the folklore of Kashmir; Sir Walter Lawrence in *The Valley of Kashmir*, (London, 1895) mentions that married women were given six annas a day and single women four annas. An inscription over the main gate of the wall reads:

Na kardeh hech kas begar anja
Tamame yaftand az makhzanash zar.

(No one, it proclaims proudly, was shanghaied into *begar*,
or forced labour, for this imperial project; each worker was
paid fully for his or her labour.)

Other public works—roads, canals, irrigation projects—were launched. Full employment was supplemented by the import of thousands of maunds of grain from Punjab. By the time the emperor left Srinagar, as winter approached, instead of famine there was festivity in the air: that year, the birth of the river was celebrated, and a good crop added to the cheer. As a gesture to the changed mood, the emperor held a durbar just prior to his departure. Mughal rule was never seriously to be disturbed again in Kashmir until it had fallen into fragments in Delhi. And then too it was not a Kashmiri who sought to overthrow the government of Delhi (where the Mughal capital had been shifted by Shah Jehan), but an Afghan.

The decent thing about peace and prosperity is that you can skip across about 150 years in a few sentences. Peace, of course, is profitable too. The revenue from Kashmir under Akbar's son Jahangir rose to 7,46,70,000 *dams*. Jahangir and Kashmir are now inextricably linked; his sheer love for the land and its people ensure that much. His memoirs are full of Kashmir; he wanted to die there, and would have done so if he had not been ordered by his doctors to return for better treatment to Delhi. He died on the way, on 7 November 1627. A Persian couplet by Tughara recalls the emperor's passion:

> *Az Shah-i-Jahangir dameh nazah chu justand*
> *Ba khawahish-i-dil guft ki Kashmir digar hech.*

> (When, it says, Jahangir was asked on his deathbed what his last wish was, he replied from his heart: Kashmir, and nothing else.)

Francois Bernier, the French physician and traveller who accompanied Aurangzeb on his sole visit to Kashmir (predictably, Aurangzeb tried to impose his puritanism, banning bare legs, opium cultivation and popular theatre; Kashmir simply ignored the edicts), describes a Kashmir at peace with itself in 1665:

> The Kashmiris are celebrated for wit, and considered much more intelligent than the Indians. In poetry and the sciences they are not inferior to the Persians. They are also very active and industrious. The workmanship of their *palkis*, bedsteads, inkstands, boxes, spoons and various other things are quite remarkable, and articles of their manufacture are in use in every part of the Indies.

Clearly, the export trade was flourishing; note too, that the Kashmiris were clearly identified as separate from the Indians. Bernier adds:

> But what may be considered peculiar to the Kashmiri, and the staple commodity, that which particularly promotes the trade of the country and fills it with wealth, is the prodigious quantity of shawls they manufacture, and which gives occupation to the little children . . .

The political equation with the rest of the subcontinent was bringing dividends in the shape of a huge market for this artistry.

More than a century of this rising prosperity ended, alas, with the death of Aurangzeb and the sensational degeneration of Mughal rule that followed. The half century of Aurangzeb, last of the six great Mughals, has, it is true, been brutalized by the bias of partisan historians, but even the admirers of Aurangzeb would not deny that his span in power was an object lesson in dismantling of empire. At the core of this was the reversal of Akbar's policies, faithfully pursued by Akbar's son, Jahangir and grandson Shah Jehan. (It is interesting that both Jahangir and Shah Jehan had Hindu mothers.) Social conflict on sectarian lines, and not restricted to merely the Hindu-Muslim divide, was encouraged rather than ameliorated; Kashmir in particular was to suffer the emperor's pronounced animosity towards Shias. There is as much to learn about India, the unity of its people, and the nature of the polity it needs for harmony, from the forty-nine years of Aurangzeb as the equally long rule of Akbar. What had seemed, and indeed was, impregnable for a century-and-a-half, could not survive the critical mistakes of Aurangzeb. Worse, Aurangzeb was followed by a succession of weak kings, and when Delhi became fragile, confused or simply lost in bitter internecine conflicts for power, a province like Kashmir became the plaything for governors released from much sense of responsibility. It was too much to expect the empire to retain Kashmir; within forty-six years of the death of Aurangzeb, in 1753, a general of Ahmad Shah Abdali, Ishaq Aqqasi, had planted the Afghan standard on the rampants of Akbar's citadel on Hari Parbat.

In these forty-six years, the throne of Delhi was occupied by no less than seven emperors, and this becomes even more pathetic if we remove Muhammad Shah from the list. Muhammad Shah lasted for twenty-nine of these forty-six years, and not because of strength in the mould of his famous predecessors, but precisely because he was weak, a permanent hostage to shifting alliances which ruled in exchange for letting him reign. Nicknamed 'Rangeela', or The Colourful, Muhammad Shah was a joke with an extraordinary fate line. The success of his ineptitude was truly phenomenal.

Kashmir saw fifty-seven governors and deputy governors in these forty-six years, as each kingmaker in Delhi added his share to the building chaos. The misrule of governors like Jafar Khan (1707–1709) or Saadat Khan (1713–1717) only compounded the hardships when nature withdrew her benevolence, and famine or flood inflicted its share of misery. If Mughal power had taken firm root thanks to the wise management of famine, it also withered under the strain of three major famines, in 1724, 1735 and 1746, whose horrors the administration was unable to check. Continuous political instability also invited inter-religious and inter-clan wars. The name of Mahtabi Khan, also known as Mulla Abdun Nabi, made chief theologian of Kashmir by Bahadur Shah, still raises a shudder or two. Hindus and Shias were this bigot's targets: the former were forbidden to practise any of their religious rites, wear *tikas* or turbans, ride horses or even wear clean clothes. By 1720, there was a Hindu-Shia revolt against Mahtabi Khan; he was seized and killed on 12 September. But his son, Mulla Sharafuddin, took his revenge, and the Shia locality of Zadibal was turned into ashes. Delhi did not wake up until Abdur Samad Khan reached Srinagar next year at the head of a special force, defeated Sharafuddin, and hanged the Mulla and fifty of his chief lieutenants on gallows erected along the one-mile road between Naid Kadal and Khwaja Yarbal in Srinagar. Kashmiri bards sang in praise of Samad:

> *Haqqa! av Samad phutran zin*
> *Na rud kuni Sharaf na rud kuni din.*

(When the just Samad came swiftly on his horse, there neither remained the leader nor his bigoted faith; the couplet has pun on Sharafuddin's name, which meant leader of the faith.)

But of course there was a shortage of Samads as the Mughals collapsed. However, even the disasters of these forty-six years were to prove nothing compared to the sixty-seven years of Afghan oppression that followed as Abdali's armies scissored Kashmir out of the Mughal empire and tucked it into their own, after Abdullah Khan Ishaq Aqqasi defeated a Kashmir-Mughal force under Abdul Qasim at Shopian, on the Pir Panjal Pass, in a fifteen-day battle. The Afghans wrought relentless havoc: that memory still haunts the Valley. This terrible chapter in Kashmir's history is distilled in a moving couplet:

> *Pursidan az kharabiye gulshan zi baghban*
> *Afghan kashid guft ki Afghan kharab kard.*

(I asked, says the poet, who laid waste this garden? With a deep sigh he replied: 'It was the Afghan.')

8

Kabul and Lahore: A Bitter Century

The *Ain-i-Akbari* has a very interesting passage on the origins of the Afghans:

> Eleven languages are spoken in this province (the Sarkar of Kabul), each nationality using its own, viz., Turkish, Mughal, Persian, Hindi, Afghan, Pushtu, Parachi, Geberi, Bereki, Lamghani and Arabic. The chief tribes are the Hazarahs and Afghans. The Hazarahs are the descendants of the Chaghtai army, sent by Manku Khan to the assistance of Hulaku Khan . . . They are divided into factions, each covetous of what they can obtain, deceptive in their common intercourse, and their conventions of amity savour of the wolf.

> The Afghans consider themselves the descendants of the Israelites. They assert that their remote progenitor, named *Afghan,* had three sons, viz., Saraban . . . Ghurghusht . . . Batan . . . It is said that Mast Ali, whom the Afghans call Mati, had illicit intercourse with one of the daughters of Batan. When the results of this clandestine intimacy were about to become manifest, he preserved her reputation by marriage, and three sons were born to him., viz., Ghilzai ('ghil' meaning illicit, and 'zai' birth), Lodi and Sarwani.

> Some assert the Afghans to be Copts, and that when the Israelites came to Egypt from Jerusalem, this people passed into Hindustan. The tradition is too long to be condensed within narrow limits, but it is noticed in passing as a fanciful digression.

A lost tribe of Jews, or wandering Copts, or whatever else might have been the truth about their antecedents, the continually squabbling tribes living amid the harsh mountains of the Hindu Kush and the Sulaiman

Range rediscovered themselves in the middle of the eighteenth century, thanks to yet another star of the kind which, when it appears, dominates the firmament as long as it lasts. His name was Ahmad Shah Abdali. A general in the armies of Nadir Shah, the Persian conqueror who devastated Delhi just thirty-one years after the death of Aurangzeb, he left service after his master was assassinated (on 2 June 1747) to return to his own country, Afghanistan.

Ambition is a self-feeding virtue. Having first established control over Kabul and unified his own country, Abdali turned his eyes eastwards. By 1752, Abdali had brought Punjab under his sway; Kashmir was now a matter of time—about a year, in fact. For sixty-six years after 1753, five Afghan governors ruled Kashmir in the name of the Abdali dynasty. Sparse patches of relief apart it was one long story of misery; mothers in the Valley still frighten their children with stories of Afghan brutality. William Moorcraft, who was one of the first British agent-explorers in the region and visited the Valley just after the end of Pathan rule in 1819, writes in *Travels in the Himalayan Provinces of Hindustan and Punjab, in Ladakh and Kashmir* (London, 1841):

> Everywhere the people are in the most abject condition. Not more than about one-sixteenth of the cultivable surface is in cultivation, and the inhabitants, starving at home, are driven in great numbers to the plains of Hindustan . . . the beauty of the scenery ill-harmonised with the appearance of the peasantry.

The Srinagar whose lofty houses were the envy of monarchs was now

> a confused mass of ill-favoured buildings, forming a complicated labyrinth of narrow and dirty lanes and having a small gutter in the centre, full of filth, banked up on each side by a border of mire. The houses are mostly in a neglected and ruinous condition with broken doors or no doors at all, with windows stopped with boards, paper or rags . . . all a striking picture of wretchedness and decay.

The simple fact of eighteenth century politics was that he who seized Punjab was going to control Kashmir. By the turn of the nineteenth century Punjab had fallen to a new power: the Sikhs, striking out under the leadership of the charismatic, one- eyed, illiterate, courageous, superstitious, generous, military genius, Maharaja Ranjit Singh. He was only twelve when he succeeded his father, Mahan Singh, as leader of the

Sukarchakia *misl*, but by 1799 Ranjit Singh had taken possession of both the great cities of Punjab, Lahore and Amritsar—the first by negotiation with the weakening Afghans, and the second by military arms. In a very short period a Sikh empire had found space between the Afghans in the west and the first conquerors of Delhi to come from the east, the British.

The *Angrez* had started as traders in Madras, and with superb opportunism financed, fought and cheated their way towards the control of most of India. The Company's sweep, with its epicentre at Plassey (the critical battle won by Robert Clive in 1757) had moved inexorably to absorb Patna, Allahabad, Varanasi and Awadh before the armies of Lord Lake smashed the Marathas under Scindia thereby clearing the road to Delhi. By 1803 the hapless Mughal emperor had been confined to a fort he could barely call his own, and the British had replaced the Marathas as the paramount power of the north. For the moment, British ambition, perhaps exhausted by its own phenomenal burst of energy, paused east of the river Sutlej. From this point to the Karakoram became the range of Maharaja Ranjit Singh's power, and the equation was formalized in the treaty of friendship signed between the Sikhs and the British in Amritsar in 1809.

For the British another worry had begun to loom, as a distant horizon began to approach at a disturbing pace. Napoleon had already reconstructed the map of Europe, and when he entered into an alliance with Persia, suddenly the prospect of a French expedition to India through the land route became credible. Charles Metcalfe went to Ranjit Singh, and Elphinstone to Kabul, both on diplomatic missions to shore up relations with the two buffer states between the Franco-Persian alliance and the British Raj. The British resumed their interest in Punjab soon after the French threat faded, but as long as Ranjit Singh was alive they had to keep their natural greed in check. Their perception of a potential threat from across the ranges was, however, to play a significant part in their Kashmir policy in that period.

Kashmir fell to Ranjit Singh in 1819, with not a little help from the Kashmiris. The last Afghan governor, Sardar Mohammad Azim Khan, began his tenure in the midst of that familiar consequence of misrule, famine. Azim Khan appointed Pandit Sahaz Ram Sapru as his Dewan, Pandit Hara Dass as his Chief Secretary, and Pandits Birbal Dhar, Mirza Dhar and Sukh Ram Safaya as his principal revenue collectors. The famine was the culmination of six years of poor crops, with inevitable loss to the state exchequer. A bad ruler blames his tax collectors. Pandit Birbal Dhar, a particular target of Afghan wrath, decided that the moment had come to ask the Lahore court to intervene.

He escaped, along with his son, and reached the palace of the Raja of Jammu, Gulab Singh, whose brother, Raja Dhyan Singh was Ranjit Singh's Prime Minister, and who arranged an audience with the maharaja. Ranjit Singh did not need much persuasion. The climate was extremely favourable for a takeover; with largescale popular discontent, and the administration in total disarray. Azim Khan himself had disappeared to Kabul, leaving the government to his brother Jabbar Khan and the treasury (with more than one crore in cash) to Pandit Sahaz Ram Sapru. The Sikhs sent a force of 30,000 led by the maharaja's heir Kharrak Singh and his best generals—Sardar Hari Singh Nalwa, Sardar Jwala Singh and Dewan Misr Chand—in command. They were joined by Gulab Singh at Jammu and took the Mughal route, through Bhimbhar, Rajouri and the Durhal Pass. The Pathans gave battle at Shopian, and were routed by the second day: on 15 June 1819, sixty-seven years of Afghan rule finally, and mercifully, came to an end.

It also drew the curtain on five centuries of Muslim rule. But it would be quite inaccurate to suggest that this was a consequence of a Hindu-Sikh conspiracy: Pandit Birbal Dhar was reflecting Kashmir's anger, not just the anger of the Kashmiri Pandits. There is enough evidence for this. After his escape, his wife and young daughter-in-law took shelter in the house of a Muslim milkman, Quddus Gojri. Pandit Birbal Dhar, in fact, only managed to escape out of the Valley thanks to the assistance of the Maliks of Kulgam, Zulfiqar and Kamgar, who were the wardens of the Devasar Pass. It was a Kashmiri revolt against the brutal Afghans, not a Hindu revolt. Similarly, there was no communal dimension to treachery either: Birbal Dhar's family was betrayed by his own son-in-law, Munshi Trilok Chand: Birbal Dhar's wife committed suicide, his daughter-in-law was sent to Kabul, and Quddus Gojri was killed along with his family. There was little squeamishness in either friend or foe in the culture of the period. Maharaja Ranjit Singh detained Birbal Dhar's son, Kak Dhar, as hostage to ensure his father's fealty during the Sikh campaign. That might seem a bit harsh on the bearer of the invitation, but care is the first demand of realpolitik. When news of victory reached Maharaja Ranjit Singh's court in Lahore, Kak Dhar was bestowed robes of honour and appropriate compensation, while Lahore was illuminated for three days. His father Birbal Dhar returned to his old job as revenue collector.

But it did not take long for hopes to wither. Sir Francis Younghusband notes in *Kashmir*:

The Sikhs who succeeded the Afghans were not so bar-
barically cruel, but they were hard and tough masters.

It was probably difficult to be worse than the Afghans, but not for lack of
trying. Moreover, a virulent anti-Muslim communalism marked the
policies of the new dispensation. After the first governor Misr Dewan
Chand had completed his mopping-up operations and left, came Dewan
Moti Ram to give Muslims a taste of what it meant to be on the receiving
end of bigotry. One of Moti Ram's first decisions was an extraordinary
insult to the Muslim psyche: the Jama Masjid in Srinagar was shut down,
and the *aazaan* was forbidden. One overenthusiastic Sikh commander,
Phula Singh, actually trained his guns on the mosque of the revered Shah
Hamadan: he wanted to blow it up on the excuse that it was constructed
on a Hindu shrine. It was only the last-minute intervention of Pandit Birbal
Dhar which prevented this outrage. Numerous mosques were seized by
the state; cow-slaughter was made a crime punishable by death; and, for
good measure, a number of butchers were publicly hanged as a display
of intent. All this took place during the fourteen months of Moti Ram,
who has been called generally fair and kind-hearted by historians. His
successor, Sardar Hari Singh Nalwa, had no time for such niceties.
Nalwa's economic rape was matched only by his personal viciousness.
When Pandit Birbal Dhar could bear this no longer and protested, he was
dismissed from service and had his property confiscated. When the truth
finally reached Ranjit Singh, he sent Moti Ram and Birbal Dhar to mend
matters, but there was not much that they could do to reverse the broad
trend of policy.

For the peasantry, Sikh rule was synonymous with the hated *begar* and
exploitation of the worst kind. Famine was inevitable. During Ranjit
Singh's son Sher Singh's term, the famine became so severe that the
population of Kashmir plummeted from eight hundred thousand to two
hundred thousand, as a result of death or migration. Sher Singh confronted
this crisis by retiring to his private chambers and drinking. Ranjit Singh
was forced to recall his son. When his successor "Colonel" Mian Singh
reached Srinagar, he could not see a single lamp lit at night nor hear a
single cock crow at dawn.

Maharaja Ranjit Singh was in decline by now, both personally and
politically. His expeditions had overextended his resources, and his
soldiers were hungry in the outposts of empire. When the floodgates of
resentment broke with the maharaja's death in 1839, the colonies began
tottering. Colonel Mian Singh was killed in a mutiny on 17 April 1841;

order only began to get restored in 1842 when the Sikhs sent their first Muslim governor, Sheikh Ghulam Mohiuddin. One of his initial decisions was to reopen the gates of the Jama Masjid, closed since 1819; in a gesture of parity, he ordered repairs to the Shiva temple on Shankaracharya hill, and the construction of a new *lingam* there. State benevolence towards the Rishis, and to cultural and religious institutions, was restored; government grain was issued at controlled prices. But it was all too late: Sikh rule was fated to end soon. As the Sikh kingdom began to disintegrate, the loss of Kashmir was inevitable; it was only a question of when. A claimant was present and waiting. He was not a Kashmiri.

The Kashmiri spirit seemed to have collapsed under the burden of nearly a century of oppression, of slavery. Moorcraft reports the social conditions of this period:

> The murder of a native by a Sikh is punished by a fine to the government of from sixteen to twenty rupees, of which four rupees are paid to the family of the deceased if a Hindu, and two rupees if a Muhammadan.

He describes life in a village:

> The people of Sugam were almost in a savage state. The men were in general tall and robust; the women haggard and ill-looking. The houses were mostly constructed of small trees, coarsely dovetailed together and coated with rough plaster inside. A flat planking was laid over the top, resting on the walls, and above that a sloping roof constructed, open at the ends, the space being either filled with dry grass, or serving to give shelter to poultry. The interior was divided by partitions of wickerwork, plastered into three or four dirty small apartments.

Once famous for the absence of both, crime and beggary were now rampant in Kashmir. Poverty reduced even the traditional artist to an object of contempt. A saying acquired currency:

> *Sini muhima sutsal, rani muhima khandava.*

> (If you cannot find any vegetable to eat, at least you will get mallow; and if you cannot find anyone to marry at least you will get a shawl-weaver.)

There is a deeper sadness here: while the weaver starved, the industry, controlled by outsiders, flourished. The fame of the Kashmiri shawl, and the carpet, had long crossed the borders of the Valley, and become a present suitable for kings and queens. Colonel Mian Singh sent Maharaja Ranjit Singh a fine green carpet bedecked with pink and pearl dots that created an impression of blossoms and dew: when the maharaja saw it, he was so delighted that he rolled along it like a child. The weavers, Fazal Jan, Jabbar Khan and Kamal Ju, were rewarded with a pair of golden bracelets each. And surely the most famous wearer of the Kashmiri shawl was the pace-setting wife of Napoleon, Josephine. There is a fascinating story of how this shawl reached her. A blind man driven by wanderlust, Saiyyid Yahya, reached Kashmir at the time when Abdullah Khan was governor; when he left he was presented a shawl by Abdullah Khan. His next stop was Egypt, and he offered this shawl to the Khedive. When Napoleon reached Egypt, the Khedive offered the French conqueror this shawl along with other presents, and the emperor passed it on to his tempestuous wife who immediately made it high fashion in Paris.

By the nineteenth century, Kashmir had been ruled by all three centres of power in northern India: Delhi, Kabul and Lahore. It was now the turn of an immediate neighbour to preside over its fortunes.

9

He Who Wishes To Climb . . .

Dogirath is a Sanskrit word meaning two lakes. As the plains of Punjab rise towards the highlands of the north, we encounter a Rajput settlement around the waters of two lakes, the Mansar and the Siroinsar, which together give the people their name—the Dogras. They are believed to have moved here from Delhi and Awadh to defend India against the Greek invader, Alexander; and the centre of their colonization became the town of Jammu, the capital of the Dogra rulers. They also were feudatories of the Mughals, but the decline after Aurangzeb had whetted their ambitions too. During the thirty-one stable and wise years of Raja Ranjit Dev, who came to power in 1750, they carefully nurtured their fortunes through any alliance which served their interests: Ahmad Shah Abdali, for example, gave them a *jagir* in reward for help against Raja Sukh Jiwan. Ranjit Dev pushed his domains up to Sialkot in the west and the hill states of the east, and it was inevitable that he would keep an eye open northwards. In 1779 he sent an army across the Banihal Pass into Kashmir, but it was ambushed and defeated, and returned in disorder.

Ranjit Dev's son, Brij Raj, was unable to hold on to his father's achievements, and bought his peace with the growing power of the Sikhs with an annual tribute of Rs 50,000 to the Sukarchakia *misl* led by Mahan Singh. At least he displayed the merit of choosing the right master, because Mahan Singh's son Ranjit Singh was destined to control Punjab's fate for half a century. The Dogras entered Ranjit Singh's service—and the real dividends came a generation later, in the time of Gulab Singh, grandson of Surat Dev, the younger brother of Ranjit Dev.

Born in 1792, Gulab Singh joined Ranjit Singh's army in 1809 as the commander of a small unit. But his abilities took him quickly up the ladder, and a pleased maharaja eventually rewarded him with his family's traditional possessions in Jammu, with the hereditary title of Raja, under the overlordship of Lahore of course. The details of the self-destruction of the Sikhs after Ranjit Singh are too complicated to be dealt with here; what we need to note is that Gulab Singh was the only person to carve a state out of the ruins of the Sikh empire. And he did it by investing in the British rather than in his countrymen.

Gulab Singh supported the British at the two critical moments when their power could have been checked. The first was at the Battle of Sobraon on 10 February 1846, described by the English general Lord Gough, as the Waterloo of India; the second was in 1857. Lord Gough was clearly referring not only to the impact of the English victory over the Sikhs at Sobraon, but also to the margin; it was a very thin victory whose fortunes were finally dictated by those who stayed out of it—by prearrangement. Gulab Singh's neutrality tilted the wavering balance decisively in favour of the British; if he had entered the field on the side of the Sikh durbar, as he was committed to do, the British tide would have been stayed for the forseeable future. Even an author as favourably inclined to Gulab Singh as his biographer K.M. Pannikar concedes in *Founder of the Kashmir State* (Allen & Unwin, London, 1953):

> Where his interest required he did not hesitate to resort to tricks and strategems which would in ordinary life be considered dishonourable.

But it must be added that, unfortunate as it was, Gulab Singh's neutrality was still better than the behaviour of Sikh chieftains like Lal Singh and Tej Singh who betrayed their standard on the field of battle. Of the most powerful Sikh nobles, four—Patiala, Jind, Faridkot and Chachrauli, gave unstinted support to the English and were duly rewarded. Of the others—Nabha, Ladwa, Allowala, Malaudh, Thaneswar, Ropar, Kheri, Mani Majra, Shahabad, Sikri, Shamgarh, Buria and Anandpur—there were a number who preferred a perch on the fence.

It is axiomatic that British interest should have preceded British rule. If nothing else then the politics of Europe was sufficient to ensure a more than healthy interest in the passes of the Hindu Kush and the borders of Tsarist Russia, then advancing south, wresting Kazakhstan, Kirghizia, Tajikistan, Turkmenia, Uzbegistan, Armenia, Ajerbaizan, Georgia and the Caucasus from the rule or influence of the Persians. In 1774 Warren Hastings sent a mission to Tibet, whose political fortunes of course were linked to adjoining Kashmir. When the Valley fell to the Lahore durbar of the Sikhs, British interest quickened. Two 'travellers', Moorcraft and Trebeck, ostensibly on a mission to study the wool trade, reached Ladakh in 1820. They were agents of the Raj, and when they obtained their much-delayed audience with the ruler, used the opportunity to warn him about Sikh intentions and offered the British hand of support as a safeguard. They brought with them the specific suggestion of a British fort in Leh. Wisely, the 'generosity' was refused. But the Raj was not going to be put off so easily; it drew a line in the mountains beyond which it was not ready to allow any Indian ruler to travel. When Zorawar Singh, acting in the name of the Lahore durbar, took his Dogra troops into Tibet in 1841, frowns were immediately visible in Calcutta. The screw was applied on Lahore, and the pressure worked. Captain J. D. Cunningham was sent to supervise the withdrawal of Zorawar Singh's army, originally scheduled for 10 December 1841. However, this intervention was made irrelevant by the annihilation of the army by the Tibetan General Shatra's troops on 12 December: only twenty-five Dogra soldiers escaped the massacre.

The British eventually imposed their will on the region by the first settlement of Punjab through the Treaty of Amritsar in 1846. The boundary of Tibet was marked as the border of Lahore's ambitions. It was this treaty which rewarded Gulab Singh's support to the English cause by confirming him as the ruler of the new state of Jammu and Kashmir, along with Ladakh and Baltistan.

Gulab Singh's links with the British went back at least to 1841, when the British suffered their humiliating rout in their first Afghan war. By this time, the three Dogra brothers, Gulab Singh, Dhyan Singh (the Dewan) and Suchet Singh (a general) were the most powerful triumvirate in the Lahore durbar. When the British requested help for their besieged garrison at Jalalabad, the durbar responded positively, and Gulab Singh personally led the mission. There he ingratiated himself with a man destined to become famous in the history of Punjab, Henry Lawrence, later to be knighted. Two of the three Dogra brothers, however, became victims of court intrigue in 1842; only Gulab Singh, away in Jammu, survived the deadly tussle for power in a rudderless court. From there he watched the growing estrangement between the Sikhs and the English, and hedged his bets. When the inevitable war came, he politely refused the honour of leading the Sikh forces into battle. He was amply rewarded by his fair friends. One could do no better than to quote the brilliant work of scholarship by Khushwant Singh. *A History of the Sikhs* (Princeton, 1963):

> Gulab Singh was acceptable to the British because of his earlier negotiations with them and because he had prevented the Dogras from joining the Punjabis. From January 1846 Gulab Singh had been in communication with the Governor General through various agents. One of

his emissaries was a Bengali physician, Bansi Dhar Ghosh, who delivered a letter from his master to Lieutenant E. Lake (assistant agent to the Governor General) on January 15, 1846. The Dogra wanted to be early in his offer of collaboration. He wrote: 'He who wishes to climb the summit of a lofty mountain, must start at daybreak; should he delay, night may close over him ere he has gained the desire of his heart; the treasure which is buried in the depths of the mountain will become the prize of that man, who is the first to reach the summit.'

Early in February 1846 Gulab Singh sent a private emissary to Major Henry Lawrence, who had taken over the Governor General's agency from Broadfoot. It seems clear that an understanding was reached between the British and Gulab Singh before the Battle of Subraon. As stated in his letter of February 19, 1846, to the Secret Committee, Hardinge gave Gulab Singh an assurance that his interests would be given full consideration.

They were, by the Treaty of Amritsar, signed on 16 March 1846. Viscount Hardinge, recalling events a year later, put the matter succinctly:

It was necessary last March to weaken the Sikhs by depriving them of Kashmir. The distance between Kashmir and the Sutlej is 300 miles of very difficult mountainous country, quite impracticable for six months. To keep a British force 300 miles from any possibility of support would have been an undertaking that merited a straitwaistcoat and not a peerage.

Of the hill regions obtained from the Sikhs, the British kept only Kulu, Mandi, Nurpur and Kangra. They sold the rest. The Valley of Kashmir was sold to Gulab Singh for just seventy-five lakh rupees.

It was at this point that Gulab Singh made a seemingly minor but historically critical error: he spoke the truth. In a phrase with gushing gratitude to the British he described himself as a *zar kharid*: a slave bought by gold. The phrase would haunt Kashmiri sentiment for many generations after Gulab Singh was dead and gone.

The maharaja himself did not seem particularly disturbed about this sentiment; if anything, his main grouse seems to have been that he was overcharged, and his aim was clearly to recover the amount from the people within his own lifetime. Prithvi Nath Kaul Bamzai, in his substantial history of Kashmir, notes with some dismay that the maharaja would personally pounce at and pocket as little as a rupee if it was held out in front of him. In return, the donor received an audience. As for the British, having installed their puppet, they now attempted to place a resident puppeteer in the court, as was their practice elsewhere. Gulab Singh was fortunate in the loyalty of friends like Henry Lawrence, who protected him. Circumstances helped too. The second Anglo-Sikh war, in 1848, eased British pressure on him; but it was Gulab Singh's decisive support to the British during the nationalist revolt, when his troops fought against the Indians in the siege of Delhi, that made the Dogras a favourite of the British.

Equitable rule over a century might have softened the memory of the original British-Dogra insult to the Kashmiri psyche, but though there was some reform and creeping progress, the injustice and oppression which the people of the Valley had to bear in these hundred years far outweighed any marginal compensations. As the turbulence of the twentieth century swept across India, and the demand for freedom and self-rule became a stirring revolution under the leadership of Mohandas Karamchand Gandhi, Kashmir too began to rise against its insensitive monarchs. The tide of growing anger threw up a young man destined to dominate the mood and politics of his land for half a century: Sheikh Mohammad Abdullah. He would become, in October 1947, the first Kashmiri to rule in Srinagar since the conquest of the Mughals in 1589—after 358 years, to be precise.

But that too, alas, was only the beginning of another stormtossed chapter in the tempestuous history of Kashmir. Peace and Paradise had clearly not been made for each other.

Love, Politics and Other Tragedies

10

A Tide, Rising at His Feet

A Colonel came to me in great distress, asking for advice.
He had just come up the river from Baramulla to Srinagar,
a journey of three days. He was paying off his boat when
the boatman demanded Rs 500, the proper fare being Rs
3.8 (*three and a half rupees; eight annas being half a rupee
in the pre-decimal age*). On his asking the reason for
extortion, the boatman calmly told him that if he did not
pay up the Rs 500 he would let it be known far and wide
that the Colonel Sahib had been living with this woman
for three days in his boat during the journey up the river.

This luminous paragraph appears in the narrative written by the good
Reverend C.E. Tyndale Biscoe (M.A.) of life in the Valley circa 1890:
Kashmir In Sunlight And Shade. One might wonder what the headmaster
of the Mission School was doing tendering advice on such problems to
Colonels in a bachelor mood; clearly Victorian missionaries were not
totally Victorian. But there is much to be gleaned about life under
British-Dogra rule from such memoirs. The privileges of power were
many and varied:

As a matter of fact, the *dhobis* are on the whole a great
comfort, for they can turn out excellent work, and then
when you come to the price as compared with English
laundries it is marvellously cheap. Up to a year ago I paid
three rupees only for one hundred garments washed — i.e.
from a pocket-handkerchief to a bedsheet.

The sahibs were obviously allowed the run of the place when they chose
to come. Annie Besant, crusading against the Mission School complained
bitterly that:

Mr Biscoe, a missionary in Kashmir, makes his Brahman
boys drag dead dogs through the city.

An insouciant Mr Biscoe replied that he cared not a whit for either the accusation or the fact that it had appeared in "forty native papers". Rest, recreation and the occasional bit of proselytization were fine, but there was more to the British interest in Kashmir than the pleasures of dancing girls in a houseboat, cheap laundry and white racism.

Gulab Singh, as we have noted, was well-rewarded for his betrayal of the Sikhs. According to Article III of the Treaty of 16 March 1846, he was allowed to "purchase" 2.5 million people spread over 84,471 square miles for

> the sum of Rupees (Nanakshahi) fifty lakhs to be paid on ratification of this treaty and twenty-five lakhs on or before the first October of the current year, AD 1846.

Governor-General Hardinge explained the rationale for such atypical British generosity in his communication to the Secret Committee on 19 February 1846:

> Raja Golab Singh, on being installed as Minister (of the Sikh Durbar), put himself in communication with us, proffering every assistance in his power for the furtherance of any ends in regard to the State of Lahore which we might have in view.

Obviously Kashmir did not much care for the status of thirty pieces of silver, and the hurt among Kashmiris was intense. A few British voices rose too in sympathy. Robert Thorp writes in *Cashmeer Misgovernment* (London, 1870):

> Towards the people of Cashmeer we have committed a wanton outrage, a gross injustice, and an act of tyrannical oppression which violates every human and honourable sentiment which is opposed to the whole spirit of modern civilisation, and is in direct opposition to every tenet of religion we profess.

But Raj policy was not noticeably influenced by either standards of honour or native sentiment. Gulab Singh's son Ranbir Singh, who inherited the throne in 1856, two years before his father's death, only intensified Dogra discrimination against the Kashmiris, Baltis and Ladakhis. However, though his loyalty to his white masters was no less crimson than his father's, the British simply could not resist encroachment—and did so in their typical wriggle-and-crawl of excuse, pretence and deceit. Though the treaty specifically allowed the Dogras complete freedom of rule, Ranbir Singh was pressurized into accepting an Officer on Special Duty in 1870, ostensibly to tend to the needs of Europeans holidaying in the Valley and the mountains, presumably like the Colonel on the houseboat. Since the British would not allow their breed of conquerors to be tried by natives, a mixed court of British and Dogra officials was created in 1872 to try civil suits. By 1877, all pretences were off; the Officer on Special Duty was placed under the orders of Delhi. The next step was only logical; the Raj wanted a Resident, which was how it kept control of the other Princely States. Its formal excuse was the threat from across the Himalayas—an expansionist Tsarist Russia. But at last, Ranbir Singh protested and a surprised Raj realized that it may have overplayed its hand. Enclosure Number One to the Secretary of State for India sent on 19 October 1885 says:

> So long as Maharaja Ranbir Singh is alive, the Government of India do not propose to make any change in their existing policy.

It became a different matter of course once he was dead. Rather crassly, the British did not waste even a minute. Pratap Singh, the new Maharaja, was still in mourning when the process was set in motion. His protests were brushed aside, and the first Resident, Sir Olivier St. John ; reached Srinagar; but it was not until the second, an aggressive officer of the Political Service, C. Plowden, arrived that classic intrigue took wing. By 1888, the British were dictating a new Constitution; by 1889, the ruler's authority had been clipped by a Council. Now Plowden concentrated on splitting the Dogra family, fomenting a power struggle between Pratap Singh and his brother Amar Singh. Plowden reported to Delhi that Pratap Singh was an imbecile, which may have been merely an exaggeration, but there was certainly no truth in the trumped-up charge that Pratap Singh was in communication with the great Raj bugbear of the times, the Tsar. But forged letters were given heavy play in the Anglo-Indian press, and the purpose was achieved. Pratap Singh's deposition acquired legitimacy in the eyes of the British establishment. An "Irshad", or edict of resignation, was prepared and accepted by a Viceroy in an unforgiving mood, who admonished:

> Notwithstanding the ample resources of your State, your treasury was empty; corruption and disorder prevailed in every department and every office; Your Highness was

still surrounded by low and unworthy favourites and the
continued misgovernment of your State was becoming,
every day, a more serious source of anxiety.

As for Pratap Singh, he was so upset at the false accusations that, he wrote
to the Viceroy,

His Highness did not take his meals for two days, he was
so much overpowered.

Two full days without food must have been a major sacrifice for the
Maharaja. Maybe Plowden was correct about the imbecility.

One of the five members of the new Council of Regency was to be "An
experienced European", third in the pecking order, below only Amar
Singh and the Prime Minister. Muslims, it needs to be noted, were not
considered; let alone such high position, they were not yet permitted to
even serve in the army. In effect, the British had begun to rule. When there
was an outcry in the Commons against this camel-and-tent policy, the
government offered the specious excuse that Pratap Singh had "resigned".
Nor could the decision be challenged in court as it was "an act of state".
However, the officers of the Raj had the merit of being candid in their
memoirs. A.P. Nicholson in *Scraps of Paper* (London, 1930) puts it
bluntly:

After we had obtained what we wanted from Kashmir, the
Maharaja (Pratap Singh) was restored to the throne in 1905
but was subject to the veto of the Resident.

The British wanted two things in the main. The first, was to bring Kashmir
in line with the other Princely States and establish their unquestioned
supremacy. The second, was to obtain Gilgit to firm up the Empire's
defences against Russia. They got both.

By 1891, Colonel Durand, at the head of Dogra and Gorkha troops, had
reached the northernmost point of British rule, Misghar, occupying Hunza
and Nagar along the way. Pratap Singh was offered the consolation of
trinkets. In 1893, Queen Victoria made him Grand Commander of the Star
of India. Well, as the Grand Commander said in a letter to the Residency
Vakil on 29 January 1895, he could not

even appoint a Tehsildar. . . Really I am quite helpless.

By 1905, Lord Curzon had stabilized relations with Afghanistan and
created the North West Frontier Province (NWFP), and the British were

ready to restore Pratap Singh to his throne. There was more illusion than power, though. The Resident's "advice" was paramount, whether on the Budget or on legislation or on the appointment of a minister or official. There was not much Pratap Singh could actually do—apart, now, from appointing Tehsildars. On 18 September 1920, he finally appealed for the restoration of his powers along with his title, citing his help in the war effort as a reason. Lord Chelmsford merely placed a purdah over the relationship in his concessions: the advice of the Resident would hence-forth be confidential. This was the situation when Pratap Singh died without a direct heir in 1925, and his brother Amar Singh's son Hari Singh became Maharaja in September. Hari Singh was the first public school product to sit on the Dogra throne, having been educated at Mayo College in Ajmer.

It was not, on the whole, a good advertisement for public schools. For a while his personal excesses provided some excellent copy to British tabloids when he was set up and blackmailed in a London hotel, but we shall restrict ourselves to the political events of his tumultuous years in power. Kashmir saw popular anger force change on a scale its people scarcely believed would happen, and its rulers never conceived was possible.

The misery of the Kashmiris, and particularly the Muslims, had now crossed every bearable limit. Sir Albion Banerjee, who resigned in 1929 as foreign and political minister out of sheer disgust at Hari Singh's indif-ference, has described the situation in an oft-quoted passage, also published in the papers of the All-India States' People's Conference of 1939:

> Jammu and Kashmir is labouring under many disad-vantages, with a large Muhammadan population absolute-ly illiterate, labouring under poverty and very low economic conditions of living in the villages and practi-cally governed like dumb-driven cattle. There is no touch between the Government and the people, no suitable op-portunity for representing grievances and the administra-tive machinery itself requires overhauling from top to bottom to bring it up to the modern conditions of efficien-cy. It has at present little or no sympathy with the people's wants and grievances.

The cultured tones of a distinguished civil servant could not contain the sheer anger, all the more vivid for being so cool. P.N. Kaul Bamzai in his *History of Kashmir* (Metropolitan Book Company, New Delhi, 1962) points out that Hari Singh did make an incipient attempt to correct the misrule of heedless generations, but

> The popularity of the Maharaja was shortlived. Very soon he came under the influence of advisers and court favourites who were neither intelligent nor had the good of the State and its people at heart. Unlike his predecessors, Maharaja Hari Singh lived in, so to say, an ivory tower surrounded by his few mean favourites having no personal contact with the people, who through centuries of suppression and misrule were groaning under the burden of heavy taxation, poverty and want.

Heavy is probably putting it mildly when it came to taxation. Lord Birdwood notes in *Two Nations and Kashmir* (London, 1956), a little in horror, that

> carpenters, boatmen, butchers, bakers, even prostitutes were taxed.

P.N. Kaul Bamzai adds:

> The proud Maharaja, ignorant of the forces that were rising at his feet, indulged in cheap pleasures of life and spent most of his time outside the State. The apparent calm and docility of the people lulled him into a false sense of security. But all was not quiet. . . . The educated classes in Kashmir were becoming restless particularly due to growing unemployment among them. And when they witnessed the appointment of Dogra Rajputs of mediocre abilities to high government posts, their frustration turned to anger.

Some spark had to ignite the crisis; it was jobs. The pressure was multiplied by a phenomenal growth in population: from the first census of Kashmir, in 1891, to the third, in 1921, the population grew from 814,241 to 1,407,086. The British only made a bad situation worse when they took effective control in 1889. Seeking to pack the government with officials who would be loyal to them rather than the Dogras, they began to empty the administration by a simple ruse: they changed the court language from Persian to Urdu, even as they began sacking officials on charges of corruption. The Dogras and Kashmiri Pandits were replaced by an influx of Punjabis. Out of this resentment emerged a slogan which was to echo long after Dogra rule had become a memory: the State's jobs for the State's people.

But at least one British stipulation had a long-term positive effect—they wanted matriculates. The initial intention was discriminatory since there was not a single matriculate among the Kashmiri youth, but need and humiliation soon propelled them to schools (including Biscoe's Mission School) and from there to university—particularly the new institution built by Sir Syed Ahmed, the Mahomedan Anglo-Oriental College at Aligarh, established in 1877 and destined to play a significant role in the fortunes of the subcontinent over the next hundred years. The government recognized this resentment early, but the first "concession" which formally defined the "Mulki" or "State Subject", was a non-event. The ownership of land was the means envisaged in the legislation, but anyone who received permission to own land could also claim "Mulki" status, making the provision meaningless. Once again, the original anger finds its impact on the present: legislation now prohibits the outsider from purchasing land in Kashmir.

When the Viceroy Lord Reading visited Kashmir in 1924, a memorial was submitted to him by Muslims demanding ownership rights for the peasantry; more government jobs; better education; abolition of forced labour and the restoration of all mosques seized by the state government. The moment the Viceroy departed, the Maharaja acted: however, instead of redressal, they got repression. The assets of the signatories were confiscated. In all these years of protest the only gain had been a very reluctant permission to open an Anjuman for the teaching of the *Quran* in 1921. The anger was bound to manifest itself in different ways. A number of Aligarh graduates began to gather regularly at the Muslim Reading Room in Srinagar; from here evolved what became known as the Reading Room Party. It was inevitable that the confrontation between an overwhelmingly Muslim mass and an oppressive Hindu government would acquire a communal tinge. Other factors too played their part. As Bamzai puts it:

> With the Muslim masses groaning under several disabilities and passing through a period of severe economic depression; with thousands of Hindu young men educated but unemployed; the administration under an inefficient and unsympathetic bureaucracy, and with the direct encouragement by the British to the agitators, the stage was set for a convulsion early in 1931.

Muslims yearned for liberation from Dogra rule; Hindu youth wanted

Mulki jobs; and the British of course were content to fish simultaneously in whichever patch of troubled water they could locate. In December 1930 the All-Kashmir Muslim Conference held its annual session in Lahore. Fired by the rhetoric, a group of young men launched an agitation in Jammu on their return home. The government got "tough". Arrests were made. A constable very foolishly taunted jailed agitators by desecrating the Holy *Quran* in front of them. A maulvi was prevented from reciting the *khutba* in a Jammu mosque. The hurt of a hundred years welled up into a slogan on the streets of Jammu "Islam in danger!" The spirit of protest travelled to Srinagar, where in March 1931, a young man, Yusuf Shah, had succeeded his father as Mir Waiz, or Chief Preacher. A student of the theological school at Deoband, Yusuf Shah had been an activist of the Reading Room Party, and organized a series of meetings through the mosque network. However, the fire of a mass upsurge was lit not by a Kashmiri intellectual or a mesmerizing preacher but by a Punjabi cook.

Abdul Qadir might in fact have never stepped into Kashmir if he had not been a cook in the retinue of a European posted to Srinagar. But once here, he seemed to discover a new identity. On 21 June 1931, this Abdul Qadir, whose oratory was clearly even more spicy than his cuisine, made a speech at the Khanqah of Sheikh Hamadani which sent passions soaring. His arrest was the match to the tinder-box. Huge crowds massed at his trial, till it had to be shifted into the Srinagar Central Jail. This only gave further impetus to popular feeling. About four to five thousand people collected at the gates of the jail on the day of the hearing, and as emotions rose they made a rush for the gates to free their hero. The police stopped them. The crowd replied with stones. Authority responded with bullets. Twenty-one died; many times more were wounded. An enraged crowd paraded the corpses laid out on charpoys through the main markets; shops were looted, Hindus attacked. It was a day of many firsts: the first popular street challenge to the Maharaja's despotism; the first mass communal violence; the first instance of police firing on an unarmed crowd.

The immediate consequence was a demand for an independent en-quiry—translate that to mean by a Britisher. Hari Singh refused. It was just the moment the Raj had been waiting for: the British Empire, after all, was the sum total of exploited opportunities. The Resident encouraged the idea of an independent enquiry. Hari Singh decided to flog the people into silence. Notification 19L, modelled on the draconian Burma Or-dinance, was issued: arrests, public flogging and police firing in city after city became the pattern. The Raj stepped in again, and this time with the firm tread of authority. It virtually commanded Hari Singh to order an enquiry and withdraw 19L, and also remedy longstanding Muslim grievances like the harsh cow-slaughter ordinance and the ban on *aazaan* and the *khutba*. Sir B.J. Glancy was named to head the enquiry commission.

Kashmir had changed. The movement for self-rule had now acquired a momentum which any establishment would find difficult to contain. Moreover, with great good sense, the leaders of the movement deliberately began to shift the focus away from the "Muslim" dimension to a larger, all-embracing Kashmiri character. The discrimination may have been communal, but the response was not. That anger flowered into a great movement only when it was harnessed to Kashmiriyat, and ploughed the trans-religious culture and identity of a country where a Sheikh could proudly call a Pandit his blood-brother and make common cause against both Islamic fanaticism and Hindu fascism. As the man whose name was to become synonymous with the Kashmir movement put it in October 1932:

> Our country's progress is impossible as long as we do not establish amicable relations between the different communities.

He was the first President of the Jammu and Kashmir Muslim Conference and his name was Sheikh Mohammad Abdullah.

Eloquence and Freedom

It is entirely appropriate that the first Kashmiri Muslim to rule the land in more than four centuries was a Pandit. All the fascinating nuances of the history and culture of Kashmir lie in that seeming paradox.

Sheikh Abdullah's grandfather was a Hindu, a Pandit. It was only in 1766 that his family, traditional Brahmins living in the picturesque village of Sorah on the shores of the lake Anchar Sar, converted to Islam under the influence of the Sufi divine, Mir Abdur Rashid Baihaqi. There was no material benefit in this conversion for there was active discrimination against Muslims under the Dogras. On 5 December 1905, a child was born in this family of shawl-weavers, the youngest of five sons and a daughter. The joy was tempered by the fact that the father, Sheikh Mohammad Ibrahim, had died two months before. It was a hard life. But his mother, Khairun Nisa, and his brothers soon realized that there was a natural talent in their youngest which deserved nurture. And so Sheikh Mohammad Abdullah escaped the illiteracy and induction into weaving which could so easily have been his fate. The family invested in his education. The foundation of his learning was laid by the Sufi, Akhun Mubarak Shah, who not only taught him to recite the *Quran Sharif* with a beauty that enraptured audiences all his life, but also infused a deep, Sufi humanitarianism that eventually shaped his future politics with an indelible conviction that would influence the history of Kashmir. Of course, he went to the local school too, for a standard education. From there he moved to Pratap College in Srinagar and Islamia College in Lahore for a graduate degree of Punjab University in 1928. For his Masters in Science, he shifted to one of India's great centres of learning, the Aligarh Muslim University. When he returned home in 1930, the ferment in Kashmir became a powerful magnet for this tall and lean twenty-five-year-old bubbling with a zeal to change his world. He was a natural for the Reading Room Party.

He got a job as a teacher in Srinagar's Government High School on a salary of sixty rupees a month but, as an M.Sc. from Aligarh he had legitimate higher expectations which were frustrated purely because of his religion. Satish Vashishth, whose book *Sheikh Abdullah Then and Now* (Maulik Sahitya Prakashan, 1968) is not particularly kind to its subject, notes:

> The State was then ruled by a Hindu Dogra. The doors of military (sic) were closed against the Muslims. The regiments of the Maharaja were formed of Dogras from Jammu, Kangra Rajputs and Punjabi Sikhs. Similarly in the civil administration higher appointments were particularly reserved for outsiders or were manned by educationally advanced and technically qualified Kashmiri Pandits. Frustration was writ large on Muslim youngmen (sic).

The Maharaja was both heedless and careless. When the Civil Service Recruitment Board rejected Sheikh Abdullah, he resigned from his school in protest and absorbed himself totally in the movement whose leadership began to quickly seep into his hands. D.N. Kaul, who later became Inspector-General of Police in Kashmir, remembers:

> ... the tall, slenderly built, fez-capped master in science would render many a scientific term into everyday Kashmiri so as to ensure quick and easy comprehension by the young, captive audience before him.

And outside the classroom:

> Soon after, through the narrow lanes of Srinagar I used to see him lead processions of arm-swinging, vociferously gesticulating and slogan-shouting men. I can still recall his sonorous, mellifluous voice in his public speeches which invariably began with recitations from the *Quran* or Iqbal's verses.

Politics was Abdullah's forte and oratory his master weapon. His first public speech, under the banner of the Reading Room Party, was made at the Jama Masjid, and he was soon recognized as the most eloquent voice of the growing movement. The eminence grise of Urdu letters, Sir Mohammad Iqbal, a fellow Kashmiri, who had become directly involved in politics by this time, gave support to the idea of a new party called the Muslim Conference and Abdullah became its first president. An agitation was launched. On 21 June 1931, came the first of many arrests which would mark Abdullah's fifty years in public life: arrests made both by bitter foes and trusted friends; arrests which often halted him and sometimes changed him but never quite defeated him. The first internment was brief. But no sooner was he out than he returned to the streets—and back to jail by 24 September.

But it was not only Abdullah's fame which grew rapidly. His thinking began to mature at an even faster pace. He realized that he had to correct the line on which he was travelling: the movement had to represent the whole of Kashmir and not just the Mussalmans; become a freedom struggle rather than just a sectarian protest. In October 1932, he told the Jammu and Kashmir Muslim Conference that the time had come to include Kashmiri Hindus into the fold. There was an immediate fallout. Even as it began to bridge the political Hindu-Muslim divide on the one side, the hawks within the Conference, led by the Mir Waiz, Yusuf Shah, broke away, creating a schism which still exists. But the stage was set for the next leap forward on the road to freedom. In March 1933, Sheikh Abdullah launched a civil disobedience movement for a constitutional government. The timing was opportune, because the Glancy Commission had created the conditions for such a demand.

With P.N. Bazaz, G.A. Ashai and Ghulam Abbas as co-members, Sir B.J. Glancy had begun his enquiry into Muslim grievances in November 1931 and submitted his report on 22 March 1932. The commission recommended the restoration of the *khutba* and the *aazaan*; severe action against any insult to any religion (an echo of the jail incident); positive discrimination towards Muslims in education as well as employment; and far stricter adherence to the principle of state jobs for state subjects. By and large these recommendations were accepted in the notification issued on 10 April 1932. This was supplemented by a Reform Conference, also presided over by Glancy, which proposed that a Legislative Assembly be constituted. In May 1932, a Franchise Committee, headed by Sir Barjor Dalal, was set up to determine the modalities. The pace of its work however created suspicions after Glancy's speed, and a call for civil disobedience in March 1933 acted as the necessary spur. Sir Ivo Elliot of the ICS was named Franchise Officer, and it soon suggested a legislature on the Morley–Minto model with a non-official majority. And thus emerged, on 22 April 1934, Regulation Number 1 of Samvaat 1991 (AD 1934) creating a Praja Sabha. It would consist of seventy-five members, but of its sixty non-official representatives only thirty-three were to be elected: twenty-one Muslims, ten Hindus and two Sikhs. It was the Barmecide's Feast once again; the Maharaja had the majority, not the electorate.

In any case, a bare three per cent of the people had been given the vote. Women and illiterates were completely excluded: Sir Barjor argued that

> the inclusion of women voters would increase the administrative difficulties of the elections.

Only those with a minimum annual income of Rs 400 were eligible for the franchise. Then, just to make doubly sure, Section 3 reserved all existing legislative, executive and judicial powers in the Maharaja himself. Section 30 further clarified that no measure passed by the Praja Sabha could become law without the Maharaja's consent, and his discretion was beyond challenge. The Army, the Constitution and the delicate but necessary matter of the Privy Purse were wholly out of the Sabha's purview. Sheikh Abdullah had no illusions about the true worth of the Assembly. On 29 January 1934, he protested:

> The people of this country did not spill their blood for such a mock show. . . . What hopes can the people of this country have in this kind of representative Assembly where the dead weight of the official and nominated majority will always be ready to crush the popular voice.

But of course, he had to prove that he represented this popular voice. He participated in the elections and won nineteen of the twenty-one Muslim seats. The Praja Sabha met for the first time on 17 October 1934 at the Rajgarh Palace in Srinagar.

Hari Singh professed great surprise that these crumbs had not been considered adequate, and condemned the popular hunger as greed. But Sheikh Abdullah, inspired surely by the sight of the British drawing up a new Constitution for India under Congress pressure, only intensified his demand for Responsible Government. Simultaneously, the growing all-community support for Abdullah began to demoralize his political opponents. Bickering broke out within the All-India Kashmir Committee of Lahore and Shimla, and its most famous member, Iqbal, resigned in June 1933. A last attempt at resuscitation, with Iqbal as President, was made the next month, but this particular organization had now nowhere to go except into obscurity. Abdullah was also strengthened by a change in the administration. Having finally extracted full control over the Gilgit Wazarat through a sixty-year-lease on 29 March 1935, the British rewarded Hari Singh by distancing themselves from the Kashmir government. By early 1936, Sir N. Gopalaswami Aiyangar had replaced Colonel

Colvin as Prime Minister, and he was far more considerate towards the politics of Abdullah than either his predecessor or indeed his mentor.

On 8 May 1936, the Muslim Conference organized Responsible Government Day. It was a splendid success with enthusiastic support from all communities following an appeal by Sheikh Abdullah. By 1937, the party had expanded its activities into the working class. Bakshi Ghulam Mohammad and Ghulam Mohammad Sadiq, two of Abdullah's most trusted lieutenants, who would also one day rule Kashmir, were at the head of the first procession of workers ever taken out, and speech after speech struck the same chord: the working class movement was above any communalism, it struggled for a better life for everyone. By the sixth session of the Muslim Conference, on 26 March 1938, the creeping nationalism had become established fact. Said Abdullah:

> We must end communalism by ceasing to think in terms of Muslims and non-Muslims when discussing our political problems. . . . We must open our doors to all such Hindus and Sikhs who like ourselves believe in the freedom of their country from the shackles of an irresponsible rule.

On 28 June the Working Committee of the Muslim Conference passed a resolution moved by Sheikh Abdullah to amend its Constitution and allow anyone to become a member "irrespective of their caste, creed or religion" after a fifty-two-hour-debate. The vote was seventeen to three. A special session of the party's General Assembly was summoned on 11 June 1939 to change the name of the party to "National Conference". The 179 delegates deliberated through the night, but by the morning there were only three votes against the change.

That was Sheikh Abdullah's finest hour. Having lifted his party into the fold of a nationalist ideology, he now led it towards the great struggle for independence under the leadership of Mahatma Gandhi and Jawaharlal Nehru. This last was a significant development, for only a year before the party had taken a considered decision to remain aloof from both Gandhi's Indian National Congress and Jinnah's Muslim League. But at its Anantnag session, held between 29 September and 1 October 1939, the National Conference formally endorsed the Congress policy towards the world war, which of course was one of the most momentous decisions taken by Gandhi in his three-decade-long challenge to the Raj. For the first time, Sheikh Abdullah spoke openly in praise of the Congress. It was the logical culmination of a decade of transition.

One of the messages that came to this first formal session of the All-India Jammu and Kashmir National Conference said:

> The Conference is meeting at a time of very great crisis in the world which will be reflected more and more in India. We cannot escape that crisis or ignore this revolutionary period of the world's history. . . All the world is on the move and India must move with it, not separately or in isolation. India must attain her full freedom based on unity. . . I trust that Kashmir will play an honourable part in the events to come. I hope that the Conference will view all these events that are happening in true perspective so that the people of Kashmir may attain their freedom in the larger freedom of India.

The crisis of course was the war looming over the world in October 1939; every political relationship across the globe, within and outside existing boundaries, would be remoulded in that furnace. Kashmir would play an honourable part: Sheikh Abdullah would launch a brilliant offensive against the philosophy of the Muslim League to keep Kashmir with the ideology of secular India in the critical year of 1947. There would be a hitch, though, when the high drama had sunk into pettier concerns. The dispute would revolve around the differing definitions of a most interesting phrase in that message: "the people of Kashmir may attain their freedom in the larger freedom of India".

The man who used that phrase in his personal message to the first session of the National Conference was Jawaharlal Nehru.

12

Nehru, Abdullah, Jinnah: The Triangle of Hopes

> It is not necessary for you to invite me to my homeland, for the desire to go there is always present within me. It is 19 years now since I went there and often long to be back, but circumstances have been too much for me and have prevented me from doing so . . . the bigger problems of India have kept me tied to this part of India. Those problems, as you know, ultimately affect Kashmir also, for the fate of Kashmir is bound up with that of the rest of India. If India is freed Kashmir will participate in that freedom.

This letter from Pandit Jawaharlal Nehru, a Kashmiri who had never lived in Kashmir, but whose Pandit blood had been zealously protected by successive generations of arranged marriages, to Sheikh Abdullah and his compatriot Prem Nath Bazaz, was printed in *The Hindustan Times* on 30 June 1936. There was a touch of diffidence about the invitation, as much as a touch of regret in the reply. Abdullah and Jawaharlal did not know each other very well then; they had met just once, in Lahore, though at the very first meeting Abdullah was deeply influenced—as he recalls in *Aatish-e-Chinar*—by both Nehru's love for Kashmir as well as his humanism. Abdullah was only thirty-odd years old then, and despite his achievements still at a formative stage of his thinking, while Nehru was the great hope, President of the Congress, leader of the masses and a natural lodestar for an idealist. But Nehru was certainly aware of Abdullah's growing reputation. His daughter Indira Gandhi recalls in *My Truth* (Vision Books, New Delhi, 1981):

> I first saw Sheikh Sahab in 1934, leading a procession. Not long after he came to be recognised as a prominent figure in our freedom movement. Like other popular leaders of

the old Princely States, he fought against the double yoke
of feudalism and colonialism. He stoutly opposed the
politics of the Muslim League and was a fine example of
the secular ideal of our nation.

That stout opposition would owe something to the influence of Nehru.
They became friends in fortuitous circumstances. In 1938, Abdullah and
his closest lieutenant Bakshi Ghulam Mohammad were in Lahore as the
personal guests of Mian Iftikharuddin, the President of the Punjab Pradesh
Congress Committee (PCC) when a phone call came to the house request-
ing the PCC chief to meet Nehru at the Lahore railway station when his
train to the Frontier stopped *en route*. Abdullah and Bakshi went along
too. Abdullah was moved by the warmth of the greeting, and the immediate rapport in the conversation—as if they were old friends. So
engrossed were they that they did not realize that the train had moved.
Bakshi got off at Shahdara, but Nehru, on an affectionate impulse, asked
Abdullah to accompany him on his Frontier tour. Abdullah was delighted.
He recalls Nehru on that tour in his autobiography:

> There was the innocence of a child in his demeanour which
> made one love him.

It was on this visit too that Abdullah met his great neighbour and
contemporary Khan Abdul Ghaffar Khan—or Badshah Khan, the King
Khan, or Fakhre-Afghan, the Pride of the Afghans. These two leaders
played a remarkable role: Badshah Khan building a fascinating Gandhian
movement among the tribes of the Frontier, Abdullah guarding the standard of secularism in Kashmir, the two challenging the onslaught of
Muslim communalism from the large sprawl of Punjab. Abdullah invited
both Jawaharlal and Badshah Khan to Kashmir during this tour, and they
readily accepted. But this invitation might also have got lost in the
pressure of great events: those were years when the whole world was in
turmoil—except that as events began to unfold, the importance of the
future of Kashmir to the destiny of the whole of India suddenly took on
a dimension of its own. When Jawaharlal did visit Kashmir, for the first
time in twenty-three years, in the summer of 1940, the politics of the
subcontinent had entered a whirlpool from which no one would escape
unscathed.

The decade beginning 1935 was to prove the most momentous in many
centuries. At the centre of that decade, both literally and metaphorically,
lay a resolution of the All-India Muslim League passed during the Lahore

session on 22-24 March 1940 which said:

> Muslim India will not be satisfied unless the whole Con-
> stitutional plan is reconsidered *de novo* and that no revised
> plan would be acceptable to the Muslims unless it is
> framed with their approval and consent. Resolved that it
> is the considered view of this Session of the All-India
> Muslim League that no Constitutional plan would be
> workable in this country or acceptable to the Muslims
> unless it is designed on the following basic principles, viz.
> that geographically contiguous units are demarcated into
> regions which should be constituted, with such territorial
> readjustments as may be necessary, that the areas in which
> the Muslims are numerically in a majority as in the North-
> Western and Eastern zones of India should be grouped to
> constitute 'Independent State' in which the constituent
> units shall be autonomous and sovereign.

Or, as Mohammad Ali Jinnah put it in his presidential address on 22 March 1940:

> The Mussulmans are not a minority. The Mussulmans are
> a nation by any definition. . . If the British Government
> are really in earnest about sincere peace and happiness of
> the people of this subcontinent, the only course open to us
> all is to allow the major nations separate homelands by
> dividing India into 'autonomous national states'.

If this logic had to work then the Muslims of these "North-Western and
Eastern zones" would obviously have to endorse the resolution by popular
consent. That was less easy than passing resolutions. Sind was indifferent,
Punjab sceptical, the Frontier antagonistic, Bengal still wary. And in Kashmir,
despite the fact that the premier popular party had emerged from the Muslim
Conference, the language of its leader Abdullah was now in harmony not with
Jinnah but with the men Jinnah despised, Gandhi and Nehru.

On 4 August 1935, the Government of India Act received royal assent
and became the basis for a new Constitution and fresh elections in British
India. But the very success of the Congress in those elections , despite the
in-built hurdles, became a problem as a defeated Jinnah stepped up the
ante by adopting the demand for a separate homeland. Nehru took on
Jinnah in speech after speech, castigating him for dividing Indians, and
accusing him of being as fascist as Bhai Parmanand of the Hindu

Mahasabha. Simultaneously, he intensified the Congress campaign in the Muslim-majority provinces.

There was one serious problem, however. Gandhi would not touch the Princely States, concentrating his political energies on British India. But Jawaharlal was in no mood for generosity towards these protectorates of the Raj. A resolution of the Congress Working Committee, held between 29 July and 1 August 1935, had finally defined the party position on the Indian States:

> The Indian National Congress recognises that the people in the Indian States have an inherent right to Swaraj no less than the people of British India. It has accordingly declared itself in favour of establishment of representative responsible government in the States and has in that behalf not only appealed to the Princes to establish such responsible government in their States and to guarantee fundamental rights of citizenship, like freedom of person, speech, association, of the press, to their people but has also pledged to the States people its sympathy and support in their legitimate and peaceful struggle for the attainment of full Responsible Government.

This resolution provided great encouragement to leaders like Abdullah then themselves demanding Responsible Government. But there was a caveat.

> It should be understood, however, that the responsibility and the burden of carrying on the struggle within the States must necessarily fall on the States people themselves. The Congress can exercise moral and friendly influence upon the States and this it is bound to do wherever possible. The Congress has no other power under existing circumstances although the people of India whether under the British, the Princes or any other power are geographically and historically one and indivisible. In the heat of the controversy the limitation of the Congress is often forgotten.

Jawaharlal set up a halfway house: The All-India States' Peoples' Conference. Delivering the presidential address in February 1939 at Ludhiana, he gave public support to Abdullah and noted:

> . . .in Kashmir, I am glad to say, a number of wise and far-seeing Hindus and Sikhs threw their weight on the side

of the popular movement and supported the 'National Demand' which asked for a responsible government.

Abdullah had already committed himself, as we have seen, to a change in Constitution and nomenclature, saying, in his presidential address, on 26 March 1938, to the Muslim Conference:

> Like us the large majority of Hindus and Sikhs in the State have immensely suffered at the hands of irresponsible government. They are also steeped in deep ignorance, have to pay large taxes and are in debt and starving. . . . The main problem therefore before us is to organise joint action and a united front against the forces that stand in our way in the achievement of our goal. This will require re-christening our organisation as a non-communal political body and introducing certain amendments in its Constitution and its rules. I reiterate today what I have said so often. Firstly, we must end communalism by ceasing to think in terms of Muslims and non-Muslims while discussing our political problems. Secondly, there must be universal suffrage on the basis of joint electorate; without these two democracy is lifeless.

Nehru and Badshah Khan came to Kashmir in May–June of 1940 as much on a holiday as to cement these bonds in the united fight against communalism. Nehru tried very hard to take Gandhi along, but the Mahatma's reluctance to interfere in Princely States kept him away. One thing is certain: if the Mahatma had gone he would have needed more than a loincloth. It was a wet summer. But Jawaharlal's enthusiasm for Kashmir was not going to be dampened by mere chill drizzles. He has left a long description of this visit, published now in *The Unity of India* (Lindsay Drummond, London, 1948). He indulged his passion for glaciers and high slopes fully. After three-and-a-half days in Srinagar the party, led by host Abdullah and followed by a small army of eager helpers, left for the higher valleys: Vernag, Acchbal, Anantnag, Mattan. By the time they reached Pahalgam they were soaked to the skin but an undeterred Nehru trotted off to Chandwari on a day trip the next morning. On the third day, they followed the course of the Liddar river, and an exhilarated Nehru moved on towards the Kolohai glacier. Everyone was bone-tired by now but Jawaharlal had acquired the energy of a liberated child. He pushed ahead towards the Sonemarg valley. Here finally the irresistible force met the immovable object:

> . . .in order to get there we had to go over a high pass,
> which was not an easy matter at that time of the year. . .
> This pass has the expressive name of Yamher—the ladder
> of death. It is covered with slippery ice, which no doubt
> facilitates the passage to the other world.

But while all this was very adventurous and so forth, there was also hard
work to be done. Nehru saw for himself the appeal that Abdullah's name
carried in the remotest corners of the state. He saw the affection the people
had for him:

> I addressed many great gatherings in Srinagar and outside,
> but I had gone to Kashmir more to learn and to understand
> than to teach. Two of the Srinagar meetings I addressed
> were held under the auspices of the National Conference,
> whose guest I was. Two others in Srinagar were held under
> the auspices of the Yuvak Sabha, the organisation of the
> Kashmiri Pandits, and one of these meetings, held at my
> particular request, was specially meant for the Pan-
> ditanis. . .   The women's meeting was an extraordinary
> sight. It rained heavily throughout , and the meeting was
> held in the open. I had imagined that the meeting would
> be abandoned. But for hours before the time of the meeting
> thousands of women gathered and stood in the pouring
> rain, and when Badshah Khan and I got there these girls
> and young women and old women were standing in ankle-
> deep mud and water. I am partial to the women of Kashmir.
> They are beautiful and full of charm. . . . It was a joy to
> meet them and see the affection in their eyes. At Mattan,
> old Kashmiri ladies came to bless me and kiss me on the
> forehead, as a mother does to her son.

The affection of the people, and the unity between the Pandit and the
Sheikh became the definitive fact which shaped Kashmir in the 1940s,
the years in which history was being forged in the crucibles of hatred.

Abdullah now took the next logical step: in 1941, the National
Conference joined the All-India States' Peoples' Conference (he would
become President in 1946). The Muslim League reacted by reviving the
Muslim Conference under the veteran, Ghulam Abbas, but there was little
popular response. Abdullah moved even closer to the Congress. When

Gandhi reawakened India with his last great movement in August 1942, Abdullah was ready to echo the Gandhian ultimatum in the Valley. Within a week of the "Quit India" resolution, the National Conference said, on 16 August 1942:

> The demand of the Congress is based on just reasons. The Working Committee condemns the reign of terror and repression which the Government of India have launched by declaring the Indian National Congress illegal, by the arrest of the leaders, and by shooting down unarmed people.

But with the Congress leaders in jail, and the world at war, the struggle for freedom went into the shadows. Abdullah, however, did not waste this time. In 1944, his maturing dream found remarkable expression in the New Kashmir Plan. The Constitution which Abdullah proposed guaranteed freedom, equality and democracy. The economic creed was socialism: land to the tiller, and full protection to the working class in order

> to perfect our union in the fullest equality and self-determination, to raise ourselves and our children forever from the abyss of oppression and poverty, degradation and superstition, from medieval darkness and ignorance, into the sunlit valleys of plenty ruled by freedom, science and honest toil. . .

The language was positively Nehruvian. Clause 12 of the New Kashmir Constitution is of particular interest given popular notions of Muslim politics:

> Women citizens shall be accorded equal rights with men in all fields of national life: economic, cultural, political, and in the state services. These rights shall be realized by affording women the right to work in every employment upon equal terms and for equal wages with men. Women shall be ensured rest, social insurance and education equally with men. The law shall give special protection to the interests of mother and child.

These ideas fired the imagination of the people even further, and a slogan emerged out of the mood:

Alyaban hallakari, dushman challakari.

(When the plough moves, it tears apart the enemy).

But the Muslim League was not ready to surrender Kashmir to the Nehru–Abdullah axis. In the same year as the New Kashmir Plan it made its most serious bid to win mass support in the Valley of Muslims. And the man who went awooing was none other than Jinnah himself. He spent the summer of '44 in Kashmir.

The National Conference did not seek a quarrel with him. In fact, Jinnah was even accorded a reception upon his arrival, and the cordial address of welcome said:

> We Kashmiris today receive you as a prominent Indian
> despite the ideological differences we have with you.

Speaking on the occasion, at Pratap Park in Srinagar on 10 May 1944, Abdullah described Jinnah as "a beloved leader of the Muslims of India". Jinnah was equally cordial. But within an hour he was at another reception, this arranged by the Muslim Conference, and here he launched the political offensive that was his purpose. He asked Muslims to join the Muslim Conference because

> Muslims have one platform, one *Kalma* and one God. . .
> I am a Muslim and all my sympathies are for the Muslim
> cause.

This Abdullah was not ready to let pass. In a sharp rejoinder he declared that the

> ills of this land can only be remedied by carrying Hindus,
> Muslims and Sikhs together.

The war had begun in earnest. Presiding over the annual session of the Muslim Conference, Jinnah called the National Conference a "band of gangsters". Abdullah responded with a series of mass meetings. At one such gathering, on 20 June, he lashed out:

> If Jinnah does not give up the habit of interfering in our
> politics, it will be difficult for him to go back in an
> honourable manner.

Nor was he averse to exploiting contradictions in Jinnah's stand. On 24 June he issued a written statement:

> As for the National Conference we certainly owe no

apologies to Mr Jinnah for our existence. Starting the Muslim Conference as a sectional organisation in 1932, we passed on to a higher stage of political evolution in 1939. Thus we passed Mr Jinnah's milestone of today over five years ago. Viewing the position from an all-India perspective, we find that Mr Jinnah has repeatedly declared that he does not extend his plans of Pakistan to the Indian States. Thus his conception of Islamic sovereignty halts at the customs barrier which divides our State from British India. Yet when it comes to giving advice, Mr Jinnah trespasses his own boundaries.

1944 was clearly a year of hectic activity, for in the fall the leader of the Hindu Mahasabha, V.D. Savarkar, came to generate support among the Pandits for a "Hindu Rashtra." Pandit S.N. Fotedar, President of the Yuvak Sabha (which had given Nehru a warm reception in 1940) very bluntly told Savarkar that Hindu fundamentalism was as alien to the culture of Kashmir as Muslim fundamentalism. Both the Hindus and Muslims of Kashmir remained with Nehru and Abdullah even as in the rest of the subcontinent the unity began to crack under the twin pressure of riots and impending freedom. Kashmiriyat survived the tests of that tragic decade.

Years later, Sheikh Abdullah still could not quite keep his anger at the politics and personality of Jinnah out of his autobiography. He wrote:

> It is one of the strange ironies of history that Jinnah became the saviour of the extremist Muslims, who wanted a separate country called Pakistan. Jinnah Sahab, by temperament and training was miles away from such people. He was not in the least interested in living like a good Muslim. He did not even have an inkling of the languages associated with Islamic culture, Arabic, Persian and Urdu. It is famous about him that he would get into all sorts of difficulties whenever he was forced to do namaaz. Despite all this he became the biggest champion of Pakistan. But I agree that without the force of his personality and his dedication to the idea, Pakistan would not have been formed.

And, it may be added, without the force of Abdullah's personality and his dedication to the faith of secularism Kashmir would not have remained in India.

But to continue with 1944. Hoping to ease the pressure, Hari Singh announced a major concession: while he could not accept the demand for Responsible Government he was ready to take two members of the Praja Sabha, one Muslim and one Hindu, into his council of ministers. The National Conference agreed to cooperate and on 19 October its nominee Mirza Afzal Beg was sworn in as Public Works minister along with Ganga Ram, a Dogra chosen by Hari Singh himself. While the latter got the Home portfolio and some respect, Beg quickly discovered that his officials would not listen to him and his colleagues would simply not recognize his presence. Meanwhile, as the war unwound, the pace of politics stepped up. The Congress leaders were released on Friday, 15 June 1945; ten days later the Shimla Conference summoned by Lord Wavell began discussions on the calendar of the transfer of power. In this environment Abdullah and Nehru were keen to publicly display the close relations between their parties. The annual session of the National Conference that year, held in the first week of August, was graced by a host of Congress leaders including of course Nehru. Maulana Azad was there too, as well as Badshah Khan: politics apart, the prospect of autumn days in Kashmir appealed to these jail-weary veterans of struggle. They were welcomed with a massive public reception, and a splendid boat procession on the Jhelum on 1 August. (The Muslim Conference threatened to disrupt the procession with demonstrators; Abdullah asked his party cadres to take care of anyone trying to create mischief—and that was the end of their heroism.) Badshah Khan told the Kashmiris:

Sheikh Abdullah is a gift of god. If you don't follow him you will be humiliated.

In his speech to the session on 4 August Jawaharlal said that he was there because it was a mass party and totally non-communal:

Its doors are open to all Kashmiris. . . Kashmir is a beautiful land and those who live here are fortunate. But real good fortune will only come on the day freedom comes to the people. . . . I hope under the wise and far-seeing leadership of the Sher-e-Kashmir, Sheikh Mohammad Abdullah, it will succeed in achieving its objective.

Nehru also made it a point to tell the Pandits on 7 August (reported in *The Hindu* of 10 August):

I advise others to join it (National Conference) in much

larger numbers and thereby influence its decisions. They must not remain passive spectators and critics. It is obvious, and even a child should know, that the Maharaja and the British will always keep you slaves if you do not line up with the masses in the land.

The enthusiasm for the Congress leaders was so great that there was almost a serious accident: a cracker hit Sheikh Abdullah in the face while he and Nehru drove towards an office of the party on 19 August. Writing to Beg on 3 September Nehru noted that both Abdullah and he could have lost their eyesight. Buoyed by the success of the August session, Abdullah sought to open a dialogue with Hari Singh, even going up to Bombay, where the Maharaja spent most of his time, to obtain an audience. He failed, and was forced to turn once again to direct action. Beg resigned from his meaningless ministership on 17 March 1946 and an angry Abdullah launched what would be his last agitation against Hari Singh. Taking his cue from the Congress he named it simply the Quit Kashmir movement. At the heart of this struggle lay a question emerging from the birth of Dogra rule: its legitimacy. Sheikh Abdullah was addressing both the Maharaja and his original and existing progenitor, the British. The logic of this demand to Quit Kashmir lay in the hated sale deed: the British had no right to sell the people of Kashmir to an opportunist for favours rendered, and the Dogras even less right to treat Kashmir as their natural property.

Abdullah's worries were increased by a statement of the Cabinet Mission which arrived in India on 24 March 1946, to try and finalize the fate of the subcontinent. The second round of talks conducted by the Cabinet Mission began on Sunday 5 May. On 12 May, the Mission issued a memorandum on the future of the Princely States:

> . . . His Majesty's Government will cease to exercise the powers of paramountcy. This means that the rights of States which flow from their relationship to the Crown will no longer exist and that all the rights surrendered by the States to the paramount power will return to the States.

Again on 3 June the British formally reaffirmed:

> His Majesty's Government wish to make it clear that. . . their policy towards Indian States contained in the Cabinet Mission Memorandum. . . remains unchanged.

There was, consequently, a great deal for Hari Singh to be pleased about and Abdullah to be apprehensive about. The present and future were volatile; the shape of post-British India uncertain. The last thing Abdullah wanted was British rule replaced by a Maharaja's autocracy; freedom would mean nothing to Kashmir until they had also won freedom from a purchased feudalism. Hari Singh, as events were to confirm, wanted to inherit an independent state out of the collapse of the British Empire just as his ancestors had carved out an independent state out of the collapse of the Sikh empire. Abdullah—and Nehru—wanted to sabotage that possibility. Abdullah took the position that whatever might be the case in other Princely States, the Dogras had no legitimacy in Kashmir. He sent a tough message to the Cabinet Mission after the 12 May memorandum, saying:

> Today the national demand of the people of Kashmir is not merely the establishment of Responsible Government, but their right to absolute freedom from autocratic rule. The immensity of the wrong done to our people by the 'Sale Deed' of 1846 can only be judged by looking into the actual living conditions of the people. It is the depth of our torment that has given strength to our protest.

If this was harsh then the speeches were acerbic. Abdullah displayed the honesty which others considered impolitic. The rulers of the Indian States, he said,

> who possess one-fourth of India have always played traitors to the cause of Indian freedom. The demand that the princely order should quit is a logical extension of the policy of Quit India. . . No sale deed, however sacrosanct, can condemn four million men and women to the servitude of an autocrat when the will to live under his rule is no longer there. We, the people of Kashmir, are determined to mould our own destiny. . .

Not having the people on his side, Jinnah was content to let any Maharaja mould their destiny. He supported the Cabinet Mission memorandum because it was certain to Balkanize what was left of India after Pakistan had been lopped off on the east and the west. The Muslim Conference, consequently, took Hari Singh's side during the Quit Kashmir movement; if ever there was a recipe for suicide this was it. It tried a clumsy cover-up, claiming in a statement on 8 June 1946 that "the direction and guidance of the present movement has definitely passed into the hands of the Hindu leaders". But this was too transparent a dodge to fool anyone.

Hari Singh's response was a crackdown. He had a new Prime Minister by now. After the resignation of N. Gopalaswami Aiyangar there had been a rapid turnover—Raja Sir Maharaj Singh, Colonel Sir K.N. Haksar and Sir B.N. Rau—until in the summer of 1945 when Hari Singh settled for a career-long loyalist, Ram Chandra Kak. Beginning as a librarian in a college, Kak had wheedled his way to minister-in-waiting to Hari Singh before landing the coveted job. He was the kind of servant who betrayed his master's interests by excess. National Conference leaders were picked up on 20 May, and it was announced that they would be tried for sedition. Kak told *The Hindustan Times* (27 May 1946):

> We have been preparing for it for 11 months and now we are ready to meet the challenge. There will be no more vacillation and no weak-kneed policy. We shall be ruthlessly firm and we make no apology about it. . .

Ruthless he was. In three days after 20 May twenty people died in police firing, hundreds were injured, and hundreds more were arrested. Such was the vehemence of popular anger that the whole of the Kashmir police revolted, refusing to lathi charge civil resisters, and three units of the State Army, on duty in West Asia, had to be flown back to deal with the situation.

Sheikh Abdullah was at Ghari, a hundred miles from Srinagar, on his way to meet Nehru in Delhi at the latter's request when he was arrested. The action was deliberately provocative, and Jawaharlal said in a statement on 21 May that though he was not aware of the specific reason for the Sheikh's arrest, it seemed part of a general pattern of repression. On 26 May he was more specific, after he had been briefed by two Conference leaders who had escaped the dragnet, Bakshi Ghulam Mohammad and Dwarka Nath Kachru. Nehru warned the Princes that "sovereignty will have to reside in the people and what follows will necessarily be according to the wishes of the people. . . What happened in Kashmir clearly demonstrates the desire of the State authorities to avail themselves of any pretext to crush the popular movement".

A phrase Nehru used—"Srinagar is almost a city of the dead. . ."— captured the essence of the moment, but the full passage bears repetition for it is excellent reportage:

> The whole of the valley was handed over to military

administration. The police, being Kashmiris, were withdrawn. A reign of terrorism and frightfulness (sic) then began. Kashmir has practically been cut off from the outside world since then and martial law prevails there. There have been conflicts with crowds and firing on numerous occasions. My information is that far more people than officially admitted have been killed. A much larger number who were wounded were sent to jails instead of hospitals. Srinagar is almost a city of the dead where movement is difficult and large numbers of people are practically interned in their own houses, apart from the many hundreds who have been put in prison. Clashes occur daily and even women have been shot down. But what is worse is the deliberate attempt, reminiscent of martial law days in the Punjab in 1919, to humiliate human beings. I understand that people are made to crawl in some of the streets, that sometimes they are made to take off their turbans to clean the streets and pavements, that they are made to shout at the point of the bayonet 'Maharaj ki jai'. Dead bodies are not handed to the relatives for burial according to religious rites, but are soaked in petrol and burnt. The mosques, including their inner shrines, have been occupied by the military. A wall of the Jama Masjid of Srinagar has been knocked down to make a passage for military lorries. A dangerous feature of the situation is the deliberate attempt to foment communal trouble.

Nehru threw a challenge to Hari Singh in the same statement:

Everyone who knows Kashmir knows also the position of Sheikh Mohammad Abdullah there. He is the Sher-e-Kashmir, beloved of the remotest valleys of Kashmir. Numerous legends and popular songs have grown around his personality. . . . Does anybody think we are going to desert him or his comrades in Kashmir because the Kashmir State authorities have a few guns at their disposal? We shall stand by the people of Kashmir and their leaders in this heavy trial that they are going through.

Jawaharlal stood by the people of Kashmir in 1946; they stood by him in 1947. Nehru set up a relief committee (treasurer: Kamalnayan Bajaj; all cheques to be sent c/o Bajaj and Company, 51 Mahatma Gandhi Road, Bombay), demanded an impartial enquiry, and prepared to lead a team of lawyers for Abdullah's defence. The Kashmir government refused permission. But a Maharaja's telegram was hardly going to deter a man whom the British had been unable to stop. On 19 June, Nehru told a press conference in Lahore *en route* to Srinagar for the trial, scheduled to start on 21 June: "There can be no peace in Kashmir unless Sheikh Abdullah is released".

He was stopped from entering at the Kohala bridge where Punjab ended and Kashmir began. The District Magistrate, Kishan Dár (also a relative by marriage; Dar's son was the husband of Nehru's first cousin) personally handed Jawaharlal the order banning his entry. Seeking to prove Heaven knows what, Kak had sent three lorry-loads of hired men, Muslim Conference cadres as well as some Pandits, to intimidate Jawaharlal with black flags and slogans. But seeing these *Bhare ke tattu* (hirelings) a group collected on the Punjab side and raised counter-slogans. Jawaharlal wrote: "Give me the Punjabi any day in a competition of shouting slogans. He has a perfect genius for inventing new slogans on the spot".

This drama went on for about five hours. Then, fed up, Jawaharlal simply began walking in the direction of Srinagar, defying the ban orders. He told the DM: "I have torn down such orders before, and will ignore it now. Nobody has ever dared to check my movements. I will enter Srinagar, though it may take me weeks. I will not go back. . ." Kishan Dar backed down, to a point. He allowed Nehru to motor to Domel and spend the night in a dak bungalow on the river Jhelum. A compromise was worked out. Abdullah's trial was postponed, and Azad provided Nehru with an exit route by a summons to return to Delhi at once for a Working Committee meeting.

The trial began on 22 July. Once again Jawaharlal made all arrangements for the defence, and decided to be personally present from 24 July. Hari Singh applied every form of pressure to prevent this, even using the Nawab of Bhopal as an intermediary. Nothing worked and Hari Singh in turn was forced to agree to the visit. Abdullah's long statement in court was jointly drafted by him, Nehru and the senior counsel Asaf Ali. It said:

> I am not interested in a personal defence and I would not have undertaken it if I had not felt that my trial for 'sedition' is something far more than a personal charge against me. It is, in effect, a trial of the entire population of Jammu and Kashmir. . . . This treatment of a people as

a commodity which can be transferred for hard cash (through the Treaty of Kashmir) has all along been deeply resented by the Kashmiris, whether Hindu, Sikh or Muslim. It hurts their national dignity.

Nehru stayed for four days, but despite all these efforts conviction was a foregone conclusion. On his return to Delhi, Jawaharlal issued a written statement:

After four brief days in Kashmir, my mind is full of impressions, painful and otherwise. I shall not say much about them now. To the authorities I have nothing to say, but I have a claim on the people, just as they have a claim on me. . . . May it be well with Kashmir and its people in the days to come and may we all in Kashmir and the rest of India achieve our hearts' desire—freedom for the people in a free and independent India.

Free. Independent. And partitioned. That became the problem.

13

A Basket of Apples

On 22 April 1947, Rear Admiral Viscount Francis Albert Victor Nicholas Mountbatten of Burma, now Viceroy of India, had "a long and friendly talk" with V.K. Krishna Menon, by then one of Nehru's chief advisers, over what was surely many cups of tea given the latter's fondness for the brew. Having let down their hair and chewed the fat and burnt some boats and done just about everything to exhaust every cliché in the language, they finally turned to less ponderous matters than the future of the Commonwealth. Pandit Nehru, now second only to the Viceroy in the Interim Government, was working too hard, Menon told Mountbatten. Relays of typists were in and out of his office; he was worrying about even the minor things, and would suffer a breakdown if he did not get some respite. Take Nehru for a brief holiday, Menon suggested. Where? Shimla?

'No,' replied Menon, 'that is too official; neither of you would stop working.'

'Where else?'

Kashmir, suggested Menon.

Mountbatten laughed: 'What would happen? I thought he (Nehru) wanted to make the Maharaja lick his boots, or alternatively that the Maharaja was likely to throw him into jail.'

Menon used the banter to turn to a serious point. Could Mountbatten persuade Hari Singh to release all the political prisoners, just as he had persuaded Dr Khan Sahib in the NWFP to do? The release of Abdullah would pave the way for an understanding between Nehru and the Maharaja. Mountbatten was sceptical, but he felt that in any case he should probably go over and see Hari Singh personally. The visit eventually materialized between 18 and 23 June. But by then it was too late to wake up Hari Singh and show him reality. Within the space of just one year, events had marched ahead at a pace which can only be generated by the feeling of disaster breathing down your neck.

The first step in the effective transfer of power had been taken in August 1946 with the formation of an Interim Government, headed by the Viceroy, but with Nehru (Minister for External Affairs and Commonwealth Relations) as the ranking Indian. After him, in order of power/importance were Liaqat Ali Khan (Finance); Sardar Vallabhbhai Patel (Home, Information and Broadcasting, and, after 5 July 1947, the States); I.I. Chundrigar (Commerce); Rajendra Prasad (Food and Agriculture); Abdur Rab Nashtar (Communications); Maulana Abul Kalam Azad (Education and Arts); C. Rajagopalachari (Industries and Supplies); Dr John Mathai (Transport); Ghazanfar Ali Khan (Health); Sardar Baldev Singh (Defence); Jagjivan Ram (Labour); C.H. Bhabha (Works, Mines and Power); and Jogendra Nath Mandal—the token Hindu in the Muslim League—as Minister for Law.

But this first and last effort in Congress–Muslim League cooperation was quickly destroyed by lack of will in the Congress and lack of interest in the League. As early as in the winter of 1946–47, Nehru and Patel privately resigned themselves to the inevitability of Partition. But there was one crucial difference between them—on Kashmir. Patel, following the logic of communal-country divide, had mentally written off Kashmir. Jawaharlal had not. Because of Sheikh Abdullah. He was the key.

Nehru showed what he thought of Hari Singh's jail sentence by naming Abdullah President of the All-India States' Peoples' Conference in 1946. He now pushed Mountbatten, as Menon had done, to go to Kashmir and try and force Hari Singh to release Abdullah. When the Viceroy did go he carried a brief prepared personally by Nehru ('A Note on Kashmir,' Enclosure to No 229 in Volume XI of *Transfer of Power*). Jawaharlal's intentions are strewn through twenty-eight long paragraphs. Witness:

> ... There is no doubt that Sheikh Abdullah himself is by far the most outstanding leader in Kashmir. . . The National Conference has stood for and still stands for Kashmir joining the Constituent Assembly of India. . . If any attempt is made to push Kashmir into the Pakistan Constituent Assembly there is likely to be much trouble because the National Conference is not in favour of it and the Maharaja's position would also become very difficult.

This is also evidence that Nehru and Abdullah had already discussed the subject and reached this decision. Jinnah, for obvious reasons, wanted to encourage Hari Singh. One day before Mountbatten flew to Kashmir, he issued a statement saying:

Constitutionally and legally the Indian States will be independent sovereign States on the termination of Paramountcy and they will be free to decide for themselves to adopt any course they like.

Hari Singh and Kak opted for evasion when Mountbatten reached Srinagar—which was perhaps the most dangerous course of all. Mountbatten reported to London on 27 June 1947:

> I had several preliminary talks with the Maharaja and with his Prime Minister, but nearly always in the presence of others. I therefore asked for an hour's interview alone with the Maharaja, to be followed by an hour with him and his Prime Minister. The Maharaja suggested this should take place on the last day, the 22nd June. I agreed and on that last morning the Maharaja remained in bed with colic and was unable to have his interview. (Sir Conrad) Corfield remarked that this was his usual technique to avoid unpleasant discussions. The same view was expressed by Nehru, who was bitterly disappointed at my not being able to discuss the release of Sheikh Abdullah.

That was an understatement. Nehru was furious. He needed Abdullah for the coming political battles on Kashmir, particularly since Kak had clearly indicated that Hari Singh was not going to accede before 15 August, the date set for independence. In Kak's words to Mountbatten:

> H.H.'s decision was that at present he could not commit himself... H.H. realised the various factors involved, but in any case was not now in any way alarmed by Pandit Nehru or disturbed by his threats.

Nehru met Mountbatten to discuss the latter's Kashmir trip between 11 and 12.30 on the morning of 24 June. The Viceroy seemed full of ideas, at least some of them unwanted—including a design for the flag of free India! ("This consisted of a Congress flag with a small Union Jack in the upper canton. Since the Congress flag consists of three horizontal stripes, the Union Jack had been fitted into the exact width of the space between the stripes which made the Jack one-sixth of the total area of the flag instead of one-quarter as in the case of Australia, etc"). After brushing aside this absurd thought (Union Jack on the tricolour!) as politely as he could, Nehru turned to Kashmir. Hari Singh's colic, he fumed, " was an old trick, which the Maharajah had played on him when he was going to meet him in Kashmir—he had on that occasion also had 'a tummy ache'". Mountbatten informed Nehru he had advised Hari Singh not to talk about independence; he should enter into a Standstill Agreement with both India and Pakistan, and eventually join "one of the two States, at least for defence, communications and external affairs". Nehru insisted that "the problem would not be solved until Sheikh Abdullah was released from prison and the rights of the people were restored". He wanted to go at once to Kashmir "to take up the cudgels on behalf of his friend and for the freedom of the people". But the Kashmir government would not entertain the idea, and Mountbatten asked Nehru not to go.

But by now Gandhi was as anxious about the drift in Kashmir as Nehru. On 26 June, Gandhi went to see Mountbatten "in high distress about Kashmir. He said either he or Nehru must go at once to Kashmir". Mountbatten eventually sold a Gandhi-visit to Hari Singh with the theory of the lesser evil; a Nehru-visit would have meant far more trouble for the Maharaja. Gandhi went on his only visit to Kashmir in the first week of August; this was his last political initiative under the British Raj. Hari Singh, however, might have been justified in wondering whether Gandhi really was a lesser evil after all; Gandhi pointedly rejected the Maharaja's offer of hospitality, preferring to be the guest of the National Conference. Gandhi made it clear that he had come to greet the people—who responded with unbounded enthusiasm. With freedom just a few days away, Hari Singh stuck to silence as a policy. Frightened by Jinnah's Islam in Pakistan and Nehru's democracy in India, he opted for procrastination. The price is still being paid.

From where he was, Nehru did everything he could to protect Kashmir for India. One of his most critical victories was achieved very quietly, in the relative shadow of private commitments.

The Partition Plan of 3 June 1947 envisaged two Boundary Commissions to run a scalpel through the east and west: Bengal and Assam-Sylhet, and Punjab. Jinnah wanted UN arbitration; Nehru rejected it as too cumbrous. It was decided that the commissions would consist of four High Court judges each, two named by Congress and two by the League, with a chairman holding the casting vote. Since the Congress and the League were unable to agree on any Indian, Mountbatten selected an Englishman, Sir Cyril Radcliffe. Nehru was apprehensive at the thought of a Tory in such a sensitive job, and Jinnah's warm endorsement did not help, but he did not press his reservations. The commissions were set up on 30 June; Sir Cyril reached New Delhi on 8 July, taking up a bungalow on the

Viceregal estate because Mountbatten thought accommodation in the Viceroy's House itself would open him to charges of influence. Those charges were made nevertheless when the Boundary Award was finally announced on 16 August. One of the most controversial decisions dealt with the Gurdaspur district in north Punjab.

The terms of reference given to Sir Cyril were that the demarcation should be on the basis of contiguous Muslim or non-Muslim majority areas—with a loose provision that "other factors" should also be kept in mind. It was the kind of open-ended clause which gave enough room for any kind of interpretation, from the logical (river lines, water works etc.), to the arbitrary, to the unstated. Gurdaspur was a Muslim-majority district. The contiguous-communal argument could have taken it to Pakistan. Instead it came to India.

There were two main pre-Partition routes to Kashmir; one via Lahore, Rawalpindi and Murree into Muzaffarabad and Srinagar; the other through Sialkot, Jammu and the Banihal Pass. Neither would be available to India after Partition as both Lahore and Sialkot were bound to go to Pakistan. There was a third route, more a dirt track than a road, via Gurdaspur. If Gurdaspur was also awarded to Pakistan, there would be no effective road link between India and Kashmir until a new road could be constructed via Pathankot. Could Kashmir remain safe unless India was able to defend it? Nehru could hardly take the risk. And so, during private meetings, he persuaded Mountbatten to leave this Gurdaspur link in Indian hands.

Pakistan was, naturally, aware of this factor. H.V. Hodson writes in *The Great Divide: Britain, India, Pakistan* (Hutchinson, 1969):

> Early in August, Lord Ismay was given a strongly worded oral message from Mr Liaqat Ali Khan that if Gurdaspur district in the north of the Punjab or any large part of it were allotted to India this would be regarded as a most serious fact by Mr Jinnah and the Pakistan Government. If it turned out that such an award was a political rather than a judicial decision, it would amount to so grave a breach of faith as to imperil future friendly relations between Pakistan and Britain.

The Boundary Commission's report on Punjab was sent to the Viceroy on the afternoon of 13 August. Mountbatten, it is true, was busy; he went to Karachi on 14 August, and 15 August was hectic enough; so there was some justification for showing the award to the political parties only at 5 p.m. on 16 August. But this delay deepened Muslim League suspicions that the award had been tampered with under pressure from Mountbatten. When Liaqat saw that Gurdaspur had been divided along the line of the Ravi, leaving India with a road to Kashmir, he was furious. This was the "political" decision he had warned about, it was a "conspiracy" without which India could never have retained Kashmir. While conclusive evidence is impossible in such matters, Nehru's pressure on his friend Mountbatten was certainly a factor. That route was to prove an invaluable asset within just ten weeks of freedom. Without that route the Indian armed forces could never have reached Kashmir in sufficient strength to turn back the near-successful first offensive from Pakistan in October 1947. As for Sir Cyril, he never made a single comment on his decisions either on or off the record.

Nehru badgered Mountbatten so often on Kashmir, and so passionately, that Mountbatten once described him in an official report as "pathological". Perhaps that was why he was relieved when Patel took charge of the Ministry of States, formed on 5 July to supervise the integration of these theoretically independent powers into the emerging Indian union. Wrote the Viceroy:

> I am glad to say that Nehru has not been put in charge of the new States Department, which would have wrecked everything. Patel, who is essentially a realist and very sensible, is going to take it over. . . Even better news is that V.P. Menon is to be the Secretary.

Mountbatten was right: Jawaharlal's ideological anger against British-sponsored royalty would have made him a poor negotiator with the Princes, so many of whom seemed unable to emerge out of their fantasies. Bhopal, for instance, was determined to get independence; the Nawab resigned as Chancellor of the Chamber of Princes and refused to attend the meeting summoned by the Viceroy on 25 July rather than hear the bad news. Indore did not even reply to this invitation. Sir C.P. Ramaswamy Aiyar, the Dewan of Travancore, had been proclaiming loudly that he wanted independence; at his meeting with Mountbatten he showed the Viceroy a sheaf of press clippings including cartoons implying Gandhi was a sex-maniac and asked if this was the rule he was being told to accept. Aiyar had even signed a trade agreement with Jinnah! Hyderabad, the biggest of the states, actually managed to retain its independence until Operation Polo of the Indian Army, under the command of Major-General 'Jimmy' Chandhuri, ordered on 9 September 1948, started on 13 September and completed on 20 September, ended the rule of the Nizam. The young and foolish Maharaja Hanwant Singh of Jodhpur, a Rajput with mostly Hindu subjects, had gone so far as to work out a deal with Jinnah for accession to adjoining Pakistan! It required some stern arm-twisting to make Jodhpur see sense. His story does not end without a dose of melodrama. When the Maharaja of Jodhpur eventually came to the Viceroy's House to sign the Instrument of Accession, he brought out an exceptionally large pen. After Mountbatten had left the room, he whipped out the nib, revealing a pistol barrel, which he levelled at V.P. Menon, exclaiming, "I refuse to accept your dictation!" Menon told him not to indulge in juvenile theatricals. When Mountbatten was told of the Prince's conduct he "gave him hell".

With such a variety of types to deal with, Patel and Menon had more than enough to do. And yet there is nothing to explain their strange indifference to Kashmir. Their very earnestness elsewhere makes their unwillingness to persuade Hari Singh to sign the Instrument of Accession stand out in sharp contrast. It is entirely logical that Patel should have doubts about bringing a Muslim-majority border state into India, but with Nehru and Abdullah ready to provide the guarantee of popular support for such an accession, it is extraordinary that the Ministry of States made no attempt to bring Hari Singh into the Indian Union either before Partition or, even more shockingly, after 15 August. Patel could easily have pressurized Hari Singh into releasing Abdullah and negotiating a settlement long before Pakistan sparked off the crisis with a sponsored invasion. The problem would never—and should never—have reached the battlefield. In fact, if Nehru had not kept up his pressure, Sheikh Abdullah may not even have been released at all until it was too late.

Mountbatten narrates the story of his meeting with Patel when he offered the latter the States Department. Patel said: 'I am prepared to accept your offer provided that you give me a full basket of apples.'

'What do you mean?' asked Mountbatten.

'I'll buy a basket with 565 apples (that was the number of Princely States in India). But if there are even two or three missing the deal is off.'

'This,' replied Mountbatten 'I cannot completely accept, but I will do my best. If I give you a basket with, say, 560 apples will you buy it?'

'Well, I might,' replied Patel.

Had Patel written off Kashmir as one of the missing apples? That is the only explanation for his attitude towards what would become India's most severe problem.

V.P. Menon recalls in *Story of the Integration of the Indian States* (Orient Longman, Calcutta, 1956) that Kak, Prime Minister of Kashmir, was in Delhi when the States Ministry was formed in July. Kak was invited on the Maharaja of Patiala's suggestion to one of the exploratory conferences taking place but did not turn up. When Menon finally met Kak at the Viceroy's House, Kak was totally evasive on the critical question of which country Kashmir would join. Writes Menon:

> I could not understand the man nor fathom his game.

Actually Menon understood the game well enough; he himself puts it succinctly:

> But the Maharajah was in a Micawberish frame of mind, hoping for the best while continuing to do nothing. Besides he was toying with the notion of an "Independent Jammu and Kashmir".

India did not even sign a Standstill Agreement with Kashmir, and this time Delhi was as guilty of dithering. Menon explains:

> Pakistan signed a Standstill Agreement. But we wanted time to examine its implications. We left the State alone. We did not ask the Maharajah to accede, though, at that time (after Partition), as a result of the Radcliffe Award, the State had become connected by road with India. Owing to the composition of the population the State had its own peculiar problems. Moreover, our hands were already full and, if truth be told, I for one had simply no time to think of Kashmir.

It is a stunning admission: the Secretary of the States Ministry had no time to think of Kashmir. Either between 5 July and 15 August or between 15 August and 27 October. Worse, Menon admits that the objective situation had been created in favour of accession by the Radcliffe Award. If Patel and Menon had put even half the pressure on Hari Singh that they put on Jodhpur, Abdullah would have been free much earlier and a tripartite settlement arranged in favour of India long before Pakistan's aggression. This is what Nehru kept pleading for. He even warned his Cabinet that Pakistan was preparing to invade Kashmir; and India should settle the Kashmir question before any such military adventure.

Hodson too is puzzled by Patel's negligence towards the third largest Princely State (only Hyderabad and Mysore were bigger). He writes in

The Great Divide:

> The States Ministry of the Government of India meanwhile
> was strictly passive. Kashmir was deliberately omitted from
> a committee of States' representatives called by the pre-
> independence States Department to discuss terms of acces-
> sion, though Hyderabad was included.

The phrase is startling: "deliberately omitted". It seems almost as if there
was a conspiracy by Patel to keep Kashmir out of India. Hodson continues:

> After independence, a representative of the Kashmir
> Government who sought a lead from the States Ministry
> on the choice between India and Pakistan was told by the
> Secretary (Mr V.P. Menon) that the Government of India
> could give no guidance in the matter, and that if a formal
> proposal for accession was received it would be con-
> sidered in the light of all the relevant factors.

For anyone who believes that Kashmir should be in India, this is appalling.
This is confirmation of the view that Patel felt it would be far better for
the ninety-six per cent Muslim Kashmir Valley to go to Pakistan. What
was an asset to Nehru was a liability to Patel; the vision of Nehru was in
conflict with the "realism" of Patel. Four-and-a-half decades later, as the
guns boom across the Valley, an interesting question also arises: was
Nehru wrong, and was Patel right? Was it wrong to believe that Hindus
and Muslims, and millions of Nehrus and Abdullahs, could march
together to fight the battles of hunger, poverty, disease and illiteracy, to
build dams and powerhouses and great factories which would lift this
nation into prosperity? Was it wrong to believe that the bitterness of
communalism could be defeated by faith and leadership? Was it naïve to
believe in a tryst with destiny? Was it sentimental to trust in the stability
of a secular India? Perhaps the answer is that Indian unity has no option
except faith in the vision of a Nehru.

However, it was this dichotomy on the part of the Indian government in
those weeks which left Kashmir becalmed in unnatural isolation until Pakistan
acted. Jinnah was encouraged by Indian indifference. He seemed to have
everything going for him in Kashmir: a Muslim majority, geographical access,
Delhi's negligence and Srinagar's vacillation. It would have been a miracle
if Jinnah had not been tempted to take advantage.

And Jinnah was in no mood to gift miracles to the nation he had just
broken.

14

Do Not Disturb

His Highness the Maharaja Bahadur Hari Singh did not want to be woken up. On 26 October 1947, after having escaped from Srinagar to his palace in Jammu, he left instructions with his ADC that he was not to be disturbed in any eventuality. His reasoning was simple. If V.P. Menon arrived then it meant that India had decided to rescue him, and he could sleep on, content. If Menon did not come, then it meant that all was over and the ADC could end the story by shooting him in his sleep.

It was perhaps the ultimate vacillation. As Alan Campbell-Johnson, Mountbatten's press attaché noted in his much-quoted diary, *Mission with Mountbatten* (London, 1951), on 28 October 1947:

> The Maharaja's chronic indecision must be accounted a big factor in the present crisis. Almost any course of action would have saved his State from this turmoil. Procrastination alone was fatal. . .

Fortunately for Hari Singh, V.P. Menon's arrival in Jammu prevented too fatal an end, but it was also too late now to avoid turmoil. It was the beginning of a nightmare that has only intensified with succeeding generations. When it could have been prevented with a little more watchfulness, the only person who was awake to the dimensions of the problem was Nehru. He wrote a remarkable letter to Patel as early as on 27 September 1947, at the height of what might be called the Stalemate Pause:

> It is obvious to me from the many reports I have received that the situation there (in Kashmir) is a dangerous and deteriorating one. The Muslim League in the Punjab and the NWFP are making preparations to enter Kashmir in considerable numbers. . . . I understand that the Pakistan strategy is to infiltrate into Kashmir now and to take some big action as soon as Kashmir is more or less isolated because of the coming winter. . .

If the analysis had come straight from a mole in the Pakistan Cabinet it could not have been more accurate. But what is astonishing is that Patel did not make any move to prepare for this predicted onslaught. Nehru was clear in his own mind about what needed to be done. He continued in his letter:

> Whether this strategy succeeds or not depends upon the forces opposed to it.

Who could they be? Not the Maharaja's army.

> I rather doubt if the Maharajah and his State forces can meet the situation by themselves and without popular help.

Who could organize the people?

> Obviously the only major group that can side with them is the National Conference under Sheikh Abdullah's leadership. If by any chance that is hostile or even passive then the Maharajah and his Government become isolated and the Pakistani people will have a relatively free field.

What did Nehru want Patel to do?

> I hope you will be able to take some action in this matter to force the pace and to turn events in the right direction. We have definitely a great asset in the National Conference provided it is properly handled. It would be a pity to lose this. Sheikh Abdullah has repeatedly given assurances of wishing to cooperate and of being opposed to Pakistan; also to abide by my advice. I would again add time is the essence of the business and things must be done in a way so as to bring about the accession of Kashmir to the Indian Union as rapidly as possible with the cooperation of Sheikh Abdullah.

There is a historic poignancy in each sentence as one contemplates the tragedies that might have been prevented if Nehru's sense of urgency had prevailed. But though Patel used his power and influence to get Abdullah released within two days of this letter (evidence, incidentally, of the clout he could wield over Hari Singh when he wanted to), nothing more happened for three long weeks. No one made any effort to go to Kashmir and get Hari Singh's signature despite the fact that Abdullah was waiting to endorse the accession and form a popular government with the whole of Kashmir safely in the Indian Union. On 4 October, he told a mammoth public meeting in Srinagar, his first after release:

> I never believed in the Pakistan slogan. . . Pandit Jawaharlal Nehru is my best friend and I hold Gandhiji in real reverence.

And when he came to Delhi he stayed with his best friend, at Jawaharlal's official residence at 17 York Road, (Nehru summoned his daughter Indira from Lucknow to improve the kitchen as the Sheikh's love for good food was famous.) But again nothing happened—until everything happened.

Pakistan began by applying an economic squeeze on Kashmir, through the land routes she controlled. Food supplies were checked, the vital Sialkot-Jammu railway service suspended; and small armed groups began probing the Maharaja's military defences. What they found there was most encouraging; Kashmir was in no position to offer any serious defence. Simultaneously, a propaganda offensive was launched to arouse Muslim sentiment against Hari Singh to fuel an uprising in the Valley which could coincide with the invasion. The horrible outburst of vicious riots as the caravans seeking refuge began crossing the new frontiers gave sustenance to the propaganda, and Jammu was a focal point of the rising hatred as the columns of stunned and betrayed and destroyed people crossed each other on the volatile Pathankot road. On 2 October, the Pakistan government cabled Srinagar that food supplies were being hampered because "Drivers of lorries, for instance, are reluctant to carry supplies between Rawalpindi and Kohala. . ." By 19 October, Karachi told Srinagar that the difficulties in transport were beyond the control of the government. That may or may not have been true. But what is beyond doubt is that the government of Pakistan was giving its full attention to organizing a different kind of transport.

The tribes of the North West Frontier Province may have been burnished by the romance of Kipling's poetry but the truth was more harsh. Poor, illiterate, controlled by wanton chieftains, outside the discipline of law, victims of a gun-culture, they were the classic fodder for a sponsored invasion. They were told to go and "liberate" Kashmir in the name of Islam; and this fervour was lubricated by the promise of booty. On 21 October, they began to assemble for the invasion at their camps, ready to roll in trucks and lorries organized by the authorities, bearing arms provided through the Muslim League as well as the government.

On 22 October 1947, between two and three hundred vehicles carrying at least 5,000 Afridis, Wazirs, Masuds, Swatis "and soldiers of the Pakistan Army 'on leave'", according to Hodson, launched the main attack along the Jhelum valley road. They were enthusiastic and undisciplined, but they were ably led—by Pakistan Army officers. The chief of operations was Major-General Akbar Khan of the Pakistan Army, using the pseudonym General Tariq. Their objective: to celebrate Id in the main mosque of Srinagar. Id that year was on 26 October: it was meant to be all over in four days, with Jinnah riding in triumph into the capital of Kashmir on the festive day. Unfortunately for him, a few imponderables like loot, rape and pillage interrupted the carefully planned time-schedule of the *jihad*.

Domel was the first city to fall. That was easy because there was no one to defend it. The first check came sixteen miles later, at Garhi, where Brigadier Rajinder Singh—appointed Chief of Staff of the State army only on 14 August 1947—organized some resistance at the head of a motley crew of about 150 men including non-combatants. It was a holding operation but a valuable one. Rajinder Singh destroyed the bridge at Uri, checking the advance, and by the time he was encircled and killed at Rampur he had served his cause with courage and intelligence. He was justly honoured with a posthumous Maha Vir Chakra when the first Indian military honours were instituted. By 26 October the raiders had only reached Baramulla instead of Srinagar.

But the main block to their progress remained a self-inflicted one: greed. They left a trail of horror along the way, raping and abducting women, looting, and murdering civilians. The incidents at Baramulla may or may not have been the worst of their kind, but they were best documented thanks to journalists who followed in the wake of the Indian Army. In fact, if the raiders had not paused to satisfy their lusts, Kashmir would probably have been secure in Pakistan's grasp. History so often turns on mistakes made at the edges of great events. Robert Trumbull, correspondent of *The New York Times,* sent this despatch, published on 10 November:

> The city had been stripped of its wealth and young women before the tribesmen fled in terror, at midnight Friday, before the advancing Indian Army. Surviving residents estimate that 3,000 of their fellow townsmen including four Europeans and a retired British Army Officer, known only as Colonel Dykes, and his pregnant wife, were slain. When the raiders rushed into town on October 26th, witnesses said: 'One party of Masud tribesmen immediately

scaled the walls of St Joseph Franciscan Convent compound, and stormed the Convent Hospital and the little church. Four nuns and Colonel Dykes, and his wife were shot immediately. The raiders' greed triumphed over their blood lust.' A former town official said: 'The raiders forced 350 local Hindus into a house, with the intention of burning it down. . .' Today, 24 hours after the Indian Army entered Baramulla, only 1,000 were left of a normal population of 14,000.

The murder of the Europeans had its own consequences. Word about Baramulla obviously did not reach the serving British military officers immediately, but they had no illusions, even in October, about what would happen to the European community and to the Mission School if the tribals ever reached Srinagar. Quietly, they made contingency plans for the evacuation of the Europeans. This, as well as their anger against the tribals, was to play an important part in the decisions that followed in rapid sequence once news reached Delhi of the invasion.

Pakistan's official line in the beginning was that this was a "spontaneous" uprising against a Hindu Raj in which the tribals had joined because they could not bear to watch the agony of their brothers and sisters in Kashmir. Doubtless if the invasion had succeeded they would have queued up in Karachi to take credit. But the failure, compounded by the reports of atrocities, made it vital for Pakistan to maintain this fiction. Pakistan kept insisting on its non-involvement with a vigour which governments only display for a lie. But it was too public an event for a lie to be sustained. Foreign journalists quickly exposed it. Alan Moorehead of the *Observer* (London) reported that recruitment for the invasion had been going on not only in tribal territory but in the rest of Pakistan too. Kingsley Martin had much the same thing to report in the magazine he edited then, the *New Statesman and Nation*. After a visit to the subcontinent, he reported in February 1948

> nor can there be any question that encouragement and aid have been given to the tribesmen in Pakistan.

On 11 January 1948, *The Times* (London) reported:

> That Pakistan is unofficially involved in aiding the raiders is certain. Your correspondent has first-hand evidence that arms, ammunition and supplies are being made available to the Azad Kashmir forces. A few Pakistani officers are

also helping to direct their operations. . . . And however much the Pakistan government may disavow intervention, moral and material support is certainly forthcoming. . .

The real hard evidence was produced by Trumbull, who secretly interviewed in Lahore an American mercenary Russel K. Haight Jr. who had served for two months in the Azad Kashmir Army:

> Mr Haight also found Pakistan Army personnel running the Azad Kashmir radio station, relaying messages through their own Pakistan Army receivers, organising and managing Azad encampments in Pakistan, and supplying uniforms, food, arms and ammunition which, he understood, came from Pakistan Army stores through such subterfuges as the 'loss' of ammunition shipments. . . Mr Haight characterized the Azad Kashmir provisional government, headed by Sardar Mohammad Ibrahim Khan, as 'Pakistan puppets'. He also deeply implicated high Pakistan government officials, notably the Premier of the North-West Frontier Province.

Then there was evidence from within Pakistan itself—inevitably. Michael Brecher in his book, *The Struggle for Kashmir* (Oxford, 1953) quotes the appeal made by the Minister of Health for Sind

> to all trained and demobilized soldiers to proceed as volunteers to the Kashmir front.

In his Budget speech, on 7 March 1949, the NWFP Premier Abdul Qayyum Khan, justifying a special grant for tribesmen, said:

> The House will recall with pride the fact that in our greatest hour of danger the Masuds responded to our call by rushing to the rescue of the oppressed Muslims of Jammu and Kashmir State.

Later, when the debate had become academic, Major-General Akbar Khan came out of the closet to explain that Pakistan had not been able to succeed in its objective only because of an old, old disease: corruption. Speaking at a public meeting in Karachi (reported in *The Pakistan Times* of 24 June 1956) he alleged that some of the guns sent for the tribals had been siphoned off and sold along the way. A familiar syndrome. Even the Khan of Mamdot, Premier of West Punjab at that time, was asked by the

Controller of Military Accounts to submit an account of his expenditure of the Kashmir Relief Fund. He replied that his answer

> might yet affect the future of Pakistan in certain matters... it was understood that the expenditure would have to be of a secret and confidential nature requiring single direction.

And on 1 August 1948, Sir A. Dundas, then governor of NWFP, told an informal meeting of the United Nations Commission for India and Pakistan (the first interim report appeared on 22 November 1948) that

> the movement of tribesmen into Kashmir had in fact to be canalized through his Province in order to avoid the serious risk of outright war with the territory of Pakistan. Further, he said that the tribesmen obtained petrol from local sources in Pakistan and made use of railways and local motor transport...

But Pakistan's official position remained the outright lie. In his letter sent on 30 December 1947, Liaqat Ali Khan told Nehru:

> As regards the charges of aid and assistance to the 'invaders' by the Pakistan Government we emphatically repudiate them. On the contrary... the Pakistan Government have continued to do all in their power to discourage the tribal movements by all means short of war.

At the United Nations their brilliant Foreign Minister Sir Zafarullah Khan kept insisting:

> We emphatically deny that the Pakistani Government are giving aid and assistance to the so-called invaders, or have committed any act of aggression against India.

The National Conference's role in this invasion is best summed up by the heroism of Mir Maqbool Sherwani, a young shopkeeper in Baramulla. It is important to remember that Sherwani was not doing anything under instructions; in fact when the invaders reached Baramulla, Abdullah was in Delhi and the party as startled as anyone else. His behaviour was the manifestation of faith in a vision. Margaret Bourke-White reports the story in *Halfway to Freedom* (Simon & Schuster, 1949):

> In Baramulla the townspeople told me of a young Muslim

shopkeeper who had sacrificed his life rather than recant in his creed of religious tolerance. His martyrdom had taken place almost under the shadow of the convent walls, and in the memory of the devoted Kashmiris he was fast assuming the stature of a saint.

When the tribesmen invaded Kashmir and terrorized the countryside, Sherwani, who knew every footpath in the Valley, began working behind the lines, keeping up the morale of the besieged villagers, urging them to resist and to stick together regardless of whether they were Hindus, Sikhs, or Muslims, assuring them that help from the Indian Army and People's Militia was on the way. Three times by skilfully planted rumours, he decoyed bands of tribesmen and got them surrounded and captured by the Indian infantry. But the fourth time he was captured himself.

The tribesmen took Sherwani to the stoop of a little apple shop in the town square in front of him with butts of rifles. Knowing Sherwani's popularity with the people, his captors ordered him to make a public announcement that Pakistan was the best solution for Muslims. When he refused, he was lashed to the porch posts with ropes, his arms spread out in the shape of a cross.

It was a curious thing that the tribesmen did next. I don't know why these savage nomads should have thought of such a thing, unless the sight of the sacred figures in Saint Joseph's Chapel on the hill just above had suggested it to them. They drove nails through the palms of Sherwani's hands. On his forehead they pressed a jagged piece of tin and wrote on it: 'The punishment of a traitor is death'.

Once more Sherwani cried out, 'Victory to Hindu-Muslim unity' and fourteen tribesmen shot bullets into his body.

If only Sherwani had lived just a little longer—till the afternoon of 8 November. That was the day the Indian Army liberated Baramulla. But Kashmir and India might never have seen this day were it not for a curious fact about the command structure of the Indian Army just after freedom.

The Indian Army, the Royal Indian Navy and the Royal Indian Air Force were also partitioned on 15 August, and many a soldier wept more at the partition of his Army than at the partition of India. Field-Marshal Sir Claude Auchinleck was named Supreme Commander until the process had been completed: and all the six Indian and Pakistani Commanders-in-Chief of the two armies, navies and air for es (all still British, incidentally) reported to him.

The British officers and officials working in Pak'stan had got wind of the impending invasion some time before it happened. A letter Sir George Cunningham, governor of the NWFP, wrote to General R.M.M. Lockhart, Commander-in-Chief of the Indian Army, before the attack ended with the postscript:

> Some people up here have been acting very foolishly. You
> will know what I mean by the time this letter reaches you.

General Sir Frank Messervy, Commander-in-Chief in Pakistan, formally advised Liaqat against such adventurism, and repeated his advice before flying to London on work. The British brass were aware, and in touch with their counterparts in Delhi across the new frontier.

Hari Singh learnt the bad news when the raiders damaged the Mohore power station on Friday the 24th, blacking out Srinagar. Finally woken up, he sent an urgent appeal to Delhi for military aid. That evening Mountbatten, now Governor-General of India to smooth the transition to Swadeshi Raj, was a guest of Nehru at an official dinner for the visiting Foreign Minister of Siam (now Thailand). Nehru took him aside and informed him. Mountbatten, on Nehru's advice, acted immediately. He summoned a meeting of the Defence Committee for 11 a.m. on the 25th. By that time on his desk lay a full brief from General Lockhart on the situation in Kashmir—possible at such short notice because the Army officers already had information. The Defence Committee learnt that Srinagar lay virtually defenceless before hordes of marauding tribesmen. Mountbatten felt that no final decision should be taken without more information. V.P. Menon, accompanied by senior Army and Air Force officers, flew to Srinagar in a BOAC plane kept ready for the evacuation of European citizens. V.P. Menon recalls in his memoirs:

> When I landed at the airfield (on the 25th), I was oppressed
> by the stillness as of a graveyard all around. Over every-
> thing hung an atmosphere of impending calamity.

From the airport he drove straight to the residence of the Prime Minister. Hari Singh had finally dispensed with Kak, but seemed to have difficulty retaining his successors: first came Major-General Janak Singh, and then, in October, Mehr Chand Mahajan. Menon found both Mahajan and Hari Singh totally unnerved and agreed that the best thing for Hari Singh to do was to get away; the Maharaja did not need any further persuasion. He commandeered all the cars he could find, packed all his valuables and sped to Jammu, leaving only one battered jeep for the use of Menon. And it was in this dilapidated vehicle that Menon, Mahajan, their aides and the air crew left for the airport before dawn on the 26th, amid rumours that the raiders had reached the city. If they had, they could have walked in. The only semblance of resistance was from the People's Militia, National Conference volunteers armed with nothing more than lathis under the leadership of Bakshi Ghulam Mohammad. As Hodson records:

> As events fell out, another hour or two's delay in holding the Defence Committee meeting of 25th October, by preventing the action that was taken on its instructions that day, might have fully vindicated such a strategy on the invaders' part—if indeed it was a strategy and not accident—by allowing them to take Srinagar airfield and so oblige any Indian reinforcements to advance by the slow, hazardous and probably ambushed land route in the teeth of impending winter.

And certainly Jinnah and Liaqat, who had witnessed such lethargy on the part of Delhi over Kashmir all this while, never expected the devastating speed with which Mountbatten and Nehru acted to save from the brink what had nearly been lost by sloth or indifference.

Despite the fact that a final decision was not yet taken, the first meeting of the Defence Committee discussed how quickly arms could be flown into Kashmir. (All these details are on record in government documents collected in the twelve volumes of *The Transfer of Power*, edited by Nicholas Mansergh and Penderel Moon). A very vital decision was also made: to shift the chartered BOAC aircraft to civilian routes so that Indian-owned civilian aircraft could be kept available for a possible airlift to Kashmir. It turned out to be the most important decision of the whole episode, since without a ready fleet of aircraft the astonishing airlift forty-eight hours later would simply never have been possible. The Commanders-in-Chief were instructed to give these orders the highest priority. Here Mountbatten's presence proved critical—because, as we shall see, the British officers in the Pakistan Army simply refused to obey Jinnah at a vital moment of this story of swinging fortunes. To prevent any future objections it was also decided that the arms could be sent to either the Maharaja's government or to any provisional government that might be formed in this crisis.

Nehru was already convinced about two things: that the raiders were part of a Pakistani operation; and that the only answer was a political-military counteroffensive in cooperation with Sheikh Abdullah. He, of course, accepted in principle that the accession of Kashmir should be ratified by the will of the people, but that could hardly be ascertained in the middle of an invasion. Mountbatten put forward the idea of temporary accession, conditional to popular endorsement later. Nehru agreed that they must ultimately abide by the will of the people, but the more pressing point was that immediate armed intervention might be necessary. Patel wanted to send the Indian Army to Kashmir whether the Maharaja signed the Instrument of Accession or not, and Nehru agreed. A final decision was postponed till Menon reported back.

Menon came with his on-the-spot version the next morning. Mountbatten now voiced the view that, legally, Indian troops could only be sent if Kashmir became a part of India and added the rider that, in view of the high percentage of Muslims, a plebiscite would have to be held after the raiders had been driven out completely and law and order restored. Nehru and Patel agreed.

Menon rushed back to Jammu to get Hari Singh's signature on the Instrument of Accession. He reached the palace to find Hari Singh in that sleep which he did not want disturbed. Menon was not in a mood for feudal niceties. The royal sleep was immediately interrupted, and the frightened Maharaja quickly signed everything. He also agreed to set up an interim government headed by Sheikh Abdullah.

Patel was waiting at the airport for Menon to return with the signed document, and both drove straight to the third meeting of the Defence Committee. They formally accepted accession, subject to a plebiscite when the situation permitted. A second decision was taken: an infantry batallion would be flown out to Srinagar by the following morning.

Mountbatten, and the chiefs of the Army, Navy and Air Force, their memories of a war they had just won still very fresh, pointed out that this was far easier said by Nehru than done by the armed forces. But there was an unspoken reason which made the British commanders lean towards intervention—the fear that the Europeans staying in the Valley would be massacred by the tribals. Auchinleck had in fact wanted to send British troops to evacuate the Europeans, but had been refused permission in a heated exchange with Mountbatten. Now, of course, the case for non-intervention had collapsed. The Governor-General wrote in his Personal

Report to the King on 7 November 1947:

> The Commanders pointed out the extreme hazards of
> flying in troops, and I added my voice to theirs. But as
> soon as I saw my Ministers had made up their minds that
> the military risks must be accepted and Indian troops sent,
> I was clear that it was essential to send sufficient and in
> time. . .

They went; and Operation JAK, as it was named, would leave even the
seasoned generals of the Second World War amazed. Instructions to get
a battalion ready were received at the Delhi-East Punjab Headquarters
(now Western Command) just after the Defence Committee meeting—at
one in the afternoon of 26 October. By midnight a battalion plus one
company had been assembled at Palam airport; by first light they were
airborne. The rest of the First Sikhs followed within twenty-four hours.
V.P. Menon writes:

> Never in the history of warfare has there been an operation
> like the airlift of Indian troops to Srinagar on 27 October
> and on subsequent days, an operation put through with no
> previous thought, let alone organised planning, and at such
> remarkably short notice. . .   In the early hours of the
> morning of 27 October over a hundred civilian aircraft and
> R.I.A.F. planes were mobilised to fly troops, equipment
> and supplies to Srinagar. The R.I.A.F. and civilian pilots
> and ground crews rose to the occasion and worked heroi-
> cally to make the airlift a success.

Menon may be said to be a partisan Indian and a civilian, but Mountbatten,
who had just been Chief of Combined Operations and Supreme Allied
Commander, South East Asia, said that

> in all his war experience he had never heard of an airlift
> of this nature being put into operation at such short notice
> and he complimented all concerned on the astonishing
> performance.

The Pakistanis had never heard of such a thing either, and they simply
did not believe a word about the "short notice". They were convinced
that it was all part of a premeditated conspiracy masterminded by Nehru
and Mountbatten. Suspicions were so pronounced that the three British
commanders had to issue "a true timetable of events" to convince

everyone that:

> No plans were made for sending these forces, nor were
> such plans even considered, before 25th October, three
> days after the tribal incursions began.

Jinnah had a great deal to be angry with the British that week. He ordered
his Army to move, and it disobeyed him.

It would have been naïve to expect Jinnah to sit back calmly and watch
Indian troops drive back his Pakistan Army-led raiders. As soon as he
heard that Indian troops had reached Srinagar, he ordered Sir Francis
Mudie, Governor of Punjab, to phone General Sir Douglas Gracey, acting
chief in the absence of General Messervey, to send the Pakistan Army at
once into Kashmir. Their instructions would be to head towards Srinagar
through the Rawalpindi-Srinagar route, as well as take the Banihal Pass
to prevent Indian reinforcements from coming by road. Gracey refused
to take orders from Jinnah. He said he would need the confirmation of
Auchinleck. Mudie, on a suggestion from Jinnah, tried to get tough.
Gracey ignored him. Auchinleck was in Delhi. He flew to Lahore on the
morning of 28 October and gave Jinnah the Mountbatten line: now that
Kashmir was legally part of India, sending the Pakistan Army would
amount to a formal declaration of war. And if Pakistan went to war,
Auchinleck said, he would withdraw every British officer serving in the
Pakistan Army. Jinnah was stumped.

It is obvious that if the Pakistan Army had intervened then, India would
not have been able to hold Kashmir. The tale of the battle in the early
stages proves as much. On the morning of 27 October Delhi was not even
sure whether the First Sikhs, posted on internal security duties at Gurgaon
and shunted at bewildering speed would be able to reach Srinagar. Lt.
Colonel Dewan Ranjit Rai, in command, had orders to land only if he was
certain that the airport had not fallen; if he had the remotest doubt he was
to fly back to Jammu and await further orders. The wireless flash that the
troops had landed reached Delhi only at 10.30 in the morning.

Rai learnt that the raiders had taken Baramulla; he decided to confront
them. Obviously he had no army transport, but Bakshi Ghulam Mohammad
delivered: he organized local buses to take Indian troops to within two miles
of Baramulla. It was only when battle was joined that Rai realized that
there was nothing primitive about the tribal attack; they were equipped
with light and medium machine guns, as well as mortars and mines, and
their commanders were fully conversant with battle tactics. He deployed
a reserve force on a hill along the main road, while another set out to probe

the enemy. Soon he discovered small parties of raiders working their way round his flanks to encircle both his groups. He immediately ordered his reserve force to withdraw in the buses, and began to disengage the rest. By the time he, with the last handful, had begun to move back, heavy fire was coming across from all sides. Lt. Colonel Rai was not destined to survive. He fell to a sniper's bullet. But his action decisively staggered the Pak advance and changed the course of the war. His heroic sacrifice was honoured with a Maha Vir Chakra. By the end of the first day, Indian troops had drawn a line at Pattan, seventeen miles from Srinagar.

The Indian Air Force had begun to mobilize too; Spitfires and Tempests arrived to provide air support. And in came 161 Brigade, led by the famous Brigadier L.P. Sen, who had won a DSO in the battle of Kangaw in the Arakan in Burma. He was given charge of all the troops, the first of many officers and jawans who were to become household names in 1947 and 1948: Major-General Kalwant Singh, Major-General K.S. Thimayya, Major-General Atma Singh, Air Vice Marshal S. Mukherjee. . . Sen was forced to pull back from Pattan as the raiders now mounted their offensive for Srinagar through four columns, from the west, south-west, north-west and north. By 3 November, the raiders had pushed back a company of the First Kumaon Regiment, and Sen had to reorganize his defences to hold a line about four-and-a-half miles to the west of Srinagar. The Pakistanis were now convinced that Srinagar would fall to a final assault. The Indian commanders had different ideas.

A squadron of armoured cars had finally completed the hazardous journey over the Banihal route, using pontoon bridges where necessary. When they drove into Srinagar, crowds lined up on both sides to cheer. By the morning of November, Major-General Kalwant Singh (who reached on 5 November to take command) and Brigadier Sen were ready to show Pakistan what war was all about. They moved towards the raiders' main position, a village called Shalteng, even as a troop of armoured cars manoeuvred to attack from the rear. Another column started down the Baramulla road to attack from the right, and the IAF provided support from the air. The battle lasted eight hours. By the afternoon of 8 November, the Indian Army had entered Baramulla, and the raiders were in total retreat, leaving at least 300 dead.

The momentum of that victory could have taken Indian troops up to Muzaffarabad, but fate willed otherwise. A shortage of petrol halted the troops, enabling the raiders to blow up bridges to stem the Indian advance. Uri,Tanmarg and Gulmarg were taken by 14 November, but by this time the initiative had stalled. Winter soon prevented any decisive operations. A large number of Indian troops had simply never seen snow before; worse, they were completely underequipped. The commanders could only plan for the spring, and there were a number of exciting successes that spring and summer, forcing Pakistan to finally give up its pretence, and formally enter the war. Thimayya, who succeeded Kalwant Singh, was confident—and he would nurse this complaint all through his life—that he would have eventually taken Muzaffarabad had he not been stopped by the politicians.

The war between India and Pakistan for the beautiful Valley of Kashmir paused a minute before midnight on the first day of 1949: precisely one year after Jawaharlal Nehru had committed what turned out to be one of the biggest blunders of his seventeen years in power. He had internationalized the dispute over Kashmir by taking it to the United Nations.

15

The Will of the People; the Wont of the Powers

"You can't build a nation on tricks."

It was one of those remarks which illuminates the future. Lord Mountbatten was speaking to Ian Stephens, editor of *The Statesman* at Government House on Tuesday, 28 October 1947, a meeting provoked by the paper's editorial criticism of the decision to send Indian troops into Kashmir. Still livid over Jinnah's underhand tactics in Kashmir, Mountbatten continued:

> Jinnah at Abbotabad. . . had been expecting to ride in triumph into Kashmir. He had been frustrated. . . . India's move on Kashmir was an event of a different order. Her readiness to accept a plebiscite had been declared from the outset. A largescale massacre, including a couple of hundred British residents in Srinagar, by tribesmen would have been inevitable if no military move had been made. The Maharaja's accession gave complete legality to the action so far taken.

The quotation is taken from *Mission With Mountbatten,* the diary of Alan Campbell-Johnson, CIE, OBE, Legion of Merit (USA), press attaché and head of the personal staff of Lord Mountbatten from January 1947 to June 1948, when Mountbatten said an emotional farewell to India. Forty years after the diary was first published in 1951, the sentence that strikes the eye most sharply is not the one about Pakistan's intentions, but India's. It is both perfectly true and perfectly logical: plebiscite began as an Indian demand, formally articulated in the first Indo-Pak talks on Kashmir, on 1 November 1947.

The invasion of the tribals suddenly lifted Kashmir out of the background and pushed it on to the front page. It also forced everyone to take a public position on a complicated problem made infinitely more complex by the first use of force in Indo-Pak relations. For the moment, however, the invasion served a very useful purpose in India: the instant and unanimous outrage melted all differences, strengthening Nehru immeasurably. Mahatma Gandhi, often taunted with the question in the war years as to how far his non-violence would succeed against a brutal invasion, now gave the answer: non-violence could wait. On 29 October he met Mountbatten for ninety minutes to display his complete support for the Indian response. What Gandhi said privately he said publicly. On the 27th itself, he had told his daily prayer meeting that he would not mind if the small Indian force which had reached Srinagar were wiped out, or if Sheikh Abdullah died resisting Pakistan: they would have fallen for a noble cause. That same day, the 27th, Sheikh Abdullah also publicly lashed out against Pakistan, telling *The Times of India* (the interview was published on 28 October) that Kashmir was in dire peril; and that the tribal incursions had to be opposed.

Pakistan had made one last attempt before the invasion to woo Abdullah. In mid-September, Jinnah's emissaries contacted National Conference leaders in Srinagar; in October, G.M. Sadiq went twice to meet the Pakistani Prime Minister, Liaqat Ali Khan. But all that the National Conference leaders would say was that Pakistan should not force the issue, and they would not support accession to Pakistan. The invasion aborted the dialogue. On 31 October, Abdullah sent a signal of peace to Pakistan. *The Hindustan Times* quoted him, on 2 November, as saying:

> I . . . request Mr Jinnah to accept the democratic principle of the sovereignty of people of our State, including as it does 78 per cent Muslims, whose free and unhampered choice must count in the matter of final accession.

That was the moral key: India was willing to stand by the option of a free and unhampered choice, Pakistan was not. Jinnah, in fact, was in a trap. He had laid claim to Junagadh, which had a Hindu majority, purely on the basis of the Nawab's right to join whichever nation he chose to. If the will of the majority of the people was not going to be a consideration in the positions Jinnah took on Junagadh or Hyderabad, he could hardly alter the rules for Kashmir. India was consistent: let the people, rather than their rulers, decide their own fate, whether in Junagadh or Hyderabad or Kashmir. In fact, the first decision by Delhi was to instal a popular government in Kashmir. On 30 October 1947 Hari Singh signed Order Number 176-H:

> We are hereby pleased to command that pending the
> formation of an Interim Government as agreed upon and
> in view of the emergency that has arisen I charge Sheikh
> Mohammad Abdullah to function as the Head of the
> Administration with power to deal with the emergency.

The twenty-three-member Emergency Council included Bakshi Ghulam
Mohammad, Mirza Mohammad Afzal Beg, G.M. Sadiq, Sham Lal Saraf,
Girdhari Lal Dogra, D.P. Dhar and J.N. Zutshi. Plebiscite was also part
of the formal commitment which Mountbatten made on behalf of the
Government of India on 27 October, in reply to Hari Singh's nine-point
acceptance of the Instrument of Accession. The relevant portion needs to
be reproduced (the full text, only slightly longer, is available in *Kashmir:
Constitutional History and Documents* by Mohan Krishen Teng, Ram
Krishen Kaul Bhatt and Santosh Kaul):

> In the special circumstances mentioned by Your Highness,
> my Government have decided to accept the accession of
> Kashmir State to the Dominion of India. Consistently with
> their policy that, in the case of any State where the issue
> of accession should be decided in accordance with the
> wishes of the people of the State, it is my Government's
> wish that, as soon as law and order have been restored in
> Kashmir and her soil cleared of the invader, the question
> of the State's accession should be settled by a reference to
> the people.

The commitment was categorical. This was precisely what Mountbatten
offered Jinnah on 1 November in Lahore. And it was Jinnah who objected!

This meeting had been proposed by Auchinleck as a sop after he refused
to order the Pakistan Army officially into Kashmir on 27 October. He
suggested a round table conference including Mountbatten, Nehru,
Jinnah, Liaqat, Hari Singh and Abdullah. Of course, after accession the
last two had no locus standi, so they were not considered by Delhi.
Mountbatten was keen on immediate talks, Nehru agreeable, but the
Sardar was violently opposed, pointing out that talks at this stage would
be akin to Munich-style appeasement:

> For the Prime Minister to go crawling to Mr Jinnah when
> we are the stronger side and in the right would never be
> forgiven by the people of India.

Patel was talking of moral strength; the military strength had not yet been proved. Nehru felt that a false sense of prestige should not sabotage a chance of peace. In any case, another factor intervened; Nehru came down with fever. (Campbell-Johnson on 28 October: "I was shocked to see how haggard and ill Nehru looked.") Liaqat would later maintain that this was only diplomatic illness. However, the meeting was finally fixed for 1 November, and the mechanism agreed upon was a conference of the Joint Defence Council (composed of representatives from both India and Pakistan) already scheduled for the first week of November. Nehru agreed to fly to Lahore with Mountbatten on the morning of the first.

But on the evening of 31 October Nehru read an official statement by Pakistan describing the accession as a triumph of "fraud and violence"; on 4 November Liaqat would repeat this phrase, still standard in Pakistani officialese four decades later, in a broadcast to his country:

> We do not recognise this accession. The accession of
> Kashmir to India is a fraud, perpetrated on the people of
> Kashmir by its cowardly Ruler with the aggressive help of
> the Indian Government.

The 31 October statement was too much for Nehru to take. He cancelled his visit, and Mountbatten went alone. Nehru's views on the Kashmir question are apparent in two statements, the first a coolly reasoned letter to the British Prime Minister Clement Attlee, on 25 October, while the problem was cascading into a crisis; the second a revealing speech in Parliament eleven months after. He wrote to Attlee:

> Kashmir's northern frontiers, as you are aware, run in
> common with those of three countries, Afghanistan, the
> USSR and China. Security of Kashmir. . . is vital to
> security of India especially since part of the southern
> boundary of Kashmir and India are common. Helping
> Kashmir, therefore, is an obligation of national interest to
> India.

Nearly a year later he would recall these tense days in an emotional speech to the Lok Sabha on 7 September 1948:

> May I take the House into my confidence? In the early
> stages. . . I was so exercised over Kashmir that if anything
> had happened or was likely to have happened in Kashmir,
> which according to me, might have been disastrous for

Kashmir, I would have been heartbroken. I was intensely interested, apart from the larger reasons which the government have, for emotional and personal reasons; I do not want to hide this: I am interested in Kashmir.

The Mountbatten–Jinnah talks of 1 November opened with wrangling over who should have informed whom about tribals and troops. Mountbatten's account (Governor-General's Personal Report No 5, 7 November 1947) records a suggestion that both sides should "withdraw at once and simultaneously". This was an interesting statement—since, by Pakistan's version of events, only one side's forces had intervened in Kashmir. For the record, Pakistan insisted that it had nothing to do with the tribals. But Campbell-Johnson recalls:

> When Mountbatten asked him (Jinnah) to explain how the tribesmen could be induced to remove themselves, his reply was, 'If you do this I will call the whole thing off,' which at least suggests that the public propaganda line that the tribal invasion was wholly beyond Pakistan's control will not be pursued too far in private discussion.

"I will call the whole thing off": at least Jinnah had the honesty to admit that he had set the whole thing on. Mountbatten now proposed a plebiscite. Hodson reports Jinnah's reaction:

> Mr Jinnah objected that with Indian troops present and Sheikh Abdullah in power the people would be frightened to vote for Pakistan.

How time has reversed the arguments! Since one man's invader is another man's liberator, the soil of Kashmir never ever became clear enough for an unambiguous plebiscite—when such a solution was still possible.

At the meeting Mountbatten introduced another dimension to the plebiscite idea; perhaps he was only offering options to a reluctant Jinnah, but he suggested a plebiscite under the auspices of the United Nations. It was the first time that the United Nations was mentioned, but then it was also the very first meeting on Kashmir. Mountbatten had no prior Cabinet sanction for this, but once again Jinnah made the suggestion irrelevant. In another massive irony, given Pakistan's persistent use of the UN later on, it was again Jinnah who turned the idea down. He suggested instead a plebiscite under the joint control and supervision of the two Governors-General Jinnah and Mountbatten. The latter saw the trap early, and slid away. He pointed out that, politically, they were hardly equals; Jinnah had real power, while Mountbatten at best held his position in trust for a few more months. But Jinnah lost a great opportunity that day, if not to go to the UN then at least to embarrass the Indian government into disowning what its own Governor-General had proposed. If only Jinnah realized what he himself was going to say on the subject of plebiscite and the United Nations about ten weeks later.

That was his irony. The Indian irony was that Mountbatten and Nehru now began to harp on a role for the United Nations. If Jinnah had reason to rue the first, then Jawaharlal had more than ample opportunity to deeply regret the second. Nehru made the involvement of the UN public in a broadcast on 2 November. Explaining why Indian troops had moved into Kashmir, he said: "Not to have taken these steps would have been betrayal of a trust and cowardly submission to the law of the sword with its accompaniment of arson, rape and slaughter". He added that once the rule of law had been reestablished India was willing to hold a referendum "under some such international auspices as that of the United Nations". V.P. Menon records this in *Story of the Integration of the Indian States*. This was obviously acceptable to the other Indian leaders, including Patel, since no one objected to the idea then.

On 3 November Home Minister Patel and Defence Minister Baldev Singh visited Srinagar; their report led to the establishment of a new divisional headquarters, signalling that India was now ready to dig in and stay. Major-General Kalwant Singh reached on 5 November, and by the afternoon of 8 November Baramulla was retaken. The now completely frustrated Pakistani leaders gave vent to their anger in statements and broadcasts: India had been as immoral as the Dogras, Abdullah was a quisling etc., etc.

Mountbatten maintained his increasingly lonely peace initiative in an environment of escalating hostility. Another meeting of the Joint Defence Council had been scheduled for Saturday, 8 November, but despite his best efforts, Mountbatten could not persuade Jinnah and Liaqat to come to Delhi to attend it. Nothing more was possible for two weeks as the Mountbattens left for London to attend the wedding of their cousin Princess Elizabeth to Lieutenant Philip Mountbatten, a nephew. But as soon as Mountbatten returned, the process was reactivated. Liaqat Ali Khan agreed to come to Delhi for a meeting on 26 November.

But once again Jawaharlal was not present. In the middle of the meeting, Mountbatten received a "Most Immediate" envelope from him, enclosing two telegrams he had received that very morning from the

Pakistan Prime Minister, along with a cryptic note:

> In view of what Mr Liaqat Ali Khan has said in these telegrams, I see no particular advantage in my discussing the Kashmir situation or indeed any other matter with him.

Mountbatten reported to his King:

> If Mr Liaqat Khan's intention had been to ruin any chance of further negotiations, he could not have phrased or timed his telegrams better. He accused Sheikh Abdullah, who, he must full well have known, was one of Pandit Nehru's closest friends, of being "a quisling and a paid agent to disrupt the Muslims of Kashmir"; and he accused the Government of India of trying to mislead the world, of evasion, of contradiction, of tyranny and of attempting to eliminate the whole Muslim population of Kashmir.

What Nehru had to say, he told Parliament on 25 November. His theme was:

> We did not want a mere accession from the top but an association in accordance with the will of the people.

The invasion, he said, reading from a prepared statement

> was an act of hostility not only to Kashmir but to the Indian Union...If we had allowed this scheme to succeed, we would have been guilty of the betrayal of the people of Kashmir and of a grave dereliction of duty to India...We cannot treat with freebooters who have murdered large numbers of people and tried to ruin Kashmir. They are not a State, although a State may be behind them.

Then Nehru promised a UN-overseen plebiscite on the floor of the House:

> In order to establish our *bona fides*, we have suggested that when the people are given the chance to decide their future, this should be done under the supervision of an impartial tribunal such as the United Nations Organisation. The issue in Kashmir is whether violence and naked force should decide the future or the will of the people.

It needs to be added that there was no objection from anyone as Nehru took this high moral ground; Patel was answering questions that day in the House, and the man who later launched a movement and a party against Nehru's "appeasement," Shyama Prasad Mookerjee, was a member of the front benches.

Despite the ill-will between Nehru and Liaqat, Mountbatten arranged a meeting between the two at four o'clock on the afternoon of 26 November. Proposals to disengage were followed up at lower levels in a series of meetings over the next two days. But within two hours of the Pakistan delegation's departure, Mountbatten attended a Defence Committee meeting of the Indian Cabinet which he called "one of the most disastrous and distressing meetings it has ever been my lot to preside over". It was a completely different mood that he witnessed within the Cabinet now. All talk of conciliation was over.

There were three reasons for this fresh burst of anger. Liaqat, who had returned home ahead of the rest of his delegation, had—instead of trying to defuse the situation—made provocative speeches saying Pakistan would never give up Kashmir, and ordered fresh batches of raiders into the Valley from their camps along the Jammu border. The information was brought to the Cabinet by Patel and Baldev Singh, who had just made another trip to Kashmir. Mountbatten records:

> Thirdly (and this affected India's Ministers perhaps more than anything else), there were the stories, which had by now become almost commonplace, of the raiders having indulged in the most ghastly atrocities, including the wholesale murder of non-Muslims and the selling of Kashmiri girls.

Jawaharlal Nehru was particularly livid. Mountbatten added:

> Pandit Nehru declared that, in these circumstances, he would certainly not talk to Mr Liaqat Ali Khan at Lahore about a plebiscite. All the Ministers were insistent on the most violent offensive military action being taken.

They wanted not only to clear Kashmir of the raiders but also a *cordon sanitaire*, or a demilitarized zone, on the Pakistan side which could be monitored from the air to ensure that the camps could never be reactivated. If that mood had been truly converted into military action right then, at least there might have been nothing called "Azad Kashmir" now. But, unfortunately for India, Mountbatten now sabotaged his own Cabinet. Hodson, a bit cheekily, exposes what transpired next:

. . . they (the Ministers) were so insistent that Lord Mountbatten had to temporize by getting the proposal referred to the Joint Planning Staff. He made sure meanwhile that the report be adverse, and so it was. The Ministers then gave up the idea without argument.

In other words, Mountbatten simply instructed the British officers to tell the Cabinet that their military aims were impossible to achieve, and they dutifully remained more loyal to Mountbatten than to the truth. Mountbatten's reluctance to see a decisive defeat of Pakistan aborted the attempt before it could even be undertaken.

He then managed to persuade the reluctant Nehru to go to Lahore for the 9 December Joint Defence Council meeting. The discussions on that day set the pattern for the next few decades: the two sides circled endlessly around their positions, occasionally stepped out to spar with each other, but there was no meeting point. The only drama was provided by unscheduled outbursts. Mountbatten recalls that at one point

> Pandit Nehru flared up and declared that the only solution was to clear Kashmir with the sword, and that he would "throw up his Prime Ministership, and take a rifle himself and lead the men of India against the invasion".

Mountbatten notes:

> I realized that the deadlock was complete, and that the only way out now was to bring in some third party in some capacity or the other. For this purpose, I suggested that the United Nations Organisation should be called upon.

The Third Party came. It settled nothing, and it is still there as an irrelevant observer. But till at least 1972, it absorbed too much time, concern and energy, and the internationalization of the dispute converted Kashmir into another playground of powerful interests. Mountbatten's motives were doubtless honourable, but he was also exhibiting the imperialist syndrome: the natives needed guidance. Interestingly, by December Nehru had begun to have some serious reservations about going to the UN. Hodson writes:

> Lord Mountbatten now bent his efforts to getting the idea of reference to the United Nations accepted. Pandit Nehru was first adamantly opposed. Under what article of the Charter, he asked, could any reference to the United Nations be made? How did Pakistan come into the picture at all?

Good questions; but why did Nehru lose faith in his own doubts? Whatever he may have said before, when the suggestion to go to the UN became serious he hesitated. But Mountbatten managed to prevail over Nehru and Patel and the Indian Cabinet finally decided on 20 December that India should take its complaint against Pakistan's involvement in the tribal invasion to the UN, under Article 35 of its Charter. Another irony: Pakistan's first reaction was an objection.

On the ground the confrontation escalated in the last days of December. By Christmas eve, the Pakistani forces had counter-attacked: the garrison at Jhangar had suffered heavy casualties, while Uri was seriously threatened—thus exposing Srinagar again. Nehru made it clear that if India became vulnerable in Kashmir it would broaden the war into Punjab—much as it was to do in 1965. Mountbatten dashed off a 2,000-word letter to Nehru urging a policy of peace. Nehru replied on Christmas Day at even longer length:

> While we ardently desire peace and the end of fighting, we must not be unrealistic. Our desire does not lead to peace unless something is done to that end. . . From the strictly legal and constitutional point of view it is our right and duty to resist this invasion with all our forces. From the point of view of international law we can in self-defence take any military measures to resist it, including the sending of our armies across Pakistan territory to attack their bases near the Kashmir border. We have refrained from doing this because of our desire to avoid complications leading to open war. In our avoidance of this we have increased our own peril and not brought peace any nearer...

He could hardly have been more categorical.

But instead of full war, the UN alternative was pursued. Disillusionment came quickly. By February, Nehru was bitterly regretting the UN decision to Mountbatten. But the fault lay with India. The leader of its delegation, Gopalaswami Aiyangar (former Prime Minister of Kashmir) bungled India's case badly. In his opening statement to the Security Council on 15 January 1948, he was unconvincingly brief, and failed to carry the argument on key issues. Perhaps the biggest mistake was Aiyangar's inexplicable failure to condemn Pakistan directly. Michael Brecher writes in *The Struggle for Kashmir*:

> Although India's complaint to the UN was raised in the

form of Pakistan's alleged complicity in the tribal invasion, India's delegate failed or was unwilling to condemn Pakistan as a *de facto* aggressor. Indeed, as noted earlier, he took great pains to differentiate sharply between Pakistan and the raiders, and by focussing the attention of the Council on the tribesmen as the culprits in the case, he lost considerable debating effectiveness in his efforts to secure the Council's condemnation of Pakistan *per se*.

Worse, Aiyangar sounded as if he was Pakistan's lawyer on the issue of plebiscite: time after time he returned to

the high-principled statesmanship of the Government of India under its present leadership. In accepting the accession they refused to take advantage of the immediate peril in which the State found itself and informed the Ruler that the accession should finally be settled by plebiscite as soon as peace had been restored.

In effect, Aiyangar seemed to question the very validity of the accession when its unquestioned legality was the very basis of the Indian intervention. Writes Brecher:

He made it appear, as if the accession was absolutely conditional upon the results of a plebiscite.

It was surprising that Aiyangar could not even present the political background of Kashmir properly. M.C. Setalvad, Attorney-General of India then, tried to repair matters but the damage was too great. And Pakistan's representative, the brilliant Sir Muhammad Zafarullah, Foreign Minister of his country, made mincemeat of the Indian position in an unprecedented five-hour exposition. He used the classic technique of changing the argument. He linked the tribal invasion to the violence elsewhere, pursuing the line that it was a natural corollary to the communal violence in Punjab and Jammu. This was completely illogical, since not a single Muslim had been touched by any Hindu in the Valley— in fact could not be, given the overwhelming Muslim majority there—but Aiyangar, instead of challenging this fake justification, agreed with it! On 22 January 1948, Aiyangar became Sir Zafarullah's biggest ally when he said:

There is no doubt that the Security Council now has before it both the Jammu and Kashmir question and situations other than this question which have been brought to the attention of the Security Council by Pakistan.

It was on 22 January, the same day, that Pakistan scored its decisive victory in the United Nations. The Security Council altered the title of the issue from "The Jammu-Kashmir Question" to "The India-Pakistan Question". From the Kashmir issue an emboldened and spirited Sir Zafarullah turned it into a *Muslim* issue, a "national" response to the "genocide" against Muslims.

Nehru made a familiar mistake; unwilling to blame Aiyangar for the collapse of the Indian case, he began to imagine larger conspiracies. Mountbatten records:

> Pandit Nehru said that he was shocked to find that power politics and not ethics were ruling the United Nations Organisation and was convinced that the United Nations Organisation was being completely run by the Americans, and that Senator Warren Austin, the American representative, had made no bones of his sympathy for the Pakistan case. . .

This may have been perfectly true, but it hardly absolved the Indian delegation of surrendering the initiative to Pakistan. K.S. Bajpai, who retired from the Indian Foreign Service as Ambassador in the United States, told the author that his father, Sir Girija Shankar Bajpai, appointed the first Secretary-General of the External Affairs Ministry, was initially selected by Nehru to lead the Indian delegation to the UN, but his name aroused too much violent opposition—Sir Girija had been one of the great favourites of the British—and had to be withdrawn. Nehru did send Bajpai to represent India later, but the damage had been done. Sir Girija would have been a far better match for Sir Zafarullah.

An angry Nehru wanted to withdraw the Indian delegation from Lake Success, but was persuaded once again by Mountbatten to stop short of such a drastic step. The Security Council resolution came on 21 April 1948. Jointly sponsored by Belgium, Canada, China, Colombia, the UK and the USA, and passed by a vote of 9–0 (the USSR and Ukraine abstaining), it created a Commission of five members, charged with restoring peace and conducting a plebiscite with the cooperation of both governments. Before Mountbatten left India on 21 June 1948, he made one final attempt at a solution. Towards the end of May, he suggested a formal partition of Kashmir. Nehru was ready to consider the idea, but

Pakistan simply ignored it, and it disappeared into the archives.

Pakistan had raised its sights by now. On 5 July 1948, Sir Zafarullah calmly informed the UN Commission in Karachi that his country had formally entered the war, with three regular Frontier Force battalions. While the fighting escalated, the Commission shifted its focus to arranging a ceasefire. One would have been possible in August if Pakistan's military ambitions had not interfered.

On 13 August 1948, the Security Council's three-part Basic Resolution called for a ceasefire; and asked Pakistan, as aggressor, to withdraw all her forces, regular or irregular, while accepting that India could retain part of her troops in Kashmir. Part Three of the Resolution, which was *not* binding unless the first two Parts had been implemented, said that

> the future status of Jammu and Kashmir shall be determined in accordance with the will of the people and to that end, upon acceptance of the Truce Agreement both Governments agree to enter into consultation with the Commission to determine fair and equitable conditions whereby such free expression of will be assured.

Pakistan refused to implement the first two Parts, thereby handing the argument back to India.

By winter, a chastened Pakistani Army headquarters had obviously realized that it would not be able to pull off any military victory. Pakistan accepted the terms of a further Resolution on 25 December 1948, and a ceasefire came into effect on 1 January 1949. Ceasefire, but no peace. The battle for Kashmir between India and Pakistan has raged all over the world, but nothing has changed on the ground. That Ceasefire Line drawn on 1 January has held through war and peace, through the decimation of one country and the destabilization of the other. The UN failed; direct negotiations, begun in August 1953, became equally pointless. Other pressures altered the dimensions of the quarrel. As military aid from the West began to flow into Pakistan, Nehru responded with the Soviet card. Kashmir was deliberately placed on Khrushchev's itinerary when he visited India in December 1955; the Soviet leader dutifully endorsed the host's position, saying

> the question of Kashmir as one of the States of India has already been decided by the people of Kashmir.

The UN continued to echo with voluminous debate, Krishna Menon making a mark during his term there. Nothing quite worked to Pakistan's advantage; neither the rhetoric of the 1950s nor the wars of the 1960s and 1970s. But over and over again, history was to prove that Delhi's real problem was not Pakistan; the invader could be and was thrown back repeatedly. The problem was at home. The politics of the Valley, tangled in the threads of ambition, were another matter. Those threads slowly wound themselves into a noose.

In the first week of November 1947, Campbell-Johnson called on Alan Moorehead, the *Observer* journalist, in Delhi as soon as he arrived. He asked: 'What is your first reaction to India?'

The journalist answered: 'It is rather like Spain. . . men sit hating each other like the wrath of God—then, because the sun is too hot, shrug their shoulders and say, "What is the use?"'

Not always, not always.

Wrapping up his diary at the end of that momentous year of 1947 Campbell-Johnson, wrote :

> 1947 ends in foreboding over the future of Indo-Pak relations generally and Kashmir in particular. It is difficult to stand back and assess the credit and debit balance of our last nine prodigious months in India. The immediate situation seems always to overwhelm our thoughts and attention. The occupational risk is to be preoccupied with the daily task. . . . My new year motto is Ismay's "Patience and proportion".

Wise words. That motto should have been burned on the mind of every player in this sensitive drama. For both patience and proportion were to be lost in the difficult years ahead.

Cold Blood

16

Clause 7, Article 370 and a Three-Nation Theory

Even in defeat Shreeman Indar Mohinder Rajrajeshwar Maharajdhiraj Shree Hari Singh was careful about the extent of surrender. Despite the panic in the air and the urgency of the moment, at least three terms in the Instrument of Accession showed evidence of some forethought. Two of these dealt with the measure of sovereignty that would reside in Srinagar. A lot, on the face of it. Clause 7 of Hari Singh's agreement with Sardar Patel said:

> Nothing in this Instrument shall be deemed to commit me in any way to acceptance of any future Constitution of India or to fetter my discretion to enter into arrangements with the Government of India under any such future Constitution.

And Clause 8 went:

> Nothing in this Instrument affects the continuance of my sovereignty in and over this State, or, save as provided by or under this Instrument, the exercise of any powers, authority and rights now enjoyed by me as Ruler of this State or the validity of any law at present in this State.

Kashmir had joined the Union of India, but not the law of India. It was still governed by the Jammu and Kashmir Constitution Act of 1939, with Delhi's jurisdiction extending only to External Affairs, Defence and Communication. From this fulcrum the friction began, with Delhi attempting to pull Kashmir into the spirit of Indian democracy and Srinagar zealously guarding the letter of the accession terms. The very use of the term 'sovereignty' created controversy. Both Hari Singh and Sheikh Abdullah were, however, agreed that by the terms of accession, Kashmir had a right to its own law, the difference being that while the Maharaja wanted the continuation of the 1939 Act, Abdullah set course for a new Constituent Assembly which would frame a modern Constitution for his New Kashmir. In June 1949, Kashmir too, like the other Princely States, sent its representatives (four) to the Constituent Assembly but after making it adequately clear that their association with India would be based only on the terms of the accession—which meant Clause 7. Such generosity had not been shown to the other former Princely States; a separate Constitution for each one would be sanction to a "legacy from the Ruler's polity which could have no place in a democratic set-up", in Patel's words to the Constituent Assembly. But Kashmir had been guaranteed special status, conceded N. Gopalaswami Aiyangar, while moving Article 306A on 17 October 1949 in the Constituent Assembly. It was Maulana Hasrat Mohani who interrupted at this point in the debate with a question, "Why this discrimination, please?" Hoping "that in due course even Jammu and Kashmir will become ripe for the same sort of integration as has taken place in the case of other States" (cheers were heard from the members), Aiyangar went on to explain why there was a difference vis-a-vis Maharaja Hari Singh's Kashmir (Clause 7 was Hari Singh's condition, after all):

> Again, the Government of India have committed themselves to the people of Kashmir in certain respects. They have committed themselves to the position that an opportunity would be given to the people of the State to decide for themselves whether they will remain with the Republic or wish to go out of it. We are also committed to ascertaining this will of the people by means of a plebiscite provided that peaceful and normal conditions are restored and the impartiality of the plebiscite could be guaranteed. We have also agreed that the will of the people, through the instrument of a Constituent Assembly, will determine the Constitution of the State as well as the sphere of Union jurisdiction over the State.

Article 306A was adopted that very day in the Draft Constitution and became Article 370 in the final Constitution. No one opposed Article 370 then. Sardar Patel justified it as willingly as Aiyangar, telling the Constituent Assembly just a week before, on 12 October 1949:

> In view of the special problems with which the government of Jammu and Kashmir is faced, we have made a

special provision for the constitutional relationship of the State with the Union on the existing basis.

The man who would lead the first major agitation against the special relationship, Shyama Prasad Mookerjee accepted it as well. Mookerjee in fact was a member of Nehru's Cabinet and resigned not on this issue but over the Nehru–Liaqat pact signed on 8 April the next year, in 1950. Article 370 was viewed then as a victory for Indian unity, and not as a problem, as is being made out by the heirs of Shyama Prasad Mookerjee.

In the meantime, the concept of Responsible Government had been strengthened by upgrading Sheikh Abdullah from Head of Emergency Administration to Prime Minister of the State, with the Maharaja given the status of a non-executive constitutional Head of State. The proclamation was signed by an extremely unhappy Maharaja on 5 March 1948. The international value of this change played its part in the decision, since Kashmir was then burning up hour after hour of the Security Council. Abdullah himself had participated in one such UN debate where he had made a spirited attack on Pakistan ("I refuse to accept Pakistan as a party in the affairs of the Jammu and Kashmir State; I refuse this point blank") and risen to Nehru's defence ("It is said that Sheikh Abdullah is a friend of Pandit Jawaharlal Nehru. Yes, I admit that. I feel honoured that such a great man claims me as his friend. And he happens to belong to my own country; he is also a Kashmiri, and blood is thicker than water").

The decision of 5 March further lifted Abdullah's spirits. He told a press conference on 6 March 1948 (recorded in *The Statesman*, 7 March 1948):

> We have decided to work with and die for India...We made our decision not in October last, but in 1944, when we resisted the advances of Mr Jinnah. Our refusal was categorical. Ever since the National Conference had attempted to keep the State clear of the pernicious two-nation theory while fighting the world's worst autocracy.

That was his refrain that year. On 29 September at another Delhi press conference, Abdullah reiterated:

> We have burnt our boats. There is no place in Kashmir for a theocratic state. Kashmir will never make a plaything of India's honour.

Id came that year on 15 October; he told the gathering at the *namaz*:

The pledge I gave to Pandit Nehru last year that Kashmir will be a part of India has now become an eternal bond.

Addressing a function of the Gandhi Memorial College at Jammu on 3 December he affirmed:

> Kashmiris would rather die following the footsteps of Gandhiji than accept the two-nation theory. We want to link the destiny of Kashmir with India because we feel that the ideal before India and Kashmir is one and the same.

In October 1948 a special session of the National Conference passed a resolution saying:

> In these circumstances, the convention, therefore, confirms the provisional accession of the State with India. It further pledges its fullest support to a final accession to India on the basis of New Kashmir, the realisation and implementation of which will be our first and foremost task. The convention strongly hopes that the Indian Government and the people of India will lend the people of Kashmir all material, moral and political support in completing this task and achieving our goal of economic and political freedom.

This last had been Abdullah's first priority from the moment he came to power. The New Kashmir manifesto began to be implemented without delay, with the biggest thrust given to land reform. But there would be a cruel twist to these egalitarian intentions. The century of Dogra rule had seen the usurpation of nearly all the land in the Valley by the ruling class, with the result that most of the 2,200,000 acres of cultivable Kashmiri land belonged either to the Maharaja directly or to his Jagirdars and the small class of landlords called Chakdars. To put it more starkly, the owners were Jammu Hindus; the tillers Kashmiri Muslims. This was enough for some elements to attribute communal motives. The onslaught on its economic power so soon after the loss of political power led to the creation of a communal Hindu organization in Jammu, the Praja Parishad, whose sole objective became the destruction of Sheikh Abdullah. This vengeance would cast a long shadow into the future.

Above Clause 7 and Clause 8 in the Instrument of Accession came Clause 6. If any evidence were needed that self-interest was always high-priority with Hari Singh, here it was. Clause 6 said:

Nothing in this Instrument shall empower the Dominion Legislature to make any law for this State authorizing the compulsory acquisition of land for any purpose, but I hereby undertake that should the Dominion for the purposes of a Dominion law which applies in this State deem it necessary to acquire any land, I will at their request acquire the land at their expense or if the land belongs to me transfer it to them on such terms as may be agreed, or, in default of agreement, determined by an arbitrator to be appointed by the Chief Justice of India.

Sheikh Abdullah was in no mood to wait for the Dominion. He may have been partly influenced by his long anger against Dogra autocracy, but he had an excellent case. Nehru or the Congress could hardly argue against land reform. He began by placing an immediate moratorium on the debts of peasants and workers, and constituted Debt Conciliation courts to ameliorate the misery of usury—perhaps the greatest crime of them all. In just one decision the quantum of debts was brought down by eighty per cent, from Rs 11.1 million to Rs 2.4 million. The rights of peasants in mortgaged property were reinstated; the tenant was now protected from ejection and his share of the crop increased from half to two-thirds, while the cost of seeds and agricultural implements was now split. But of course the real challenge was redistribution of land.

In April 1949, Abdullah appointed a Land Reforms Committee. But his impatience was such that he did not wait for the report; he announced his intended reforms from a party forum—and the legislature only approved of it later. The maximum landholding was put at 22.75 acres; the rest went to tenants. Jawaharlal publicly applauded this decision. But for Maharaja Hari Singh this proved the final blow. On 9 June 1949, citing reasons of health, he handed over office to his young son, Yuvraj Karan Singh, and left to settle down in Bombay. He would never return to Kashmir. These land reforms further consolidated the peasantry's ties with India because they understood—and Abdullah told them so—that such reform would never be possible in a Pakistan which protected feudalism and landlordism. Michael Brecher writes in *The Struggle for Kashmir*:

> The vast majority of Kashmiris have benefited from these reforms and many of those interviewed by the author expressed the fear that in Pakistan, where no comparable land reforms have taken place, the land recently given to them might be returned to the landlords or, in any event,

that further implementation of the 'New Kashmir' programme will be impossible.

In October 1950, the National Conference, after sniping at UN generosity towards Pakistan, asked for

> Immediate steps for convening a Constituent Assembly based upon adult suffrage and embracing all sections of the people and all constituents of the State for the purpose of determining the future shape and affiliations of the State of Jammu and Kashmir.

This Assembly would simultaneously function as a legislature, one seat representing an average of 40,000 voters. On 1 May 1951, Dr Karan Singh issued the necessary proclamation. Abdullah's handpicked candidates won all the seventy-five seats in the August polls, a result not greeted without scepticism. If there was no serious controversy about this one-way avalanche it was largely because no one doubted Abdullah's popularity, manifestly more substantial than that of anyone else. The Constituent Assembly met on 31 October 1951; Sheikh Abdullah called it a "day of Destiny. A day which comes only once in the life of a nation".

In his opening address to the Constituent Assembly on 5 November, Abdullah outlined the four great tasks that lay before it:

- To frame a Constitution for Kashmir;

- To decide on the fate of the royal dynasty;

- To decide whether there should be any compensation paid to those who had lost their land through the Land Abolition Act;

- To "declare its reasoned conclusion regarding accession".

The first was an obvious task; the second was a foregone conclusion—there could be no dynasty; and the National Conference had decided that it would not pay compensation, further angering the landed Dogras who were behind the Praja Parishad. It was the last issue which was the definitive one. Abdullah dwelt at length on all the options before the framers of the Constitution, including the option of an "Eastern Switzerland", or a Third Nation on the subcontinent.

He began by comparing Pakistan and India as potential "partners" of

Kashmir. The former was clearly the aggressor in the brutal recent war, while the legality of the accession was beyond doubt. So there was no question of equating the two. But what was the balance of advantage and disadvantage? Accession to India, Abdullah argued, would ensure that there could never be any return to feudalism since India was committed to secularism and democracy. In a forceful passage, he said:

> The real character of a State is revealed in its Constitution. The Indian Constitution has set before the country the goal of a secular democracy based upon justice, freedom and equality for all without distinction. This is the bedrock of modern democracy. This should meet the argument that the Muslims of Kashmir cannot have security in India, where the large majority of the population are Hindus. Any unnatural cleavage between religious groups is the legacy of imperialism. . . . The Indian Constitution has amply and finally repudiated the concept of a religious State, which is a throwback to medievalism. . . . The national movement in our State naturally gravitates towards these principles of secular democracy.

As for Pakistan, it did not even have a Constitution, and feudalism was flourishing there. Dismissing the economic arguments in favour of Pakistan, he turned to the core of the whole case for Pakistan:

> The most powerful argument which can be advanced in her favour is that Pakistan is a Muslim State, and, a big majority of our people being Muslims the State must accede to Pakistan. This claim of being a Muslim State is of course only a camouflage. It is a screen to dupe the common man, so that he may not see clearly that Pakistan is a feudal state in which a clique is trying by these methods to maintain itself in power. . . . Right-thinking men would point out that Pakistan is not an organic unity of all the Muslims in this subcontinent. It has, on the contrary, caused the dispersion of Indian Muslims for whom it was claimed to have been created.

He then examined the independence option:

> We have to consider the alternative of making ourselves an Eastern Switzerland, of keeping aloof from both states

but having friendly relations with them.

But within a couple of sentences he had exposed the weakness of this seemingly attractive position:

> I would like to remind you that from August 15 to October 22, 1947 our State was independent and the result was that our weakness was exploited by the neighbour with invasion. What is the guarantee that in future too we may not be victims of a similar aggression.

It was a long brief for accession to India, and a convincing one. There was just one caveat—a very important one:

> Certain tendencies have been asserting themselves in India that may in the future convert it into a religious state wherein the interests of the Muslims will be jeopardised. This would happen if a communal organisation had a dominant hand in the Government, and Congress ideals of the equality of all communities were made to give way to religious intolerance.

It was a remarkably prescient statement, given the history of the 1980s and 1990. Sheikh Abdullah already had begun to feel the heat of one such tendency in his own backyard, the Praja Parishad of Jammu. And its campaign was being strengthened by the support it had begun to receive from powerful organizations like the Rashtriya Swayamsevak Sangh (RSS).

Marginalized by the awesome anger that swept India after the assassination of Mahatma Gandhi on 30 January 1948 by one of its faithful, the RSS took a little while to re-emerge into public life. Given a reprieve by Sardar Patel, who lifted the ban on the organization, the RSS—and similar movements—began searching for a leader who could articulate their ideology, a party which could become a vehicle for their political thrust, and a cause which could provide them with a re-entry point into popular sympathy. They were fortunate to find Shyama Prasad Mookerjee, who launched the Jana Sangh in 1951. The first national committee of the Jana Sangh met from 21 October 1951, and the first manifesto announced a four-point programme for "strengthening" the unity of India:

- an educational system based on "Bhartiya culture";

- the use of Hindi in schools;

- the denial of any special privileges to minorities;
- full integration of Jammu and Kashmir into the Indian Union.

It was but logical that a party that demanded denial of any special privileges to minorities should make Muslim-majority Kashmir under Article 370 its first political target. The party went to the general elections on this platform. Although Mookerjee could win only three seats in the first Lok Sabha (two from his native Bengal), he managed to cobble together a bloc of thirty-two MPs, which took the name of the National Democratic Front. All of them came to the second annual session of the party, held in December 1952, and heard Mookerjee announce the two issues on which his party would launch its first movement: the condition of the refugees from Pakistan, and Article 370. The Jana Sangh, RSS and the Hindu Mahasabha decided to expand the agitation into an arc from Jammu to Delhi through Punjab—where they picked up an incongruous ally, the Akali Dal led by Master Tara Singh. All that Mookerjee and Tara Singh had in common was a passionate dislike of Muslims and of Nehru, but that was sufficient for the moment. They coined a slogan:

> *Ek desh mein do Vidhaan*
> *Ek desh mein do Nishaan*
> *Ek desh mein do Pradhaan*
> *Nahin chalenge, nahin chalenge.*

(Two Constitutions in one country, two flags in one country, two heads of state in one country, are unacceptable.)

The flags in particular were an emotive issue. But Kashmir had been given the right to fly its own flag, although not in competition with or in supremacy to the tricolour. It was part of what is known as the Delhi Agreement of 1952.

Early in 1952, Revenue Minister Mirza Afzal Beg led a Kashmir delegation to Delhi for talks with the Union government to obtain agreement for the various bills that the Kashmir Constituent Assembly was getting ready to pass. The consensus came to be known as the Delhi Agreement. Its main points were:

- Commitment to Article 370;
- Kashmiris would be citizens of India, but the State

Legislature would be empowered to confer the special
rights on 'state subjects' won in the struggles of 1927
and 1932;

- The President of India would be the head of State of the
  whole of India, including Kashmir;

- Kashmir would be allowed its own flag, but not as a
  rival to the tricolour, which would be supreme;

- The Sadar-i-Riyasat (Governor of the State), although
  elected by the State Legislature rather than nominated
  by the Centre, could not assume office without the
  consent of the President of India;

- The Supreme Court would, "for the time being," have
  only appellate jurisdiction in Jammu and Kashmir;

- An internal Emergency could only be applied with the
  concurrence of the State Legislature.

As in virtually any compromise, neither side left the negotiating table
without taking with it the seed of suspicion, and both became bitterly
protective of each comma of their respective interpretations of this
agreement. Suspicion is an easy weed to nourish.

The name of B.N. Mullik, Deputy Director of the Intelligence Bureau
(IB) from September 1948, with charge of Kashmir, and later Director of
India's premier internal intelligence service, is now inextricably linked to
the politics of Kashmir in the 1950s and '60s, playing as he did a starring
role through the Nehru era. In his book *My Years With Nehru* (Deep
Publications, Agra, 1971), Mullik tells an interesting story about his first
visit to the Valley, a ten-day tour in August 1949. Reports, partly
motivated, had begun to float through Home Ministry corridors in Delhi
that Abdullah's private views were less savoury than his public pronouncements. Some of his advisers had been feeding him the line that the
Muslims of India had already been reduced to second-class citizens, and
that communalists within the Congress were seizing control of key points
in the system. G.M. Ashai, Registrar of Kashmir University, had just
finished a tour of India and planted the first doubts in Abdullah's mind
about Jawaharlal's ability to hold to a secular course.

There was reasonable basis for such suspicion. In 1949 and 1950, the
communal lobby within the Congress made a very determined bid for
power. It knew that the Prime Minister's office was beyond its reach or

influence, but it also felt that Nehru could be surrounded.

When Mountbatten finally left India on 21 June 1948, Nehru made C. Rajagopalachari the interim Governor-General of India, pending the assumption of office by a President on 26 January 1950 when the Dominion would become a Republic. Nehru wanted Rajagopalachari to be India's first President but—to his utter surprise—he discovered that he had been ambushed by Rajendra Prasad who, with the help of Patel, had organized a majority in the Congress Parliamentary Party. Nehru had to swallow that particular pill, but he was not going to admit defeat. Prasad displayed his predilections when he objected to the passage of the Hindu Code Bill. Nehru wrote to N. Gopalaswami Aiyangar on 22 September 1951:

> I regret to say that the President attached more importance to his astrologers than to the advice of his Cabinet on some matters. I have no intention of submitting to the astrologers.

September was a bad month for Nehru. He suffered a very major setback when Purushottam Das Tandon, a candidate he had personally accused of being communal, was elected (once again with Patel's assistance) President of the Congress. In an unprecedented indictment Nehru released a statement on 12 September saying, "Communal and reactionary forces openly expressed their joy at the result". He initially even refused to serve in Tandon's working committee. It took him a full year before he could force Tandon out and become party chief himself. This was a phase when some of Nehru's closest and dearest comrades like Rafi Ahmed Kidwai left the Congress in protest against the rampant communalism within. The Hindu Code Bill only sharpened the anger of the conservatives and obscurantists promoting the line that Nehru's socialism only meant appeasement of Muslims and betrayal of Hindus.

Instead of stepping out to help Nehru in this ideological battle, Abdullah only retreated into his Kashmiri shell—and opened fire on Nehru from his flank, for not doing enough against the chauvinists. A lesser spirit than Nehru's would have become a victim of the crossfire. As for leaders like Patel, they interpreted Abdullah's withdrawal as the beginning of the drift towards secession. As events were to prove soon enough, no one was able to escape from this complex web spun between misunderstanding, mistakes and mischief. Sardar Patel began to openly encourage doubts about Abdullah's integrity among the seniormost officers of the Home Ministry. The case of Mullik was a classic play.

The Deputy Director, IB, reported to his Director after his first visit to Kashmir that there was intense local feeling against Pakistan, and that the Sheikh's ideological commitment to India had not weakened. The report was passed on directly to Nehru, who handled Kashmir affairs personally, and he was so pleased that he sent copies to all Indian embassies. But, Mullik writes in *My Years With Nehru*:

> Sardar Vallabhbhai Patel was unhappy. This report of mine apparently went against the views which he had held about Kashmir in general and Sheikh Abdullah in particular. . . . A few days after I had sent the report, the Home Secretary informed me that the Sardar did not agree with my assess-ment and had taken exception to the fact that I had sub-mitted this report without first consulting him. . . . I got a summons to see Sardar the next day. He was not well and was seated on his bed. . . (After hearing Mullik out) the Sardar then gave me his own views about Sheikh Abdullah. He apprehended that Sheikh Abdullah would ultimately let down India and Jawaharlal Nehru and would come out in his real colours; his antipathy to the Maharaja was not really an antipathy to a ruler as such, but to the Dogras in general and with the Dogras he identified the rest of the majority community in India. In his slow voice, he firmly told me that my assessment of Sheikh Abdullah was wrong. . .

Mullik did not change his report, but that conversation certainly began to change his mind. He writes: "That day I came back to my office wondering whether I had really made a mistake in my assessment of Kashmir and whether what the Sardar had said was not right after all".

What developed was a fascinating evolution of truth chasing suspicion. Having prejudged the Sheikh's loyalty, a hardline element in the Govern-ment of India kept baiting him, and when he rose to the bait, declared its suspicions well-founded. The Sheikh, vacillating between arrogance and anger, often played into their hands. Doubt always seeks evidence, and evidence so often is merely a matter of interpretation. The stress of events took their own toll; prejudice breeds quickest under pressure. Voices are raised, a sentence uttered, a response offered, a motive questioned, and all the goodwill of the past gets buried in the coffin of cynicism or despair. No one is to blame, and everyone is to blame. Sadly, by 1953, the distance between Nehru and Abdullah widened to a point where the unthinkable first became thinkable, then possible, then inevitable. The starting point of this cycle was probably the meeting between Abdullah and US Ambassador Loy Henderson in the spring of 1949, when the former got his first firm impression that the West could support the idea of an independent Kashmir. S. Gopal, in his excellent three-volume biography of Nehru (Oxford University Press, New Delhi, 1974) notes:

> It has recently been suggested that some Indian leaders believed that it was Mrs Loy Henderson, the wife of the United States Ambassador, and some CIA agents who encouraged Abdullah to think in these terms.

Gopal's source of reference was Volume Five of *The Papers of Adlai Stevenson* edited by W. Johnson. The breaking point was probably the speech Abdullah made at Ranbirsinghpura on 10 April 1952. By this time even some of his closest comrades had begun to doubt his intentions and were mentally ready to leave him if he went too far.

The first split in the National Conference ranks had come as early as in 1949, when Ghulam Mohiuddin Karra, the efficient underground "dictator" of the Quit Kashmir movement left in a huff after being denied a place in the Cabinet. By 1950 the IB, which had vastly expanded its network, began sending reports to Delhi that the National Conference had begun drifting into two camps on the critical issue of accession: one, led by Abdullah and Beg, advocating the maximum distance within the terms of Article 370; and the other, consisting of Bakshi, Sadiq, Dhar, Saraf etc. working for greater integration with India. Soon, Nehru also began to get direct evidence of this. As Prime Minister he simply could not ignore what had begun as Abdullah's ambivalence and flourished into intransigence. By the summer of 1950, Abdullah had even begun hinting at the independence option to Sir Owen Dixon, the UN representative. Nehru summed up his dilemma in a letter to his sister Vijaylakshmi Pandit on 10 May 1950: "The most difficult thing in life is what to do with one's friends." The tension began to creep into the Nehru–Abdullah correspondence. When Abdullah publicly rebuked Delhi for advising him on matters outside Defence, External Affairs and Communications, Nehru wrote on 4 July 1950:

> I greatly regret that you should have taken up a position which indicates that you do not attach any value to any friendly advice we might give and, indeed, consider it as improper interference, of which you take a grave view.

Abdullah's reply of 10 July 1950 was a carefully constructed threat:

> It is clear that there are powerful influences at work in
> India who do not see eye to eye with you regarding your
> ideal of making the Union a truly secular state and your
> Kashmir policy. . . . While I feel I can willingly go down
> and sacrifice myself for you, I am afraid as custodian of
> the destinies of 40 lac (sic) of Kashmiris, I cannot barter
> away their cherished rights and privileges. I have several
> times stated that we acceded to India because we saw there
> two bright stars of hope and aspiration, namely, Gandhiji
> and yourself, and despite our having so many affinities
> with Pakistan we did not join it, because we thought our
> programme will not fit with their policy. If, however, we
> are driven to the conclusion that we cannot build our state
> on our own lines, suited to our genius, what answer can I
> give to my people and how am I to face them?

By 1952, Abdullah was ready to step up the confrontation with Delhi.
He took a stand when Gopalaswami Aiyangar attempted to extend the
jurisdiction of the Comptroller and Auditor-General to Kashmir. All his
pent-up frustration, anger and indeed ambition came bubbling out in
words when he spoke at Ranbirsinghpura on 10 April 1952. He rejected
the full application of the Indian Constitution to Kashmir as "unrealistic,
childish and savouring of lunacy". Why? India's *bona fides* were suspect.

> Many Kashmiris are apprehensive as to what will happen
> to them and their position if, for instance, something
> happens to Pandit Nehru. We do not know. As realists, we,
> Kashmiris, have to provide for all eventualities.

Nehru protested and Abdullah realized he had crossed his limits. He made
amends, using the press as the scapegoat: he had not been quoted accurately, he complained. On 18 April he tried to mollify Delhi a little more,
saying in a speech that there was no reason for Pakistan to be happy about
anything, as it had only disappointments in store. On 25 April he reaffirmed that the accession would be finally settled by the Constituent
Assembly. On 23 July 1952 he even came up to Delhi to clear doubts
about the Ranbirsinghpura speech in front of Congress MPs. At the
Congress session at Madras in 1953, he told a public meeting on 21
January that independence was a foolish idea for a tiny Kashmir
surrounded by Big Powers.

But by 1953, Abdullah had begun the dangerous practice of tailoring his nuances to fit the needs of his audience. Nehru analyzed him well in a letter to Maulana Azad on 1 March 1953:

> I fear that Sheikh Sahib's mind is so utterly confused that he does not know what to do. All kinds of pressures are being brought to bear upon him and he is getting more and more into a tangle. There is nobody with him who can really help him much, because he does not trust anyone fully, and yet everyone influences him. . . . My fear is that Sheikh Sahib, in his present frame of mind, is likely to do something or take some step, which might make things worse. . .

He did. More than one. Between 1 and 3 May Abdullah met Adlai Stevenson for three days of talks, including a seven-hour conversation on the last day at which no one else was present. At once rumours of Anglo-American support for Kashmir's independence filled the air, so much so that Government of India had to clarify on 10 July, on the eve of the Karachi round of Indo-Pak talks, that the independence of Kashmir was neither on the agenda nor an option Delhi was ready to consider. But undeterred by this statement, Abdullah said in his Martyrs' Day speech of 13 July that

> Kashmir should have the sympathy of both India and Pakistan. . . . It is not necessary that our State should become an appendage of either India or Pakistan.

That was the straw which broke Nehru's patient back. It was deliberate and crass provocation, not merely because of what was said but also because of the political context in which it was uttered. For by July, Abdullah had lost too many friends outside Kashmir, and quite a few inside it. And as if, the statements were not provocative enough, the Jana Sangh leader Shyama Prasad Mookerjee died while in detention in Srinagar on 23 June.

Mookerjee's promised agitation concentrated on three points: Kashmir's status, the condition of the refugees from Pakistan and cow-slaughter. To an extent Kashmir was only an excuse; Mookerjee's real target was Nehru. As he wrote to Jawaharlal on 3 February 1953:

> It is through your mistaken policy and your failure to understand the viewpoints of those who differ from you,

that the country is being brought to the brink of disaster.

What was worse was that old socialist comrades of Jawaharlal like Jaya Prakash Narayan had given support to such a communal campaign, their ire against Nehru being their predominant compulsion. But foes apart, Nehru's handling of this agitation dismayed even his friends. A kind of hatred was being whipped up which could have thrown the north of India back into the havoc of Hindu-Muslim riots, but Nehru seemed transfixed into helplessness. His biographer S. Gopal writes:

> Such potential danger called for quick and firm action at many levels; but nowhere was Nehru fully successful, and in consequence the crisis mounted beyond control. His orders that every attempt at disturbance within India should be suppressed were carried out only half-heartedly. The Home Ministry was at this time in the hands of Kailas Nath Katju, a loyal follower of Nehru but long past his prime; and his doddering ineptitude was accentuated by the tardiness of many officials whose communal sympathies were barely concealed.

Nehru ordered largescale arrests of Jana Sangh volunteers, and even suggested banning the party, but the Home Minister seemed simply incapable of doing anything. When Mookerjee was eventually arrested he won release from the Supreme Court on technical grounds, which was tardy mismanagement by the Home and Law ministries to say the least. Mookerjee returned to the fray with emboldened vigour. To provoke Nehru and Abdullah even further, he decided to cross into Jammu and Kashmir even though he did not have permission to do so. Mookerjee was of course also seeking to drive home the point of the Supreme Court's jurisdiction: he was free where the Court's writ ran, and detained where it did not.

Abdullah showed none of Nehru's hesitation. On 8 May 1953, Dr Shyama Prasad Mookerjee tried to cross the Madhopur bridge on the Jammu border. He was promptly taken to Srinagar and placed under house arrest. A dangerous agitation in the north; talks between Abdullah and Adlai Stevenson; Mookerjee under arrest; concern about Kashmir in the whole of India: the complications were mounting. Nehru decided to take the initiative. A special session of the National Conference had been called to discuss the Basic Principles (that is, the accession) between May 16 to 21, and Nehru decided to visit Kashmir then. He tried every form of persuasion and argument, but Abdullah now insisted that there was no middle line between full integration and full autonomy—and of course Kashmir had to get the latter. Autonomy had become a code word for independence. A dejected Nehru returned and sent Azad to try and persuade Abdullah. The Maulana was no more successful than the Pandit; Azad, in fact, returned an angry man. A mood was now building up in Delhi for Abdullah's dismissal. But before he took any extreme step Nehru preferred to wait. He had to leave for London on 28 May 1953 for the coronation of Queen Elizabeth and the Commonwealth Conference; it would be a long trip, with Nehru returning only on 27 June. In the National Conference there was now quite an·open split over accession between what was known as the Inner Eight: Sheikh Abdullah, Bakshi Ghulam Mohammad, Mirza Mohammad Afzal Beg, G.M. Sadiq, Maulana Masoodi, Girdhari Lal Dogra, Shamlal Saraf and Budh Singh. Bakshi proposed they defer a decision till Nehru returned. And there matters might have rested, but for 23 June. The death of Mookerjee was attributed by Abdullah to natural causes and ill-health. The immediate reaction was disbelief. Dr B.C. Roy, family physician of the Mookerjees, shot off an angry telegram demanding to know why he had not been informed that Mookerjee was ill. Nehru was in London when he heard the news; his reaction was that the uproar would only harden attitudes on both sides, and he was right.

By this time Abdullah had also realized that Bakshi was being wooed by Delhi (including through Mullik), and that he might have difficulty mustering a majority for a completely anti-Delhi stand. Ministers like D.P. Dhar, concerned about this dangerous drift, had been in regular and secret communication with the Sadar-i-Riyasat, Dr Karan Singh, who though still a young man of twenty-two, played a major role in that crucial phase, keeping Delhi in touch with the situation in the power centres of Kashmir. In July D.P. Dhar visited Delhi and briefed Rafi Ahmed Kidwai: the Sheikh, he reported, was preparing to throw the whole Bakshi group out of the government and the party. Kidwai tried to phone Abdullah. When he was rebuffed he went to see Nehru along with Dhar. Nehru was finally ready to act. And yet, as Dr Karan Singh recalled, his style was careful; he indicated the broad direction, but kept himself out of specifics in front of politicians. However, the signal had come. At the political level, Karan Singh, Bakshi and D.P. Dhar had to ensure that the operation remained a complete secret; they believed that Abdullah could even have arrested them in a pre-emptive move, and thrown Kashmir and India into a major constitutional crisis.

In Delhi officials began preparations to ensure that the fallout was controlled. The Prime Minister summoned Mullik and told him to strengthen the IB and police. D.W. Mehra, Deputy Director, IB, was posted to Srinagar. On 31 July, Nehru told Mullik and Mehra at a closed-door meeting that he hoped it could be done peacefully but they should be ready for violence if it came to that. Mullik describes the scene:

> At this point Pandit Nehru was nearly overwhelmed by emotion. Both of us, who had known him for some years, had never seen him in such a disturbed mood before. We realised that he was on the point of uprooting a plant which he had nursed with great care. At the end he wished Mehra good luck and wanted to be kept informed regularly. For this purpose, we could call him up even in the night.

Rafi Ahmed Kidwai was given charge of the operation in Delhi while A.P. Jain was sent to Srinagar for on-the-spot supervision.

On 6 August, Abdullah gave Delhi the opportunity it was seeking: he ordered Saraf to resign from the Cabinet. Saraf called on Dr Karan Singh and the Sadar-i-Riyasat encouraged him to defy Abdullah. Saraf refused to resign. Bakshi and Maulana Masoodi began to mobilize support for Saraf, in the Cabinet and the party. On the morning of 8 August, the Sheikh suddenly left for Gulmarg. IB reported to Delhi that he had gone to establish secret contact with a representative of Pakistan. True or false, this was the excuse to make 8 August D-Day. That evening Dr Karan Singh dismissed Abdullah and invited Bakshi to form the government. At this point Bakshi Ghulam Mohammad suddenly lost his nerve.

Nehru and Kidwai were at an official dinner at Hyderabad House in Delhi when, at eleven, Mullik brought the message that Bakshi was refusing to take charge. They left for the PM's house as quickly as was polite, spoke to A.P. Jain on the telephone and learnt that Bakshi had refused to take the oath until he was absolutely certain that Abdullah was behind bars. At midnight Dr Karan Singh gave orders for Abdullah's arrest. Bakshi rediscovered his courage only at around four in the morning when he had verified that a police party, led by L.D. Thakur, DIG, had actually left for Gulmarg. Even after that Bakshi Ghulam Mohammad needed the restorative powers of a large shot of brandy, obligingly offered by the Sadar-i-Riyasat, to improve his spirits. Before dawn he became the second Prime Minister of Kashmir.

There were widespread disturbances that day, but with Abdullah behind bars Bakshi's courage began improving in leaps and bounds. It took nearly three weeks to bring the situation under control; about sixty persons lost their lives. But when peace returned it did so for a decade. Bakshi grew with the job, and although he was later tainted by corruption charges, his contribution has been too easily dismissed in the romance of the Abdullah story. India had a good deal to be thankful to Bakshi for.

Blame is a very easy thing to distribute; but if it is of any satisfaction to anyone, then in this case we can at least share it between the two towering idealists. Jawaharlal could argue that a broken heart was preferable to a broken nation, but his incomprehensible surrender to his unmemorable Home Minister is inexplicable. Perhaps he was leaning in the other direction after having successfully stopped the Rajendra Prasad–Tandon lobby. Abdullah's growing flirtation with that chimera called independence hardly helped. But this much at least is clear: he never wanted to join Pakistan. As late as in June 1953 he arrested Ghulam Mohiuddin Karra for advocating accession to Pakistan in a public speech. For nearly eleven years, with a brief pause prompted by Nehruvian guilt in 1958, the Government of India tried to prove Abdullah's complicity with Pakistan. Time has made the details of the detention without trial and then detention with trial more of a personal tragedy, but there was a sense of vindication when Sheikh Abdullah was unconditionally released in 1964. Those were the lost years, and they ended too late. Together, Nehru and Abdullah could truly have made Kashmir the stabilizing force of secular India; their failure had consequences which shaped events long after they had passed on the responsibility to their heirs.

What Nehru lost by arresting Abdullah was the moral argument, and it troubled him deeply. Unable to reconcile himself to the fact that Abdullah had still not been brought to trial, he ordered his friend's release on 8 January 1958. But the Sheikh, now swayed by the halo of martyrdom, used the opportunity to stoke another confrontation and was rearrested on 30 April 1958. One reason for rearrest was Exhibit No. P-169 of the Kashmir Conspiracy Case launched against him. It was the draft of a resolution of the Plebiscite Front, dated 7 April 1958, calling on Kashmir to break its ties with India, on the grounds that accession without plebiscite was null and void. The resolution said:

> In the opinion of the committee the Jammu and Kashmir State has not yet acceeded (sic) with either of the two dominions and therefore the question of aggression by Pakistan on Indian territory is not a 'reality' but only an excuse for India to maintain her forced occupation on a

part of the State.

The typed draft had been overwritten in places in the Sheikh's hand. But the story of Kashmir has too many paradoxes to display too much patriotic horror at this. From the shadows of the historical record emerges one more startling fact. Within a fortnight of arresting Abdullah for asking too much of Delhi, Jawaharlal Nehru completely reversed India's position and offered Pakistan a plebiscite!

The Prime Minister of Pakistan, now Mohammad Ali, came to Delhi on an official visit. In the talks Nehru suggested that after the two Prime Ministers had finalized the preliminary issues, a plebiscite administrator could be named by April 1954. He even told Mohammad Ali that voting could be done in the whole state rather than separate Hindu or Muslim regions, and if this meant the loss of the whole Valley, he was prepared for it! The offer was confirmed in a letter to Mohammad Ali on 3 September. So shocked was Bakshi that he threatened to resign. Nehru calmed him with a letter on 18 August 1953 in which he said:

> In particular, we have to look a little ahead and think of the future. . . . We have to choose the lesser evil and we have to choose a path which not only promises the greatest advantage but is dignified and in keeping with our general policy.

The only condition Nehru placed was that the American UN nominee Admiral Nimitz be replaced as Plebiscite Administrator by someone from a smaller country. Deeply suspicious of the US, he did not want this superpower's hand in the plebiscite.

Now the second startling surprise. Rather than grabbing at the offer—as Pakistan would surely do today if anyone in Delhi was foolish enough to make it—Pakistan made Admiral Nimitz an issue, insisting that he should not be replaced; and raised small and imaginary issues needlessly blocking a settlement on plebiscite. It all seems unbelievable now, but that is what the record shows. With Abdullah in jail, and a popular upsurge in the Valley, Pakistan was being virtually handed Kashmir. If there were any doubts about Nehru's sincerity in those years about the plebiscite commitment, then surely they should have ended with this proposal. But soon after this Pakistan went ahead with her military alliance with the United States and Nehru withdrew his offer. The chance was lost. The paradox of course is this: a formal position of the Government of India in August 1953 can hardly become treason by April 1958.

Or, can it?

Delhi argued that the ratification of the accession by the Constituent Assembly during Bakshi's rule had closed this particular chapter, but Abdullah of course could not accept the legitimacy of a House in which he.was not present. He had won the election; he had the mandate; he had the support of the people. And he proved it. By the surge of the welcoming crowds during his brief release in 1958. And, far more significantly, during a strange episode which took place while he was still in jail in December 1963: the theft of the greatest treasure that the people of Kashmir possessed, a Holy Relic kept in the mosque from where the Sheikh himself had launched so many historic movements, Hazratbal.

A strand from the beard of the Prophet of Islam, Peace Be Upon Him, suddenly disappeared from its resting place at Hazratbal, and then suddenly reappeared. It was an incident which shook the subcontinent, taking Delhi to the edge of panic before there was an almost magical solution. And it finally ended the decade of jail which Abdullah suffered not under the rule of any Maharaja, but under the rule of his friend, Jawaharlal Nehru.

17

The Puppets of Allah

It was a strange cauldron of reasons for the release of a man jailed for a decade; a sudden turn in a story which began more than three hundred years before. A family quarrel in the holy city of Medina; Aurangzeb's ruinous ambitions in the Deccan; a chance friendship between an exiled, penniless Arab and a prosperous Kashmiri trader; and two dreams which gave the people of Kashmir their greatest treasure, a relic they have revered and loved since the first year of the eighteenth century when it reached them by divine will. And then suddenly on 26 December 1963 it got stolen. The facts were mysterious, but there was a wonder to perform.

In the year 1635 a traveller in search of a home named Syed Abdullah reached the then powerful kingdom of Bijapur. He told the ruler that he had been the principal Mutawalli of the main shrine at Medina until he fell out with his cousin, Syed Hashim, and became a victim of court intrigues thanks to the latter's machinations. He preferred banishment to the Sultan's justice. Claiming direct descent from the Prophet himself through his grandson Hazrat Imam Hussain, Syed Abdullah announced that he had brought with him a priceless family relic, a strand of hair from the beard of the Prophet, the Mo-e-Muqaddas. He was believed, honoured and rewarded with a *jagir*. The rest of his life was peaceful, but his son, Syed Hamid, had to face the turbulence of Mughal aspirations. In 1686 Bijapur finally fell to Aurangzeb and Syed Hamid was forced to flee. He stopped at Jahanabad, where he was befriended by that familiar Kashmiri, the trader, in this case a man called Nooruddin Ashwari. Soon Nooruddin learnt of Syed Hamid's heirlooms, and asked for the Mo-e-Muqaddas. Hamid, of course, refused. But that very night, Hamid had a dream in which the Prophet himself told him to hand it over to Nooruddin. Hamid did so the very next day. Now Nooruddin was told in a dream to take the Mo-e-Muqaddas to Kashmir and find a home for it on the banks of the lake. Nooruddin shut down his business and set off for his native land at once. But all along the way Nooruddin kept displaying the Holy Relic to excited people, and as its fame spread word reached Aurangzeb. Suspecting him to be a charlatan, the emperor sent Nooruddin to prison and ordered the Mo-e-Muqaddas to be brought before him. When he had the hair tested, he became convinced that it was genuine. Now his doubt turned to concern; he felt that such a precious memento was too valuable to be left with an individual, and sent it to the shrine of Sheikh Moinuddin Chishti at Ajmer Sharif for safekeeping. But as soon as it reached Ajmer, Aurangzeb had a dream—the Prophet told him that the destination of the Mo-e-Muqaddas was Kashmir. Nooruddin, in the meanwhile, had died from shock and grief. Aurangzeb entrusted the Relic to Nooruddin's servant, Medanish, and he eventually reached the Valley in 1700, where he was received with royal ceremony by the Governor, Mir Fazil Khan. The Mo-e-Muqaddas was first kept at Khanqah Naqshband, but it proved too small for the eager crowds who thronged for a view. It was finally taken to the Bagh-e-Sadiq Khan, built in Shah Jehan's time on the banks of the Dal Lake, and the place came to be known as the Asar-e-Sharif (Shrine of the Relic), and then Hazratbal (the Lake of the Hazrat, or the Prophet). The original command had been that it rest beside the lake and that is where it found its home. Hazratbal became the symbol of the people of Kashmir, and Sheikh Abdullah made it a brilliant counterfoil to the Jama Masjid of Srinagar after he broke with the conservatives in the 1930s. His own mellifluous oratory became a staple at the prayers in the mosque of Hazratbal. The heirs of Nooruddin became the hereditary custodians of the Holy Relic, and are known as the Nishan Dez— or, the persons authorized to protect it and put it on public display on ten special days in the year, all connected with the Prophet's life. Placed within a five-inch quartz container, it can be seen only from one side. The strand, its top curved a little, is held upward in a tube, which, when not on display, lies in a bag embroidered in gold which in turn is kept in a walnut box. This box is kept double locked within a small room on the first floor of the Hazratbal mosque.

The 20th of December 1963 was a day of "Deedar" (viewing), and the Mo-e-Muqaddas was, as usual, brought to the balcony by the Nishan Dez and displayed to fervent crowds. On the evening of 26 December, Rahim Bandey, the senior Nishan Dez, organized a private viewing, locked up the Relic, and went home. It was a bitterly cold night and Hazratbal was deserted. In the early hours of 27 December, Rahim Bandey discovered that the door of the room holding the Mo-e-Muqaddas had been broken into. At some point between the time he had left at night and early morning the Mo-e-Muqaddas had been stolen.

It was freezing, and grey, and the Valley was choked with snow, but word spread at the speed of fire. By the afternoon, completely spon-taneously, thousands were marching through the streets of Srinagar demanding that the culprits be identified, caught and punished. The shops shut in an impromptu *hartal* and the shopkeepers said they would not reopen until the beloved Relic had been recovered. The mood of anger began to swell, and one incident suddenly burst open a decade-long volcano. A nephew of Bakshi Ghulam Mohammad, Bakshi Abdul Rashid, appeared before the emotional crowds and began exhorting them to disperse. A rumour started, and quickly became belief: the Mo-e-Muqaddas had been picked up by some of Bakshi's men, who had taken it to the Bakshi home to satisfy his ailing mother's wish. Rashid had to be rescued from the people, who then set fire to a hotel and a cinema hall owned by the Bakshi family. Three persons died in police firing. In revenge, the Kothibagh police station was torched. Perhaps it was fortunate that the man who had taken over when Sheikh Abdullah was sent to jail a decade and three months before was no longer Chief Minister of Kashmir, having just been divested of his chair in the most unusual circumstances.

Sadar-i-Riyasat Dr Karan Singh had set one formal condition when swearing in Bakshi in the summer dawn of August 1953: "The con-tinuance in office of the new Cabinet will depend upon its securing a vote of confidence from the Legislative Assembly during its coming session". Bakshi went towards this goal step by step. By the end of August he had brought the demonstrations under control. On 13–15 September he called a convention of the National Conference, attended by about 400 delegates, which resolved that the change of government was "inevitable in the interest of the country and the national movement". The legislature then met on 5 October 1953 and gave Bakshi a unanimous vote of confidence: an unanimity encouraged by the fact of Abdullah and his loyalists in jail. Now Bakshi turned his attention to sewing up the threads of accession. On 20 October 1953 a Basic Principles Committee and an Advisory Committee on Fundamental Rights and Citizenship was set up. Its recom-mendations, based on the Delhi Agreement, were adopted by the Jammu and Kashmir Constituent Assembly on 6 February 1954. A Drafting Committee worked out the letter of the law by 12 February, and it was passed on 15 February 1954. An argument that had raised so much commotion for three years was—a trifle wordlessly—closed. The Con-stituent Assembly had formally ratified the accession of Jammu and Kashmir to India, thereby providing the legitimacy of popular sanction to the agreement signed by Hari Singh. As far as Delhi was concerned, this also ended all discussions about a plebiscite; Nehru's offer to Pakistan a few months before, consequently, was literally the last offer. But Abdullah of course was not going to close this chapter so neatly: after his arrest, in his view, the Constituent Assembly no longer represented the will of the people. In his logic, the demand for a plebiscite had become even more justified by the events of 1953 and 1954. But Bakshi and Nehru went ahead, giving practical shape to the integration. The customs barrier between Kashmir and the rest of India was lifted on 13 April 1954; in the same month Dr Rajendra Prasad made the first official visit by a President of India to Kashmir. On 14 May 1954, Prasad signed the order, using the authority of Article 370, endorsing Kashmir's constitutional relationship with India. On 26 January 1957 Kashmir approved its own Constitution, and the legislature could move towards the next milestone: elections for a normal Legislative Assembly. Its strength was kept at a hundred members, with two additional seats reserved for women to be nominated. Twenty-four of the seats were kept vacant for Pakistan-Occupied Kashmir. In March 1957 elections were held, and Bakshi was now—for the record—an elected Chief Minister.

Those elections also became the cause of yet another split in the National Conference. There were no principles involved this time, just power. A dispute over distribution of seats ended with the group led by G.M. Sadiq (and including D.P. Dhar, Mir Qasim and Girdhari Lal Dogra) launching the Democratic National Conference. The split and departure of experienced administrators not only weakened the quality of government seriously, but also brought to the fore elements who would contribute substantially to the destruction of Bakshi's reputation. By the spring of 1962, when the next elections were held, Bakshi was palpably unpopular. But he retained the support of Nehru, who bartered stability for corruption. The only way Bakshi "won" the 1962 elections was by total rigging with the help of Delhi officials. Jawaharlal sent him a sardonic message in his letter of 4 March 1962:

> In fact, it would strengthen your position much more if you lost a few seats to *bonafide* opponents.

To others Nehru was defensive. As he wrote to P.N. Bazaz on 7 August 1962: "It is true that political liberty does not exist there in the same measure as in the rest of India. At the same time there is much more of it than there used to be". A very poor excuse, and Nehru was conscious of it. In April 1962 he had tried to get Abdullah released, but was again blocked by the Bakshi–Mullik combination who kept promising imminent success in the conspiracy case against Abdullah. If Nehru had succeeded perhaps the volatile events of the winter of 1963–64 would not have taken place.

However, there was first the trauma of the winter of 1962 to suffer. The military humiliation by China in 1962 shattered Nehru, the Congress and the country. In June 1963— coincidentally, in Srinagar—the young and dashing confidant of Nehru, Biju Patnaik, proposed a strategy to revitalize the Congress by sending some of its most senior leaders back to where they had started from, the grassroots. Nehru did not bite at once, and it was only in August 1963 that what came to be known as the Kamaraj Plan (named after the then Congress president) was put into effect. A whole range of Cabinet ministers and chief ministers sent in their resignations. Among the more enthusiastic ones to offer to leave was Bakshi. But bitter wrangling broke out in Srinagar over not merely the chief minister's chair, but a lot of less important furniture as well. The net result was that a complete outsider, Shamsuddin, ended up as Bakshi's heir in September. Unfortunately for him he also began his tenure with the unsavoury reputation of being Bakshi's stooge.

And so when the rumour raced through Kashmir that Bakshi's people were behind the theft of the Mo-e-Muqaddas, it was implicitly assumed that Shamsuddin simply did not have the will or the ability to have interfered with Bakshi's plans.

Shamsuddin was in Jammu on 27 December 1963; he rushed to Srinagar by the evening. When he saw the hostile mood, he shut himself indoors. And remained there. By the 28th restive crowds were preparing to attack the All India Radio station for broadcasting what they said was false information about the culprits behind the theft; Pakistan Radio, of course, discovered a flourishing market for its disinformation. An Action Committee was set up under the chairmanship of Maulvi Mohammad Sayeed Masoodi: and for the first time since the break in the 1930s the pro- and anti-Abdullah forces shared the same platform. Two young men, both named Farooq, entered the limelight as members of this Action Committee. One was Mir Waiz Maulvi Farooq; the other was Sheikh Farooq, later to become more famous as Farooq Abdullah. Posters sprouted on the walls demanding the arrest of Bakshi. With the state administration dormant, and the agitation turning more aggressive by the hour, Nehru decided to send in his favourite Kashmir policeman, B.N.Mullik, and made a special broadcast to Kashmiris to tell them that Mullik was coming to recover the Relic.

Mullik left the next morning, the last day of 1963, by an Indian Air Force Viscount. At the airport to receive him was *his* favourite policeman,

Lakshman Das Thakur, now Inspector-General of Police—the same officer who led the party to arrest Abdullah on the night Bakshi needed sustenance before taking his oath of office. Their conclusions after investigations were: the locks had been broken between midnight and three in the morning; and that it was an inside job by someone whose presence would not cause any surprise on the Hazratbal premises.

By the new year, the agitation had spread not only to other parts of the country, but across the borders too. Pakistan was deliberately trying to create communal riots in East Bengal on the issue. Not surprisingly, it succeeded, leading in a short while to another exodus of Hindus into India, hysterical headlines in the West Bengali press, and a burst of anti-Muslim rioting in Calcutta, the like of which had not been seen since 1950. There was careful planning in the simultaneous conflagration. In Kashmir the agitation had reached every village; people from the interior were trickling into Srinagar, and free food was being distributed from *langars*. Every speech from every corner now demanded not just the arrest of Bakshi, but also the release of Sheikh Abdullah. Fresh posters called for United Nations Security Council intervention, and an announcement of a panel of judges from three Muslim countries to try the accused: Indian courts were obviously too full of infidels for the Action Committee. The crescendo was peaking to a dangerously high emotional pitch. On 3 January, Sheikh Abdullah pitched it even higher by sending a long letter to President Radhakrishnan from jail demanding a review of the Kashmir policy since 1953, which he said was at the root of these tragic events. Abdullah noted: "It is quite possible that the motive behind this sacrilege is purely political". Abdullah was hinting at Bakshi, but there was more than one kind of politics being played. Bakshi was only a scapegoat. However, preferring discretion to valour, Bakshi quietly left the Valley on 4 January, a day of high excitement. Dr Karan Singh reached Srinagar that morning sparking rumours that he was going to dismiss Shamsuddin and take over. That was not the reason why he had come, but he was to play an important role in managing the situation. He visited Hazratbal and was greeted warmly by the people—proof that it was not communal anger, but simply the cry of the heart of the Kashmiri. Karan Singh organized prayers in all the temples for the recovery of the Mo-e-Muqaddas. Delhi, by now, did want to replace Shamsuddin as soon as possible, but no one was in a mood for gifts that morning. Mir Qasim turned down an offer to take over. Perhaps he may have accepted it if he had known what was going to happen early in the evening of 4 January.

Mullik and Thakur cleared Hazratbal of all policemen, including plainclothesmen. They had tracked down the theft and made a deal with those responsible: the Mo-e-Muqaddas would be quietly replaced at some point that evening. They were tense, of course, for things could still go wrong. There were no higher stakes, and a deal is always vulnerable to any new motivation. A little after five in the evening, Mullik and Thakur walked into Hazratbal and went to the first floor. The Mo-e-Muqaddas was resting in its familiar wooden box, now broken of course. In relief and triumph Mullik picked up the Holy Relic, placed it reverently on his head, walked to the balcony, and announced to the excited throng that Kashmir's symbol of Islam had returned to its people. The telephone line to Delhi had been dead most of the day, but perhaps Mullik's sheer eagerness psyched it into life. By six, Mullik was talking to Nehru on the phone. His excitement, and the poor line, both came in the way, and it took a few extra sentences for him to convey to the Prime Minister that the Mo-e-Muqaddas had been recovered. "God bless you, Mullik", replied Nehru, "you have saved Kashmir for us".

There were those, of course, who did not want it to be saved for Mullik, Nehru, Bakshi and India. If the people of Kashmir welcomed the news with unrestrained joy, the Action Committee was not in a mood to surrender so easily on an issue which could potentially change the destiny of Kashmir. Mullik and Thakur had taken all the precautions they could, making members of the Nishan Dez confirm publicly on 4 January that this was indeed the genuine Mo-e-Muqaddas. But the Action Committee immediately charged that it was a fake planted by Indian Intelligence Bureau (IB) officials led by Mullik and sent by Nehru. They demanded a special Deedar, or a special public viewing, by respected and holy men selected by them. The political implications were obvious enough; the pot had to be kept boiling, till the larger aim of Abdullah's release had been achieved. The government also understood this much. All that these preselected men had to do was to declare the Mo-e-Muqaddas a fake, and there would be the near uprising which was their goal.

Pakistani subversives were ready to supplement this anger. Pakistan's temptation was easily understandable. India had never been so vulnerable as she was in the winter of 1963–64. Militarily weak, politically fragile and economically depressed, the nation was under the kind of pressure which comes but rarely. (In just about two years' time, famine would rage through the north, and a dangerously frustrated youth launch a violent uprising in the name of Mao's revolution, the Naxalite movement.) And in January 1964 came a severe setback which threw the country into an unstable spin. On the morning of 6 January, on the opening day of the

Congress session at Bhubaneshwar in Orissa, with riots raging in nearby Calcutta, Jawaharlal Nehru suffered a stroke.

It was a moment made for Pakistan. Its Kashmir propaganda intensified with its perception of Nehru's and India's deepening ill-health. The clamour for a special Deedar was orchestrated into a major campaign when the administration made the mistake of stubbornly refusing this demand, damaging the credibility of its own claim. A dangerous tilt was given to the rising anger with the allegation that Hindus had dared to fake something as sacred as the Mo-e-Muqaddas; it was an insult to no less a person than the Prophet Himself. On 7 January, the Action Committee formally met Dr Karan Singh and put forward these demands.

Once again it needed Nehru to restore sense. Having recovered slightly, and been briefed, he immediately ordered that the special Deedar be permitted. As his personal emissary he sent Lal Bahadur Shastri on the afternoon of 30 January 1964 to oversee the special Deedar, and ensure that the officials, who were very upset by the decision, did not sabotage it. The date was fixed for 3 February; the time, two in the afternoon. By prearranged terms the Action Committee was supposed to let the government know the names of its Holy Fourteen in advance, but—obviously to guard against any pressure—this was not done. The Delhi bureaucrats were now in deep depression. They were convinced that despite their successful recovery they had been finessed by Pakistan. Even Mullik lost all hope, except for a little flicker at the back of his mind which did not seem rational enough to trust.

Shastri, along with Shamsuddin and the officials, reached Hazratbal at one o' clock. Half-an-hour later the Action Committee arrived. Masoodi opened with a long speech in which he enjoined the witnesses, by all that was holy to them, in the name of Allah and the Prophet, to be totally honest. Shamsuddin sat in a corner, praying silently; Shastri sombrely in front; Mullik against a far wall. Masoodi made each of the Fourteen take an oath by the Holy *Quran*. The chief Nishan Dez was Nooruddin; it was a name that echoed back to the origins—the ancestor too was faced with the problem of proof before the world. Nooruddin Bandey brought the Holy Relic out from a Godrej safe; the seal was broken by the District Magistrate. A complete and silent tension had gripped every single person present, whether actor or audience. The witnesses examined the Relic intensely, taking it close to their eyes. Suddenly a murmur broke out among the Kashmiri officials near the witnesses, and a few of them broke and ran towards Mullik. His first reaction was that they were coming to protect him from the fury that was about to burst. Then, in a moment, came the joyous cry, *"Mubarak ho!"* Congratulations! In seconds they had lifted Mullik on their shoulders and were dancing with joy.

The decisive verdict came from a saintly divine, over eighty years old and the most respected Pir in the Valley, Faqir Miraq Shah. He raised the crystal tube, looked at it for an endless moment, and then pronounced judgement in a clear and firm voice: *"Al Haq."* (It is the truth.) Thirty-seven days of tension melted into joy. Coincidentally the weather too changed that day, the *Bara Kalan* (Great Winter) softening into *Bacha Kalan* (Small Winter).

For Mullik this was no longer coincidence; he had begun to believe in the divine power of the Mo-e-Muqaddas himself. If he had that glimmer of hope before the Deedar it was because he believed that the Divine would intervene again to corroborate the Relic's authenticity, this time through a dream for Faqir Miraq Shah. He narrates a mystic experience he himself underwent in *My Years With Nehru*:

> A strange thing happened. One evening, while I was at the Guest House, a Muslim Divine came to see me. I had never met him before. He did not even introduce himself to me. He came up to me and said that he had come to congratulate me on the recovery and restoration of the Mo-e-Muqaddas. He further said that the Mo-e-Muqaddas could only ride on the shoulders of an honest man and it was remarkable that it did not find any suitable person in Kashmir Valley and chose me—a person of another faith and coming from another part of the country—as its vehicle. He left immediately, after invoking Allah's blessings on me. The Guest House *khansamas*, from whom I enquired, said that they had not noticed this Faqir. . . we who worked in the cause were only puppets in the game. Glory to the Mo-e-Muqaddas!

But of course the questions of the sceptics would never completely go away, more so since neither Mullik nor L.D. Thakur have disclosed how precisely they recovered the Mo-e-Muqaddas and from whom. Home Minister Gulzarilal Nanda named three men in connection with the theft: Mutawalli Abdul Rahim Bandey, Abdul Rashid and Kabir Butt, but there was no follow-up action. Mullik teases us in his memoirs: "This was an intelligence operation, never to be disclosed". Thakur, who probably played a greater role for his country than Mullik in this episode, has maintained a loyal and disciplined silence in the belief that the truth could even now be inflammatory. But did the intimate friendship between Mullik and Bakshi, as well as their close political cooperation, have anything to do with the recovery? It is an interesting fact that Bakshi, who had rushed to the Valley from Delhi on hearing the news on the 27th, quietly left Kashmir on the morning of 4 January, the day the Mo-e-Muqaddas was recovered.

A more political question: what were the real motivations of the Action Committee in this movement? Was it only the restoration of Sheikh Abdullah, a legitimate enough cause for one of the members, his son Farooq, or was it playing Pakistan's game through the other Farooq, whose uncle, Yusuf Shah, had crossed over to the other Kashmir. Partisans will interpret the past according to their current needs, so it is best to quote the independent judgement of Dr Karan Singh (*Sadar-i-Riyasat*, Oxford University Press), who describes his dialogue with the Action Committee on 7 January 1964 thus:

> These demands were moderate and sensible, and despite the virulent propaganda from Pakistan in its press and radio ever since the disappearance of the Relic, the Action Committee did not allow the movement to fall into anti-national hands. While their distrust of the Shamsuddin government was total, their appeal was not to any outside power but to the Government of India. In this, the role played by the veteran Maulana Masoodi was crucial and praiseworthy. A deputation led by him and including Dr Farooq Abdullah, Maulvi Farooq, Mufti Jalaluddin, Maulvi Mohammad Yasin, Mohammad Abbas and Ghulam Rasool met me on 7 January and was with me for over two hours.

A postscript is necessary. Twenty-six years later, when Maulana Masoodi was largely bedridden by age, a Pakistan-trained terrorist shot him in cold blood.

The whole episode finally convinced Nehru that he had been wrong to succumb repeatedly to Bakshi and Mullik's advice, and he began clearing the path for Abdullah's release. Shamsuddin had to go, of course; he was both too identified with Bakshi and too incompetent. He was replaced by G.M. Sadiq. On 5 April 1964 Sadiq issued a press statement from Srinagar saying that the conspiracy case against Abdullah would be withdrawn immediately. That afternoon Nehru explained to a Cabinet Committee (Gulzarilal Nanda, T.T. Krishnamachari, Lal Bahadur Shastri and

A.K.Sen) that if fifteen years after freedom the people of Kashmir could rise against the government like this, then there was something radically wrong with their Kashmir policy. With his bureaucrats Nehru was less polite. His last Foreign Secretary, Y.D.Gundevia, who had been sent along with Shastri on the Deedar trip, reports a conversation between Nehru and M.J.Desai, Secretary General in the external affairs ministry. Desai was once again repeating the litany of doubts when Nehru, furious, turned upon him and said, "You look after them. If a damned thing can't be proved in four years, in six years, there's obviously nothing to be proved".

On 8 April 1964 Sheikh Abdullah was finally free. President Radhakrishnan called the release of Abdullah and fourteen of his colleagues "an act of faith in which we expect the Sheikh and his friends to justify our faith".

On 9 April Abdullah held his first press conference and declared, "I am neither a Pakistani agent, nor an Indian agent. I am a servant of the people of Jammu and Kashmir". He stressed one point: the problem should be settled in Nehru's lifetime, and there was no time to lose, for Jawaharlal's health was failing. Nehru had wanted Abdullah to come up to Delhi immediately after his release, but Abdullah, legitimately, wanted to visit Kashmir first. Perhaps he should not have spent three weeks in Kashmir. He ran out of time.

Abdullah reached Delhi on 29 April: with him were his lieutenant Mirza Afzal Beg and his eldest son—just blooded in politics through the Action Committee—Farooq, then a medical graduate. He stayed of course, with Nehru; the two old friends spent many hours in discussion, but Nehru also wanted Abdullah to talk to the full spectrum of the country's political leadership. He set up a three-member team for morning briefings to bring the Sheikh up-to-date: Gundevia, Badruddin Tyabji, and the current Indian High Commissioner to Pakistan, a man who would play a major role in a historic decision a decade later, G.Parthasarathi. Abdullah named this combination of a Parsi, a Muslim and a Tamil Brahmin, Nehru's Three Musketeers. The briefings had almost immediate impact, softening the Sheikh perceptibly. On 2 May he told newsmen:

> My friends here have been obsessed with this accession business. It is a very minor point. It is only a means to an end. . . .

What was the end? Peace on the subcontinent. How could it be achieved? Abdullah's mind was already casting in fresh directions, but how were the newsmen to know that yet? Abdullah left Delhi to call on three great stalwarts: Acharya Vinoba Bhave, Jaya Prakash Narayan and C. Rajagopalachari. When he returned he placed his idea before Nehru: a Confederation of India, Pakistan and Kashmir. The thought was hardly absent from Nehru's mind, though he had seen too much to be optimistic. But if there was even a remote chance he would not stand in the way. Abdullah was determined to pursue the chance, however remote. On 6 May he received an invitation from President Ayub Khan to visit Pakistan. He accepted as cordially as it had been sent. Nehru went through the motions; Dr Krishna Rao of the Legal and Treaties Division was assigned to examine every corner of international law on confederations. On 15 May at the All India Congress Committee session in Bombay, Nehru explained, "He (Abdullah) does not believe in the two-nation theory which was the basis of the formation of Pakistan". Then, without mentioning it specifically, he floated the three-nation theory:

> Nevertheless he hopes that it should be possible for India, holding on to her principles, to live in peace and friendship with Pakistan and thus incidentally to put an end to the question of Kashmir. . . If Sheikh Abdullah can help in bringing this about, he will have done a great service to both the countries.

A little carried away by his enthusiasm, the Sheikh seriously considered going to Pakistan by crossing the Ceasefire Line in Kashmir on foot, and even got Nehru's approval, before the romanticism was grounded by Gundevia and Parthasarathi. The bureaucrats were realistic; leave fanciful notions like Confederation aside, if Abdullah managed to get Ayub to accept even the Ceasefire Line as a practical solution that would be achievement enough. Sadly it would take two extremely expensive wars, and another partition of a country, to reach this point.

On Saturday 23 May, the Sheikh left for Rawalpindi. Parthasarathi flew off the same day to Karachi, to await word from Abdullah and then brief Nehru through embassy channels. The Sheikh was given a heroic welcome at Chaklala airport at the start of what was scheduled to be a sixteen-day peace visit, being received by no less a person than Foreign Minister Bhutto himself. But public spirits soon dampened as Abdullah began praising India's secularism. *The Dawn* pouted: "Sheikh Abdullah's statement and his references to India's so-called secularism have caused a certain amount of disappointment among the public in general, and the intelligentsia in particular". That was only the most respectful comment. On his side Abdullah had even greater reason for disappointment. Ayub did not waste a minute before he dismissed the idea of any Confederation. The Sheikh then bargained for a minimum of an Ayub–Nehru summit in June. Having obtained Ayub's consent, Abdullah announced on 26 May that this step should be sufficient cause for satisfaction for the moment. Parthasarathi telegraphed C.S. Jha, then Commonwealth Secretary; Jha promised he would be in touch as soon as he met Nehru, who had returned from Dehra Dun only on the evening of the 26th. Nehru's consent lay on Parthasarathi's table in Karachi on the morning of 27 May.

That was the morning the world learnt that Pandit Jawaharlal Nehru had passed away in his sleep.

The last chance of a peaceful solution to Kashmir probably died that day. Yet another journey had only begun; there were so many difficult miles to go, but the one man who had the moral stature, the political will and the unique vision to take us there closed his eyes forever on us that day.

India and Pakistan have not been overly blessed with giants; but there is no shortage of pygmies and scavengers busy burying hope wherever they find it. Pakistan had too many petty minds locked in the most childish fantasies, but very representative of the simulated mythology that had spawned the country itself two decades previously. Tinpot generals, their chests ablaze with self-inflicted valour, went around promising that they would plant the Pakistan flag on Delhi's Red Fort after they had made mincemeat of the hordes of cowardly, dhoti-clad Hindu soldiers. India's air was shrill with the vulture-squawk of communalists determined to resurrect the fire and blood of the Partition riots. S.Gopal quotes in his biography of Nehru a memorably chilling stanza from Bertolt Brecht to describe the time:

> This was the thing that nearly had us mastered,
> Do not rejoice in his defeat, you men;
> Although the world stood up and stopped the bastard,
> The bitch that bore him is in heat again.

Pakistan treated Nehru's death not as tragedy but as encouragement, and began planning to complete its war of 1947. India was too weighed down by its internal crises to lift its eyes across any border and notice what was happening. Abdullah returned to the stump, flogging plebiscite again for what it was worth. Delhi continued its process of integration. In early January 1965 Articles 356 and 357 were extended to Kashmir, making Governor's Rule possible without the consent of the State legislature. This was followed by the announcement that the Indian National Congress would be formally launched in the State on 26 January 1965, which it was. Abdullah seethed at these encroachments upon Kashmir's status and his preserve. In an angry speech at Hazratbal on 15 January 1965 he even hinted that his continuing agitation might not remain peaceful forever. On 29 January he called for a social boycott of those who had joined Congress, and taunted Shastri as a weakling from whom nothing could be expected. There was anger in Delhi and pressure to stop Abdullah from his next mission: a Haj trip which would also embrace visits to a number of countries other than Saudi Arabia. Shastri very correctly did not make an issue over a religious journey. Abdullah, however, had no qualms about mixing politics with religion. He was openly provocative, quite blatantly using Pakistan embassy facilities and wooing Arab-Muslim sentiment for Kashmiri "self-determination". Delhi by and large ignored Abdullah's tour in the beginning, preferring to concentrate its attentions on the Valley. On the night of 6–7 March, for instance, about 200 Plebiscite Front activists were arrested. The process of integration continued. Another symbol of difference, the title of Sadar-i-Riyasat for the equivalent of the Governor, went, and Kashmir came on par with the rest of the country after 10 April 1965. By this date Abdullah had set off an uproar in India by hobnobbing with the two principal foes of the country.

It was Zulfiqar Ali Bhutto who broke the news at a banquet for his visiting Chinese counterpart in Karachi: there would be a meeting between Sheikh Abdullah and the Chinese Premier Zhou En-lai, and China would invite Abdullah for a visit—almost as if Abdullah were head of a government in exile. The two met on 31 March at Algiers at a get-together obviously designed for the purpose. China publicly supported "self-determination" for Kashmir and Abdullah welcomed this support. Shastri spoke of taking "drastic steps" in Parliament; Abdullah's passport was cancelled, and when he reached Indian soil on 8 May he was promptly arrested at the airport. It would mean another thirty months of prison, but it was at least a gilded cage. Abdullah was taken to a guest-house in the southern hill resort of Ooty, and then to Kodaikanal. Pakistan protested, calling the arrest "reckless", and even lodged a complaint with the UN Security Council on 20 May. But that was only the official face of its response. Convinced that this time the people of Kashmir would cooperate rather than confront it, Pakistan speeded up the timetable for its second major military adventure in the Valley of Kashmir.

The collapse of the Holy Relic agitation had caused severe disappointment in Pakistan. Our source for such a statement is authoritative enough: General Mohammad Musa, Commander-in-Chief of the Pakistan Army in 1965 writes, in *My Version* (ABC, New Delhi, 1983):

> . . . the unrest among the people of the occupied valley, caused by the theft of the Holy Relic in Hazratbal in 1963, too, petered out, in sheer frustration the (Pakistan) Government asked the Intelligence Bureau to keep the flickering flame alive by throwing occasional crackers in occupied Kashmir.

He added in the following paragraph that the arrest of the Sheikh provided the spur which finally set a pre-planned war effort going.

A strong lobby headed by the young Foreign Minister Zulfiqar Ali Bhutto, and including Foreign Secretary Aziz Ahmed and Major-General Akhtar Husain Malik, commander of the troops in Pak-held Kashmir, were exerting strong pressure on Ayub to strike as early as possible. Indians had seen Bhutto's talons during the long-drawn-out peace talks of 1963 (the talks failed; so what else was new?); the hawk had now become convinced that he could take on his prey. In early 1964, a secret Kashmir cell was set up by Pakistan with the Foreign Secretary as chairman; no record was kept of its proceedings. By December 1964 Ayub Khan had given approval to the Army to organize guerrilla raids. Bhutto sent in his assessment to Ayub on 12 March 1965: "India is not at present in a position to risk a general war of unlimited duration for the annihilation of Pakistan". The Pakistan Army brass was not so sanguine. However, after Abdullah's arrest the raids began in earnest, while the Pak GHQ were told to prepare two battleplans: one, for all-out warfare; the second, for low-key operations. The second was abandoned in the optimism generated by Pakistan's extraordinary success in the dummy-run war which took place in the summer of 1965.

The fighting began in the early hours of 9 April 1965 at the opposite end of the India-Pakistan border from Kashmir—the southern tip of Gujarat, the Rann of Kutch. Pakistan attacked and soon had the territorial advantage which it held through a prolonged and desultory confrontation, until an agreement brokered by British Prime Minister Harold Wilson ended the fighting on 30 June. Ayub Khan was content. He felt confident now about the success of his two-pronged strategy for Kashmir: the Gibraltar punch backed up by the Grand Slam knockout. In the first, trained raiders would immobilize and weaken the Indian Army in Kashmir; in the second, the regular Army would decapitate the Valley from the rest of India. Now he only had to wait for operations weather.

The 7,000-strong Gibraltar Force began to slip into Kashmir in twos and threes from 7 August 1965. Their objectives: sabotage, disruption, distribution of arms and initiation of a guerrilla uprising. These were trained men, organized groups with regular command levels, equipped for mobility, speed and communication. On paper, they could not fail. In practice, Gibraltar fell on its face. The Kashmiris who were supposed to rise as one against India, rose instead against the raiders—precisely as they had done in 1947: truth to tell, probably to the equal surprise of both Rawalpindi and Delhi. Kashmiriyat was clearly still alive and well. Gibraltar was reinforced by a second wave of infiltrators along the 470-mile Ceasefire Line, but with the people indifferent or hostile the hunters became the hunted. The Indian Army now moved to block the passes through which the raiders had come. On 24 August 1965 they crossed the Ceasefire Line at Tithwal and occupied Pir Sahiba at 9,000 feet. On 26 August, a force under Major Ranjit Singh Dayal, displaying extraordinary heroism, moved towards the vital Haji Pir Pass and took it by the 28th. By 10 September Indian forces held a line from Uri to Poonch.

But if Gibraltar had met with surprising failure then Grand Slam sped along with surprising success. On 1 September, Pakistan expanded the war. Moving in from Bhimbar, the forces commanded by Major-General Akhtar Husain Malik (who had also drafted Gibraltar) raced up to the shallow Munawwar Tawi river, and reached Chhamb. The bridge over the Chenab lay in front of 7 Division, and Akhnur was there for the taking. Jammu was at Pakistan's mercy; and the road links to the Valley through Pathankot could have been in Pakistani hands, trapping the Indian Army in Kashmir. The psychological effect itself would have been devastating. At this point, someone's prayers worked. An inexplicable change of command took place; Malik was sent to Kargil, replaced at the head of 7 Division by Major-General Agha Mohammad Yahya Khan (a man, incidentally, destined to defeat his own side again a few years later). There was delay, confusion at the top, and sheer mismanagement of signals. Witness Musa's memoirs:

> General Malik was not in his own headquarters when I visited the battlefield on 2 September. . . Our forward troops had moved on after capturing Chhamb but stopped west of the Tawi and were awaiting receipt of the code-word for crossing the river. The divisional commander did not seem to be aware of this development.

Or again:

On my way to Chhamb, I went to see the staff officer. To my amazement, he couldn't brief me on the latest situation. He didn't know it himself, being out of touch with his divisional commander for several hours and was trying, in vain, to establish contact with him when I arrived there.

Indian troops fought back stubbornly, relieved at the respite. The Indian Air Force went into action from 1 September; the Gnat jet fighter was to make its reputation as a lethal little insect in this war. The stalled Pakistani offensive reached Jaurian only on 5 September; Akhnur was still totally vulnerable, but once again Yahya Khan came to India's rescue; despite specific orders to take Akhnur as quickly as he could, he delayed. He was not going to get another chance.

At 0330 hours on 6 September Indian troops crossed the international boundary from Sialkot to Kasur, and what was called the "All-Out War" began. Abruptly the nature of the war had changed. Lahore was under threat. There were some massive tank battles, but the eventual outcome was that each side managed to stop the other's advance. A ceasefire was the logical conclusion, particularly with ammunition running low in both armies. On 23 September 1965 a ceasefire under the aegis of the UN Security Council came into effect. For the record, India had about 740 square miles under occupation, against 210 square miles by Pakistan, but the strategic balance was even.

The Tashkent talks which gave the two neighbours their territories back—and where Shastri tragically passed away just when he was coming into his own—are now a matter of detail. The two conclusions relevant to history are: Pakistan's second war for Kashmir added not an inch to what it had seized till 1948; and the Kashmiris had proved that even if they had much reason to be unhappy with India they were in absolutely no mood to surrender their unique culture and identity to Pakistan. Kashmiriyat survived the war of 1965.

Field Marshal Ayub Khan wanted to go down in history as the man who broke India. Instead, his failure set off a sequence of events which ended in breaking up his own country. 1971 saw yet another partition on the subcontinent: the partition of Pakistan. A little after the 1965 war was over, Ayub Khan's regime began to come apart. Disillusioned and frustrated, the people took to the streets: corruption, prices, and army despotism became the issues that rallied people from Peshawar to Karachi. From Foreign Minister of Ayub Khan the sharp-nosed Bhutto quickly escaped to become the Messiah of democracy. A more genuine one appeared in the East: Sheikh Mujibur Rahman. The Army bought time, switching the dictatorial Ayub for the suicidal Yahya Khan. Yahya's only contribution to Pakistan was to hold the first honest election in its history; such was the impact of the truth that it split the country. A chauvinist West Pakistani establishment, whether composed of generals in uniform or Bhuttos in civvies, refused to hand over power to the legitimate victors of the general election simply because they were Bengalis, and therefore worthy only of contempt. Anger in East Pakistan became an uprising; and then a revolt; and then a war. An eager India interfered. An isolated Pakistan Army was besieged within and without in the East; and the war of 1971 saw a triumphant Indian Army march into Dhaka to liberate a people and usher in a new country.

That war of 1971 was the first in which India and Pakistan did not fight over Kashmir. Maybe that is why it created the conditions for almost two decades of peace in Kashmir. Perhaps history is nothing but Allah writing fiction, and watching that fiction become truth.

18

An Answer to Their Prayers

"I hear a voice from the darkness."

The sentence seems consciously crafted for a historic moment; however, Indira Gandhi uttered it spontaneously. But there was no doubt about the fact that it was an hour in which the history of the subcontinent was being refashioned, in the aftermath of the first decisive war between India and Pakistan. The armed forces of India had done their duty in the ricefields of Bengal in the winter of 1971; the politicians were now busy in the drawing rooms of Shimla in the summer of 1972.

A summit is an interesting bit of conspiratorial playacting. Bureaucrats spend months defining the outcome, and then leave enough disagreement for their heads of government to argue about when the Big Moment arrives. Since stagecraft and position-play are the very stuff of summitry, the stars also enjoy squeezing out every last opportunity for histrionics. A dip; a signal of collapse; a dramatic meeting; a rescue. . . The Shimla Summit had fallen into one such dip-depression by 29 June. At seven in the evening the Prime Minister of India and the President of Pakistan decided to take matters into their own hands: they met alone, without their delegations. When they emerged forty-five minutes later, the flashbulbs lit up the evening. It was a woman journalist who elicited the quoted response from Mrs Gandhi. She did not add anything more of political significance, for although she had prevented a collapse of the talks there was still some way to go before a structure of peace could be announced to the people of India and Pakistan. And it had not been easy to hear that voice in the darkness. For the man Mrs Gandhi was dealing with, had created an extraordinarily successful political career on a hate-India momentum. His name was Zulfiqar Ali Bhutto.

Bhutto was the ultimate protégé. In 1958, at the remarkably young age of thirty, he was picked up by the general who introduced martial law in his country, Ayub Khan, and made Minister for Commerce. But virtually from the beginning all his energies were directed towards becoming Foreign Minister; he saw India as his mission. His ambition was fulfilled when Mohammad Ali died in January 1963, and Ayub Khan gave Bhutto the vacant chair. It was not a little ironical that the first assignment that came to the man of war was a search for peace. Under pressure from the West, peace talks had opened between India and Pakistan in December 1962; they would go into six rounds before spluttering into failure in the early summer of 1963. Success would have been difficult in any case, but Bhutto ensured that the minutest chance of it was extinguished. Obviously the hitch was Kashmir. India wanted the Ceasefire Line to become the *de facto* border around which a settlement could be finalized. Bhutto in his counter-proposal placed virtually the whole of the Valley into Pakistan's control. When the Indian side pointed out that this was hardly reasonable, Bhutto chortled: "You are a defeated nation, don't you see?" Whatever the Chinese may have made of the consequences of the 1962 war, Bhutto had convinced himself that India was now ready to be taken apart. Such immaturity certainly did change the map of the subcontinent but not quite in the manner which Bhutto might have wished: instead of gaining Kashmir, Pakistan lost half of herself. When the sixth round of talks ended in failure in 1963, Bhutto said, with obvious satisfaction, that all peaceful processes had now ended. At his post-talks press conference, Pran Chopra recalled in a special article for *The Hindustan Standard*: "He showed—or put on, I do not know which—a hair-trigger temper, and a tongue dipped in poison". The peace option finally closed, Bhutto could now freely indulge his search for war.

He played a crucial role, of course, in ensuring it took place in 1965. And when it ended in ceasefire instead of triumph, no one was more bitter than him. Some of that rancid emotion found its way into his intemperate speech at the United Nations that September when he promised a thousand years of war with India and threatened to leave the UN if the world body did not do him the service of solving the Kashmir problem—by which he presumably meant handing the Valley over to him on a personalized platter. Peace with India was anathema to him, and he could never reconcile himself to the 1966 Tashkent talks. Ranajit Roy, who covered the event for *The Hindustan Standard*, reported:

> The Tashkent Declaration was signed in the conference hall of the Uzbek government by Mr Shastri and Field Marshal Ayub and witnessed by the host, Mr Kosygin. Mr Bhutto sat through the half-hour function glum-faced. His hostility to the Declaration was writ large on his face.

Ayub Khan finally sacked him in June 1966—and Bhutto made that into the launching pad for the second phase of his political career. (The first phase ended in dismissal; the second in the glory of the oath of office of President; the third with prison and the gallows.) Bhutto, of course, had never let modesty interfere with his ambition. In the foreword to his book *The Myth of Independence* (Oxford University Press, Karachi, 1967), Bhutto writes:

> I confess that this book has been written in haste, in circumstances over which I had no control, in a race against time which is dragging Pakistan, with giant strides, to the crossroads whence all ways but one lead to destruction.

In the moment of Pakistan's self-destruction lay Bhutto's triumph, and on 20 December 1971 he was sworn in as President of Pakistan by an unstable Yahya Khan. At least this time the rhetoric could be explained in terms of the need to preserve a brave face, but there was a familiar edge to his first broadcast when he said that India would face "an implacable enemy" in Pakistan and warned India's Defence Minister: "Mr Jagjivan Ram should know that this is not the end of the war. This is the beginning of the war, of a new state of affairs. He should not gloat over temporary military victories". Perhaps more important than the rhetoric was a significant decision taken by Bhutto: to bring Aziz Ahmed, his old colleague from the 1965 days, into the foreign ministry.

India's victory in the war of December 1971 was an embarrassment of riches. India not only created another country, but a whole army fell into its lap: something like 94,000 PoWs, one of the largest single takes in military history, thanks to the surrender of all the Pak forces in East Pakistan. The battle on the western front was largely a struggle to maintain the *status quo*. In any case, the Americans had drawn the line: Henry Kissinger had made it clear that while the US was no longer in a position to prevent the emergence of Bangladesh it would not allow the break-up of West Pakistan. But Pakistan *was* a shattered nation in December 1971: physically, emotionally, ideologically; its moral basis had crumbled and its confidence was brutally shaken. If ever India had control over the situation it was in 1972. Such opportunities do not recur; neither do they last too long; it was a different story, for instance, by 1973. But in 1972 the agenda was in the control of Indira Gandhi and her advisers—the closest of whom, incidentally, happened to be Kashmiri Pandits: P.N. Haksar, her brilliant Chief-of-Staff (his official bureaucratic nomenclature of Principal Secretary is inadequate), D.P. Dhar, now Chairman of the Policy Planning Committee but much else besides, P.N. Dhar, Secretary to the Prime Minister, and T.N. Kaul, Foreign Secretary.

Obviously Bhutto had to make the first move: a message came through a third party that the issue of prisoners of war should be discussed. Delhi sent back the cool reply that the PoWs were under the joint command of India and Bangladesh, and discussions would have to include the government in Dhaka. In other words, Pakistan would have to recognize the new country. But a slightly warmer signal was also sent to Bhutto by Haksar, who was to play an influential role in the peace process. If Pakistan was interested in discussing a range of substantive matters, then there could be some point in opening a dialogue. But Bhutto first had to accept that he would come to India for talks; there would be no Tashkent this time. Bilateralism was going to be the only basis of relations; it would be the pivotal element in any future deal.

On 14 February 1972, India wrote to the Secretary General of the United Nations offering to hold direct talks with Pakistan "at any time, at any level and without preconditions". On 4 April Mrs Gandhi went public with the information that she was in direct touch with Bhutto: a letter had been sent to the Pakistan President saying that emissaries should begin preliminary discussions. On 25 April D.P. Dhar left for Islamabad to discuss "all subjects under the sun". The talks began the next day at the pretty hill station of Murree: an appropriate enough place—stand amid the rising pines on the eastern slopes of Murree, look a little towards the north and you see the mountains of Kashmir ranged across the horizon. On 30 April, the two countries announced that Indira Gandhi and Zulfiqar Ali Bhutto would meet for a summit. On 10 May, Mrs Gandhi suggested specific dates in a letter; on 12 May they were finalized. Bhutto and his delegation would reach India on 28 June. The talks would be held in the summer capital of the British Raj, Shimla. On 8 April 1950, Liaqat Ali Khan and Jawaharlal Nehru had signed the first major agreement between the blood brothers on the rights of minorities. In 1953, Mohammad Ali, blinded by suspicion, failed to understand what Nehru was offering, and another opportunity on Kashmir was squandered. Nehru visited Pakistan between 19 and 23 September to sign the Indus Canal Waters Treaty—and the situation deteriorated so much after that that the next summit could only take place on soil foreign to both countries, Tashkent. Another chance for peace had come on 28 June 1972.

Bhutto gave a twenty-three-minute speech over Radio Pakistan on the eve of his departure to India. There were the traditional noises, of course, but some careful interjections too. He said:

We are prepared. . . to make a new beginning, if the Indians are prepared for it. . . The search for peace is long and arduous. We will have to move forward step by step with sincerity on both sides. We cannot with one stroke clear past suspicions.

But. One point was non-negotiable: "self-determination for Jammu and Kashmir".

The war had been over Bangladesh. The peace talks were over Kashmir. Bangladesh was now a settled fact. There was nothing, in truth, to negotiate: Pakistan was bound to recognize the country at some point, and normalize. Seventy-five nations already had embassies in Dhaka. The whole subcontinent was only waiting to see how India and Pakistan would deal with Kashmir.

"I will never let you down," Bhutto told his people on the airwaves. To his credit, he did not.

Indira Gandhi told India that she was not going to Shimla as a victor. Perhaps she should have.

The perfect hostess that she was, Mrs Gandhi reached Shimla by a Russian built M.I. helicopter a day before the summit was due to begin. That day the host in her took over from the leader. She went on a personal inspection tour of the accommodation being readied for the eighty-five-member Pakistani delegation. When she reached Barnes' Court, now renamed a boring Himachal Bhavan, and took a look at the suite for Bhutto and his young daughter, Benazir, on her first political journey outside Pakistan, Mrs Gandhi lost her temper. Aesthetics and government have never been too fond of each other, but this was blatant divorce. Horrified at the garish furnishing, Mrs Gandhi angrily ordered the Chief Minister of the state, the ageing Y.S. Parmar, to change it all, and at once. Knowing what government was all about, she returned in the evening to check. Her anger doubled. It had become worse. This time she gave precise instructions, about the cloth, colours, curtains, furniture, flowers. . . But the shops had shut. Shopkeepers were gently but firmly told to open their backdoors; six tailors were commandeered to serve through the night so that the Bhuttos' Oxford-Sind tastes might be protected from the excesses of Public Works Department decor.

Zulfiqar Ali Bhutto reached Shimla by helicopter at 10.25 the next morning, an hour behind schedule. The summit began on a note of tragedy, when D.P. Dhar had to be hospitalized with heart trouble. On a more tragicomic note, T.N. Kaul stomped off, possibly because of an imagined slight; he would return. But centrestage was firmly held by Haksar and Foreign Minister Swaran Singh; later Mrs Gandhi asked her senior Cabinet colleagues, like Jagjivan Ram, Y.B. Chavan and Fakhruddin Ali Ahmed, to come over. One very noticeable absentee from the Shimla scene was Dr Karan Singh. Logic suggested that the man who had been Governor of Jammu and Kashmir for eighteen years, who certainly represented the Jammu–Dogra interest, and who had been inducted into the Cabinet by Mrs Gandhi herself, should have been somewhere in that very large picture. But he was neither involved in the preliminary talks nor the summit; and since the Shimla Pact was never placed before the Indian Cabinet, he was not involved in any talks at all. Dr Karan Singh never hid his resentment, and still believes that it was the "gang" of Kashmiri Pandits who finessed him. Dogra suspicion of the Pandit runs deep. Hari Singh's advice to his son used to be to trust anyone before a Pandit. Dr Karan Singh did not quite believe he would ever have reason to recall such memories, but perhaps Karan Singh was kept out because belligerence was not on the agenda. A Dogra Yuvraj may not have been the best advertisement for peaceful intentions.

It was obvious that if there was failure at the talks it would be because of Kashmir. A participant who would not allow his name on the record recalled that the first day's talks were long and complex, with bureaucrats in charge. The second day was marginally better, but progress stumbled each time on the Great Claim. It was a matter, everyone realized, for the two leaders to decide; no one else had the authority to negotiate the line of limits. It was at this stage that the Bhutto who had promised a thousand years of war turned on his persuasive charms. He mixed emotion with extremely subtle deference, and switched his pitch from the give and take of politics to a higher morality. Only a person as strong and popular as Mrs Gandhi could take that generous extra step for peace; he could not return to Pakistan with the stigma of surrender, he would be destroyed politically. And so on and so forth. Bhutto told her that Pakistan was now convinced that it could never win a war with India, that Kashmir was lost. But he could not commit that on paper. "*Bharosa keejiye*", Bhutto pleaded; trust me. "He played this particular card beautifully", was the sentence used to describe Bhutto's virtuoso performance.

Mrs Indira Gandhi trusted him. On 3 July, after the two signatures had been affixed, an official spokesman of the Government of India answered doubts by saying:

Our impression of Mr Bhutto is that he is sincere, genuine

and anxious to improve the relations between the two countries. He has reciprocated Mrs Gandhi's desire for a durable peace and it will not be right to doubt his *bona fides*.

There was much simulated euphoria then, and an impression was sought to be created that the Kashmir issue had been solved. But within weeks the External Affairs Ministry realized—although it was not yet telling—that India had been sold a pup, and a nasty little mongrel at that.

Delhi went to Shimla seeking to pin Pakistan down to the position it had been hawking since the 1960s: that the dispute should be closed on the basis of the Ceasefire Line of 1 January 1948. Pakistan would neither concede a final settlement of the Kashmir problem nor agree to ending the UN role. India was determined that after Shimla, Kashmir would always be only a bilateral matter. But with nearly 94,000 PoWs in her camps, with 5,139 square miles of territory in Punjab, Kutch and Sind in her control; and with Pakistan on its knees, India let slip the opportunity to impose, if necessary, an unambiguous settlement of the Kashmir problem. On the other hand, Pakistan sought and received formal recognition for its positions on Kashmir in the Shimla Agreement. And that, as far as India was concerned, defeated the whole purpose of the pact.

However, in the beginning, India announced a great diplomatic victory thanks to two paragraphs. The first was Point Two of Clause 1:

> That the two countries are resolved to settle their differences by peaceful means through bilateral negotiations or by any other peaceful means mutually agreed upon between them. Pending the final settlement of any of the problems between the two countries, neither side shall unilaterally alter the situation and both shall prevent the organization, assistance or encouragement of any acts detrimental to the maintenance of peaceful and harmonious relations.

The second paragraph of Indian pleasure said:

> In Jammu and Kashmir, the line of control resulting from the ceasefire of December 17, 1971 shall be respected by both sides without prejudice to the recognised position of either side. Neither side shall seek to alter it unilaterally, irrespective of mutual differences and legal interpretations. Both sides further undertake to refrain from the threat or the use of force in violation of this line.

For some time Indian diplomats went around congratulating themselves on how they had changed the Ceasefire Line (CFL) into Line of Control (LOC) till it became a bit of a joke. Pakistan played along, looking suitably dejected until it had managed to re-arm itself and reorganize its forces. Then Pakistan began to draw attention to the sentences which Bhutto had absolutely insisted on retaining as the price of an agreement. It pointed out, for instance, to the opening commitment in the pact:

> That the principles and purposes of the Charter of the United Nations shall govern the relations between the two countries.

So where was the question of the issue being withdrawn from the United Nations agenda, asked Pakistan? A paper in circulation, and easily available from any embassy of Pakistan (particularly the one in Delhi) gleefully hammers home this point. And as for the Shimla Pact ending the Kashmir dispute for all practical purposes, Pakistan's answer once again lies in the text of the agreement, in fact in the very last paragraph, just above the signatures of Indira Gandhi and Zulfiqar Ali Bhutto:

> . . . the representatives of the two sides will meet to discuss further the modalities and arrangements for the establishment of durable peace and normalization of relations. . .(including) a final settlement of Jammu and Kashmir.

And so these days Pakistan accuses India of obstruction in solving the Kashmir problem! Witness this paragraph in the Government of Pakistan document published in 1990:

> The Simla Agreement placed an obligation on both Pakistan and India to hold negotiations for "a final settlement of Jammu and Kashmir". Pakistan has on several occasions expressed its readiness to have a dialogue on this issue. However, for the past 18 years India has refused to enter into any negotiations taking the plea that the Kashmir issue was already settled. Furthermore, India violated the Simla Agreement when in contravention of the stipulation in Article 1 (ii) viz. that "pending the final settlement of any of the problems between the two countries, neither side shall unilaterally alter the situation", it forcibly occupied positions in the Siachen. India continues to hold these positions to this day.

So much for the Shimla Agreement. Just to rub it in, Pakistan also points out that India has agreed to discussions "through bilateral negotiations or by any other peaceful means mutually agreed upon between them", to quote the terms of the clause Delhi used to flaunt as a great diplomatic victory. Now a look at the Pakistan Government's booklet:

> However, should bilateral negotiations fail to resolve the problem, the Simla Agreement does not make extinct Pakistan's right to take recourse to other methods of peaceful settlement of disputes.

The glaring fact of Shimla 1972 was that Pakistan had outmanoeuvred India from a hopeless position. The only justification that old Shimla hands can provide is that Bhutto could not have survived any other kind of agreement, but while such generosity may take you a little closer to a Nobel Peace Prize, it is not necessarily healthy for a nation-state. This is not to question the motives of those who inspired the Indian position. They were liberals in the finest tradition of that spirit. It often takes more courage to negotiate a peace than to unleash armies. A man like P.N.Haksar believed in the risk of trust; he had the strength to seek the high position, and ability to encourage the adversary to look up at hope rather than stare at the mire of wars. It may not be his fault that the hope was betrayed, but the cold truth is that it was trampled, and crudely, the moment Pakistan felt strong enough to do so. Pakistan has now gone so far as to say that it does not consider the Shimla Agreement to be a check on its right to promote secession in Kashmir.

However, there was at least one significant immediate positive gain from the signals that flew out of Shimla, and then Delhi and Islamabad while the ink of the agreement was still wet. From the very outset, Mrs Gandhi was clear that with the 1971 war behind her she could finally fashion a settlement with Sheikh Abdullah. After Shimla Zulfiqar Ali Bhutto helped her to do so. For Mrs Gandhi, and P.N. Haksar, 1972 was a year in which nothing seemed impossible.

*

Mrs Gandhi became Prime Minister in January 1966. By July 1967 she had shifted Abdullah to a bungalow in Delhi in Kotla Lane. Irritation and anger against what seemed the interminable detention of Abdullah was growing in the country, and one person who articulated these feelings was another doyen of the freedom movement, a man once considered by

Jawaharlal as a potential successor: Jaya Prakash Narayan. On 23 June 1966, Narayan sent a long, "strictly confidential" letter to Indira Gandhi (first published in Bhola Chatterjee's *Conflict In JP's Politics*, Ankur, Delhi). A few extracts provide the core and trend of his argument:

> We profess democracy, but rule by force in Kashmir—unless we have auto-suggested ourselves into believing that the two general elections under Bakshi Sahib had expressed the will of the people, or that the Sadiq government is based on popular support except for a small minority of pro-Pakistan traitors. We profess secularism, but let Hindu nationalism stampede us into trying to establish it by repression. Kashmir has distorted India's image for the world as nothing has done. There is no nation in the world, not even Russia, which appreciates our Kashmir policy, though some of them might, for their own reasons, give us their support. . . that problem exists not because Pakistan wants to grab Kashmir, but because there is deep and widespread political discontent among the people. . . Whatever be the solution, it has to be found within the limitations of accession. It is here that Sheikh's role may become decisive. . . Why do I plead for Sheikh's release? Because that may give us the only chance we have of solving the Kashmir problem. . .

Whether, as Prime Minister, she considered it wise to say as much or not, this was precisely Mrs Gandhi's own thinking. Abdullah too, used this chance to convey distinct signs of change. He explained away his meeting with Zhou En-lai in Algiers, for instance, as an opportunity to question the Chinese leader about the Sino-Pak border agreement by which 2,000 square miles of Kashmir territory in Pakistan's control had been gifted to China. This was hardly the full truth, but that was not important; Abdullah's conciliatory tone was what Delhi wanted to hear. Abdullah added that he had briefed the Indian ambassador in Algiers fully about this conversation. Along with Narayan, Abdullah also began to take a very welcome interest in national issues, particularly communalism. In an effort to revive the spirit of Gandhi, the two launched the Khudai Khidmatgars, using the name of the great movement created by the Frontier Gandhi, Badshah Khan, in the 1920s and 1930s. Such good intentions petered out because India simply did not want to be reminded of Gandhi just then. In October 1968, Narayan and Abdullah sought to give a fresh thrust to the Kashmir problem with a six-day All-Kashmir States' Peoples' convention; its burden was greater autonomy for all states. In these moves one can discern both Narayan and Abdullah edging back towards the political mainstream from their respective isolations. (In an interesting coincidence both would peak in 1975—though from completely different directions.)

Pakistan went into a spin by the end of the '60s. As we've seen Ayub Khan was virtually toppled by a mass uprising; the Army generals who replaced him thought elections would both release the pressure on them and allow them to manipulate a hung Parliament. Instead Sheikh Mujibur Rahman won a majority in his own right. The Army, in collusion with Bhutto, could not countenance this, and war became inevitable.

Mrs Indira Gandhi prepared for this war not merely at the military level, but even more seriously at the political level. Her intense international campaign on the plight of refugees who had been forced across from East Pakistan by Army repression, created tremendous sympathy all over the world for the idea of an independent Bangladesh. Her diplomats lobbied hard with any government that could be weaned away from the hard pro-Pakistan line of Washington, while the Indo-Soviet treaty secured India's base as she got ready to solve the East Pakistan problem on the battlefield. These were all moves in the open. There were also quieter efforts, as Mrs Gandhi worked brilliantly and imaginatively to protect the Indian cause on every front. It was obvious that any war with Pakistan was not going to be restricted to just the East; there would be war across the Punjab border and the Ceasefire Line in Kashmir too. She wanted to be certain that Pakistan would not get any clandestine help in the event of war. And so, through D.P. Dhar, she opened the door of a possible settlement by encouraging secret talks with Abdullah and Mirza Afzal Beg, both of whom were staying at 3 Kotla Lane in New Delhi. Dhar, in turn, used his confidants. M.L. Fotedar told the author that he had five meetings with Afzal Beg, the last one being in the last week of November, barely seven days before war broke out. Fully aware that the rooms were bugged, Beg took Fotedar for a walk on the lawns. The message he sent was that while he himself was now convinced that Kashmir's accession to India was beyond change, and he was ready to accept this publicly, Abdullah wanted to see how the impending war turned out. The war, of course, turned out to be a dream triumph for the Indian forces, from their tactical planning to their fighting quality. "Everything in war is quite simple", said Carl Clausewitz, "but even the simplest things are very difficult". Sam Manekshaw, Jagjit Singh Aurora and J.F.R. Jacob—to name only three of the many officers who deserve praise—proved that with planning and courage difficulties could be reduced to negligible proportions. By 18 December India had liberated Dhaka, and a new nation was born on the subcontinent—to the applause of much of the world. Indira Gandhi had proved Clausewitz right in at least this much: that war was an extension of politics. The politics of Kashmir became an extension of the 1971 war. In February Beg told the press that Abdullah and he were ready for a dialogue. The two had been banned from entering Kashmir since 9 January 1971; the restriction was lifted on 5 June 1972. In another twenty-three days, the post-war President of Pakistan would set foot on Indian soil to see whether Kashmir could be settled in peace after the fate of East Pakistan had been sealed in war.

Abdullah's reaction to the Shimla Pact was a guarded welcome. Obviously, he first picked out what was most favourable to him, noting that the text confirmed that the "future of Jammu and Kashmir still remains to be decided". But, as he told a public meeting at Sopore just after the pact, the

> final arbiters of the destiny of the State are its people, and not India or Pakistan. We will not permit outsiders to divide our home. We are its rightful owners.

Yes, but the lease was with Delhi, by Abdullah's own consent, and part of the home had been forcibly occupied by Pakistan. What could Abdullah do about that? Peaceful negotiations, he suggested at Sopore, in the Shimla spirit. But the real value of Shimla lay not so much in its effect on Mrs Gandhi's dialogue with Abdullah, but in its effect on Bhutto's attitude towards Kashmir till around 1975. At Hazratbal on 23 June 1972, Abdullah formally announced that he had given "full authority" to Mirza Afzal Beg to discuss with Delhi any "greater autonomy formula for Kashmir". It was, in fact, not so much Shimla as the defeat of Pakistan in 1971 which convinced Abdullah that there was no longer much joy to be had from across the border. Naturally he was castigated in Pakistan-Occupied Kashmir for his "surrender" to India, but that was really tokenism for the record. The first move for reconciliation had been made by the government while Abdullah was still in detention, and he had responded. His release and the nomination of Beg for talks were part of the process. The person Mrs Gandhi chose as her negotiator was the lean, soft spoken man of few words, G. Parthasarathi.

His task was not easy. A new goodwill might exist, but often goodwill is not good enough. Mrs Gandhi had to legitimize in the eyes of the people a settlement with a man who had been jailed for attempting secession by every Prime Minister of India, from his friend Jawaharlal in 1953 to his friend's protégé Shastri in 1965 to his friend's daughter Indira. On his side, Abdullah had to carry the people of Kashmir, who lionized him precisely because the word surrender was not available in his dictionary. It was as part of the effort to persuade the people that peace was now the only option left that Farooq Abdullah, living then in London, visited the Kashmir occupied by Pakistan in 1974.

His hosts were the Plebiscite Front, the occasion was a convention at Mirpur, a small town in the Jammu region near the Line of Control. He stayed there for two weeks, visiting the Poonch area, Muzaffarabad, Kotli, and a number of other places. At the convention, where his status was that of an observer, the view he heard repeatedly was that Kashmir would vote for independence in a plebiscite and not for Pakistan—and they wanted this conveyed to Indira Gandhi and Abdullah, who were then in the thick of negotiations. Among those seated on the dais at Mirpur were Hashim Qureshi, Maqbool Butt and Amanullah Khan—unknown then, but to become infamous in India after their Jammu and Kashmir Liberation Front (JKLF) became famous. Farooq, of course, did not have the remotest idea then that one day a decade later this would be flaunted as an anti-Indian sin; at that point, whatever he was doing had in fact the implicit support of Delhi, because his next stop would be Delhi, to meet no less a person than Mrs Gandhi herself.The most significant meeting during that tour however was with Bhutto. In an interview to the author, Farooq revealed:

> When I went to Rawalpindi in 1974 from England the entire bureaucracy of Pakistan and Bhutto's secretary himself told me that a final solution has been arrived at; there can be nothing more. What we (the Pakistanis) have got (in Kashmir) we are keeping, what they have got they are keeping, and that is how it is.

Bhutto confirmed this. Farooq flew to Delhi, where he briefed Mrs Gandhi in the presence of P.N. Dhar—by now her Principal Secretary. He then left for Srinagar to meet his father.

Two people who played a key role in the eventual settlement were D.P. Dhar and P.N. Haksar. In a note dated 28 December 1973, Dhar told the Prime Minister that Abdullah was likely to propose an election in March 1975 as the mechanism for becoming Chief Minister. But the route became simpler thanks to the sagacity of the man who had taken over after Sadiq's sad death in the midst of the 1971 war, Syed Mir Qasim.

Qasim offered to step down, and lend the support of Congress legislators to an Abdullah government in Srinagar. For Abdullah the plebiscite phase was finally over; he accepted the ratification of the accession by the Jammu and Kashmir Assembly under Bakshi. In the talks with Delhi, the focus shifted now to the legal and Constitutional changes made after 1953. Beg began by asking for the transfer of the Fundamental Rights provisions of the Constitution of India to the Jammu and Kashmir Constitution, removal of the authority of the Election Commission, and modification of Article 356 to prevent arbitrary imposition of President's Rule. As Mrs Gandhi told Parliament on 24 February 1975: "It was not found possible to agree to any of these proposals". But she added:"I must say to the credit of Sheikh Abdullah that despite his strong views on these issues, he had accepted the Agreed Conclusions".

These Conclusions, signed by Beg and Parthasarathi, left only one area in dispute. Five points of agreement were:

- Article 370 would continue;

- Residuary powers would remain with the Jammu and Kashmir Assembly; Delhi would retain control of any legislation dealing with the sovereignty of India;

- Kashmir could alter or modify any future provision, but only with the consent of the President of India;

- The State could review legislation after 1953 on the concurrent List, and President's assent "would be sympathetically considered":

- Article 356 and the power of the Election Commission would remain as they were;

- "No agreement was possible" on the question of the nomenclature of the Governor and Chief Minister; Abdullah wanted a return to Sadar-i-Riyasat and Wazir-i-Azam.

Eventually, the clock remained stuck in the pre-Abdullah accord era even on this last point. When Mrs Indira Gandhi announced this agreement in the Lok Sabha at four in the afternoon of 24 February 1975, there was an immediate roar of protest from the Opposition—predictably led by the Jana Sangh member from Gwalior, Atal Behari Vajpayee, but also backed by the socialist MP from Uttar Pradesh, Janeshwar Mishra. The Jana

Sangh target was Article 370, and Mrs Gandhi made a brilliant impromptu defence of this controversial provision:

> So far as Article 370 is concerned, you know that Jammu and Kashmir is the only State which had constituted a separate Constituent Assembly for the State to determine its Constitution and the sphere of Union jurisdiction over the State. It was left to that Assembly to decide whether Article 370 should remain or be modified or abrogated. That is reflected in Clause (3) of that Article. That is why Article 370 was called temporary, as the Constituent Assembly for that State had not given its decision by 1950. That Assembly completed its work in 1956, but it did not suggest the deletion or modification of Article 370, which, therefore, became a permanent part of our Constitution since 1956.

Mrs Indira Gandhi was at her best that day, and during the full debate on Kashmir which took place a week later. Her opening remarks on 24 February established her approach:

> In pursuance of government's policy to secure the active cooperation and involvement of all democratic, secular and progressive forces in the country it was considered desirable to have a dialogue with Sheikh Mohammad Abdullah.

It was this cardinal recognition, that Abdullah was still a champion of the secular and progressive forces, that he was still an asset to India's present and future, that underlay what, in the view of this writer, was Indira Gandhi's finest achievement. She did not put the clock back. But she picked it up and wound it again; and it was because of her that Kashmir saw a wonderful decade of freedom and peace. There was great joy in the nation at the news. When she opened the debate a week later, she began:

> My task has been made easier because of the warm and widespread welcome. . . And, with the exception of groups which have had a closed mind on Kashmir (or which do not like the government to do anything right) the reaction has been one of relief and rejoicing. Why have the people welcomed this accord? Because they feel that a controversy, which had been with them for two decades and which had caused so much misunderstanding and

defied solution, has now ended through an act of reconciliation. Any act of vision and statesmanship appeals to
the people, especially the people of India. It is particularly
praiseworthy that Sheikh Abdullah, overcoming whatever
bitterness he might have had, should have clasped the hand
of friendship extended to him. He has done this in the
larger interest of Kashmir and of the country as a whole
and of the cause which is dear to him, namely the
strengthening of democracy and secularism.

Indira Gandhi's life was full of speeches. But there were few which
captured the flavour, philosophy, generosity and sheer delight of a
democratic and secular India like this one in the Lok Sabha. She taunted
Bhutto, who was now feeling confident enough to challenge India again
and had ordered a *hartal* in his Kashmir in protest against the accord; and
she ridiculed the Jana Sangh, clubbing minority and majority fundamentalism in the best traditions of her father. Nehru would have been very
proud of Indira that day. She ended with a perceptive remark:

> . . .it is not so much the legal niceties involved in the accord
> which matter as much as the substance of the achievement
> which Sheikh Abdullah has described as the re-estab-
> lishment of trust and confidence. We believe we have
> established a solid foundation for mutual cooperation.

This mutual cooperation was in fact meant to be far less distant than
eventually transpired. This is yet another of those ifs which could have
given the history of Kashmir a totally new direction. For Sheikh Abdullah
had agreed to head a Conference–Congress coalition government in
March 1975. If that had happened then, the future would have taken a
totally different turn, and obviously one for the better. The reason why it
did not happen is so petty that it can only be totally true. Congress leaders,
including Mir Qasim and Mufti Mohammad Sayeed, actually sabotaged
the idea because of their personal rivalries. When Mir Qasim realized that
a relative whom he was promoting was not going to be given a berth in
the Abdullah coalition ministry, he encouraged the National Conference
to keep power for itself rather than share it with the Congress; when Mufti
learnt he was not going to be made minister, he too cooled to the idea.
Beg, who in any case was unhappy about the fact that Sheikh Abdullah
had agreed to a coalition, pounced on this opportunity to sink the suggestion. It never rose again in the lifetime of the one man who could have

convinced the people of Kashmir that a Conference–Congress alliance was in their interest. Indira Gandhi never forgave Mir Qasim for this.

Alas. History was being kind in March only to be cruel a little later. Too much was happening outside Kashmir in 1974 and 1975; the nation was in great turmoil over corruption, in despair over a failing economy, in disgust at political chicanery. A court judgement against Indira Gandhi in June 1975 invited a response which was deeply resented: the Emergency. A steep decline began as ideology and institutions were manipulated to preserve power. And when Mrs Gandhi finally went to the people in 1977, the north of India ensured the first Congress defeat in a general election. But opportunism was not a disease restricted to the Congress; the anti-Congress coalition which formed a government under Indira Gandhi's *bete noire* Morarji Desai began to preen and collapse in alternate phases. India suffered, and Kashmir paid her part of the price. And to think that the new beginning had been so rapturous. . . In the summer of 1975, Sheikh Abdullah recreated that wonderful mood of the past, of 1940 and 1950, when he organized for Indira Gandhi the traditional welcome for a beloved leader from Delhi—from the time of the Emperor Akbar downwards, a procession of boats down the Jhelum. It was truly a new beginning.

Sheikh Abdullah went by road from Jammu to Srinagar in March to take over as Chief Minister. Farooq Abdullah, who came down from London for a fortnight and accompanied his father, recalls:

> There were scenes of tremendous jubilation all through Jammu. Then when he entered the Valley through the tunnel, there were crowds all along the road up to Srinagar. It was the first week of March and bitterly cold. He gave a hard-hitting speech at Lal Chowk that day; he said Pakistan must not interfere in our affairs. He added, "No one should feel either victorious or defeated. There is a difficult task ahead and this can only be achieved by mutual trust. If that trust does not exist, this task cannot be completed."

That trust, unfortunately, came under strain all too soon. Not because of Mrs Gandhi, and not because of Mir Qasim, but because of a plethora of Congress underlings, who could not bear the thought of surrendering the lucrative privileges of power. They kept on provoking Mrs Gandhi to change her mind about Abdullah, but she kept them at bay. These Congressmen kept their spirits alive with just one macabre hope: that Abdullah, already ill, would not survive too long. Abdullah disappointed them. And before anything could happen to him, Mrs Gandhi lost the general elections in March 1977.

Now another invidious game began. Local Congressmen began hawking the idea that the resurrection of the party in the north could begin from its base in Kashmir where the party had a majority in the Assembly already; it could withdraw support from Abdullah, form a government of its own, and relaunch Mrs Gandhi by getting her elected from a Lok Sabha seat in the state. Sheikh Abdullah was quite willing to cooperate with the last part; he offered to vacate the Srinagar seat won by Begum Abdullah in the 1977 elections for Mrs Gandhi, despite strong opposition to the idea from his son-in-law, Ghulam Mohammad Shah, who was a force in the National Conference. It was an offer which would have had extremely beneficial consequences for the future, but Mrs Gandhi, uncharacteristically uncertain, depressed by defeat and a gathering revolt in the Congress sponsored by the very people who had been sycophants a few months before, preferred bad advice from her minions, and did not stop what might be called the Phoenix Plan put into operation by the Congress chief in the state, Mufti Mohammad Sayeed. There was enough ash around, but that Phoenix was not destined to rise. Its wings were smartly clipped by a neat counter-manoeuvre. The moment Congress withdrew support, Abdullah recommended dissolution of the House and fresh elections. L.K. Jha was governor then, Morarji Desai Prime Minister, and Jaya Prakash Narayan the father figure of the Janata government. No one was in a mood to make Mufti Chief Minister by these furtive methods. Mufti's ambitions were rudely punctured by the announcement of fresh elections. Of course he knew as well as anyone else that the Congress did not have the slightest hope of victory. Mufti Mohammad Sayeed would turn out to be a man with a very long memory, and a very keen sense of revenge.

But at least the Congress had some basis for hope, however thin it might be. What was quite astonishing about the 1977 elections was the manner in which the fledgling Janata Party began to prance and generally behave as if its fortuitous presence in power in Delhi was enough to make it a legitimate contender for power in Srinagar. Instead of coming to terms with Abdullah—a reasonable proposition after the Congress withdrawal of support—it set up a slate of candidates and mounted an electorally immature, potentially dangerous and personally virulent campaign. It was not merely the old Jana Sangh element which went around "promising" abrogation of Article 370; no less a person than Charan Singh, Home Minister of the Union of India, announced that his government would withdraw Article 370. There was boorishness too. Three days before voting, the long-expected illness struck; Abdullah had a heart attack. Instead of offering any sympathy, Jagjivan Ram, Defence Minister in Delhi, said that those who had suffered a heart attack should now rest. To rebut this was easy; Ram's own heart was less than foolproof. But this concerted political assault on Abdullah from all sides gave him the opportunity to pinpoint to his people what the election was all about. From his sickbed he recorded a speech on a cassette, and that speech unleashed a storm of emotion in Kashmir, the like of which had not been seen. He told Kashmiris that this election had become a referendum on their self-respect; they had the opportunity to show the world that they were masters of their own destiny, and that no one from Delhi could dictate their future.

Sheikh Abdullah symbolized Kashmiriyat: a spirit of independence and secularism joined by free will to a larger comity. He rejected slavery, either through force or favour. He challenged the least sign of hegemony, and he even spurned the largess of subsidized food for the Valley as the gold by which the soul of Kashmir was being purchased by Delhi. The people rallied around him with tears in their eyes. The National Conference won an overwhelming victory. The Congress became a rump force; the Janata Party disappeared into a corner. Extremist parties like the Jamaat-e-Islami, which openly advocated allegiance to Pakistan, were virtually wiped out, their five seats of 1972 being whittled down to a measly one. And not even the vanquished could pretend that there was anything unfair in the 1977 elections: in fact, those summer polls have often been called the only truly fair elections for the Kashmir Assembly.

If Kashmir in 1977 suddenly seemed safe, Indian democracy triumphant, and Indian nationalism vindicated, then the credit must be given to two persons: Indira Gandhi and Sheikh Abdullah. Together in 1975 they charted a course which could have, should have, made what Abdullah and Nehru had once dreamt of: Kashmir as the stabilizing force of secular India. The very magnitude of this triumph makes the descent to 1984 a deeply saddening story. And after their heirs, Rajiv Gandhi and Farooq Abdullah, went out of office in 1990, the descent degenerated into a gory, bloodstained collapse.

Both the Congress and the Janata seemed to realize their mistake after the 1977 elections. Morarji Desai reined in his hawks; and the Congress' scope for mischief of course had been reduced. But habits die hard, particularly in parties which become addicted to power. When Mrs Gandhi swept back as Prime Minister in 1980, the anti-Abdullah coterie took sustenance from the patronage of the new *enfant terrible*, her younger son Sanjay Gandhi. This lobby was reinforced by the arrival on the political scene of a Sanjay cousin, the sharp-eyed, quick-witted, arrogant and over-certain Arun Nehru. However, Mrs Gandhi, wiser, with more understanding of the complexities, checked this unnecessary drive to plant the Congress flag on every state capital, democratically where possible, and forcibly where required.

But time was catching up with a large heart; the man who towered above two generations in five decades of battle was finally surrendering to the one enemy which must always win. In June 1982, Abdullah refused to listen to the advice of his doctors and insisted on going through with an official visit to the very underdeveloped region of Doda, where a Cabinet meeting had been convened to sanction funding for the region. The helicopter ride itself led to a relapse of his heart condition. Very calmly, on his return to Srinagar, he told his family and his party to prepare for his death. As word spread, the *mazars* and mosques filled with Kashmiris come to pray for the life of their *Sher* who had lifted his people from cowering subjugation to the centre of the world's attention. *Bakras* were slaughtered in their thousands in sacrifice, promises made to Allah in a trade for time. In August, the cardiac problem became worse; the heart was no longer compensating; he was getting short of breath all the time. But his spirits remained cheerful: when life had not defeated him, death was hardly likely to. L.K. Jha met him just before the end. He recalls in the Commemoration volume published by Kashmir University:

> The last time I saw him alive was only a few days before his death. He knew and so did we all that his end was near. But there was no trace of self-pity in his conversation. He spoke with affection of our happy association and one could only sense the feeling of contentment in him which only comes to those who have spent their lives well, with a sense of devotion to God and His children on earth.

On 8 September, Farooq Abdullah went to Khanyar, to the shrine of Pir Dastgir Sahib to pray. While there, he received a message: father is unwell. The son knew that the worst had occurred. He rushed back. Sheikh Mohammad Abdullah had passed away as dusk began to mask his beloved Valley. There were two political decisions he took in his last days, one practical, one symbolic. He inducted his son Farooq Abdullah into his Cabinet as Health Minister. He was, of course, signalling the succession. There was naturally no question of anyone daring to challenge the Sheikh on his deathbed, but one breast burned in fierce envy—that of G.M. Shah, his son-in-law, husband of his daughter Khalida and a man who considered himself the real heir of the clan. The second was a gesture: his last important public function, just three weeks before he left the world. The doctors, as usual, forbade him, but Abdullah was now beyond caring too much for medicine men. For it was 15 August, the day thirty-five years ago his friend Jawaharlal looked up and saw the tricolour flutter against a rainbow across the evening sky. This man who had witnessed so many seasons change wanted to salute the flag of India for the last time in his life. He had been born an Indian and he would die an Indian.

*

Mrs Indira Gandhi was informed immediately about the Sheikh's death; she was very clear that there must be no sense of vacuum, and Farooq Abdullah should take over even before the people of Kashmir were told the news. That nipped any possible last-minute resistance from Shah. It was, in fact, Shah himself who proposed Farooq's name at the emergency Cabinet meeting. D.D. Thakur seconded the proposal. These names shall return to our story, dipped in acid.

Farooq Abdullah became Chief Minister of Jammu and Kashmir at ten at night. He went immediately on radio and television. The next afternoon, Sheikh Abdullah's body was taken to the Polo Gardens for the people pouring in from the villages to take a last look. *Hum pe Karbala guzar gaya hai. . . Aase gao Karbala*, they cried. There is no greater sorrow in Islam than the martyrdom at Karbala. And once again there was apprehension in the sorrow. Lions are not readily replaced; cubs need experience. Farooq had the love of the people, but only time could create trust.

To assess the life of Sheikh Mohammad Abdullah is to tread softly through a minefield of regrets. One is numbed by the sheer waste that ate up the two decades between 1953 and 1975. Sheikh Abdullah could have been Chief Minister of Jammu and Kashmir without a pause from 1947 to 1982. What a role he could have played at the crisis points along the way—1962, 1964, 1965, 1969, 1971, 1975, 1977, 1980. He would have been a symbol of continuity with 1947 as the generations turned; and India would have benefited. His own excesses, as much as Delhi's inhibitions, destroyed that possibility. What he meant for his own people cannot be easily encompassed by words. He was one of those men who add up to much more than the sum total of their actions; there is that magic of heroism which Thomas Carlyle saw in men who had dipped into some secret well of truth; men who of course make mistakes but do not lie to their souls. They embody the chemistry of aspiration; they symbolize the collective will of the people. Abdullah was both the Gandhi and the Nehru of Kashmir, the ideologue as well as the practitioner. And perhaps that is where the problem lay, for events often placed these two selves in conflict. Should a Gandhi ever exercise power?

Badruddin Tyabji, who knew and worked with Sheikh Abdullah, summed up his life in the Commemoration volume:

> Sheikh Sahib's greatest achievement was in restoring to a substantial extent in the Kashmiri people their lost sense of identity and self-respect. They had lost both in the course of the long sad history of their region. After the break-up of their indigenous Sultanate, they had progressively been more and more dominated and exploited by people from outside—Muslim and non-Muslim by turns, it did not matter which. What did matter was that they were ruled and dragooned, not by Kashmiris but by outsiders who treated them with contempt and distrust. This continuous domination over them for centuries by what was basically alien rule and partially alien culture, debilitated them morally, physically and economically. It deprived them of their self-confidence, sense of manliness and capacity to stand on their own feet. Even their high artistic skills, craftsmanship and quick intelligence brought them hardly more than bare subsistence. This developed in them an almost paranoiac distrust of the 'outsider'. Sheikh Sahib, the extrovert that he was, larger than lifesize, with abounding physical courage and self-confidence, and above all, of their own flesh and blood, was literally an answer to their prayers.

The Kashmir of 1930 could have been taken for granted, but not the Kashmir of 1982. That was the difference that one man's life made. Sheikh Mohammad Abdullah had given Kashmir back its pride; you could not wound that pride and hope that silence would again be the only response. Sheikh Mohammad Abdullah had set the *chinar* on fire.

19

Thorns

It was getting late; the glorious sunlight of the August afternoon had slipped into the haze of evening. Try as he might, Sheikh Abdullah could not keep the emotion out of his voice as he told his son in front of the overflowing crowd at Iqbal Park:

> This crown that I am placing on your head is made of thorns. My first wish is that you will never betray the hopes of your *qaum*. You are young, Farooq Abdullah, young enough to face the challenges of life, and I pray that God gives you the courage to fulfil your responsibility to these people whom I have nurtured with such pride, and to whom I have given the best years of my life.

The crowd roared: "Aameen!" The Sheikh pinned the badge of the President of the National Conference on to the breast of his son.

That speech of Sheikh Abdullah on 21 August 1981 as he passed on the burden of responsibility trembled with a lifetime's passion. In the waves of red party banners that rippled through the park he saw the blood of the martyrs who had given their young lives from 1931. In front of his eyes swam the picture of that *ghazi* (warrior), in his ears echoed the cry of his faltering voice, who on 13 July 1931 had died in front of him in the courtyard of the Jama Masjid, saying, "Sheikh Sahab! I have done my duty. Now it is your responsibility". That, said the Sheikh, was the moment of truth for him. Fifty years of service to Kashmir had gone by since that July; today he wanted to hand over the dreams of the martyrs to the generation of his son, as Motilal had done in 1930 for Jawaharlal. He was proud that the son of that "*daanishmand* Brahmin" had honoured his father's trust. Now it was Farooq's turn:

> *Hamaare qabeel-e ka dastoor qurbani pesh karne ka hai,*
> *aur aap ko apne khoon ki sadaqat sabit karna hogi.*
> *Khuda-e bartar aap ke aza-em mein almas ki si sakhti ata*

karey aur aap ko fatah wa nusrat se hamkinar kare.
Aameen Sum Aameen!

(It is our practice to offer sacrifice, and you will have to
prove to the people that your blood is true. May God give
you the strength of a precious stone and reward you with
victory.)

And he warned:

Woh waqt bhi dekhe hain taarikh ki ghariyon ne
Lamhon ne khata ki thi, sadiyon ne saza paai.

(History, he said, has seen such times, when the crime was
committed by a moment, but the punishment was suffered
by centuries.)

The story of the 1980s would be dotted with such crime, the future clouded
with punishment.

Farooq did not seem temperamentally suited to martyrdom. There had
never been the smell of prison in his life, and when in 1964, after Nehru's
death and his father's return to prison, a few eyes in Delhi began staring
at this hero of the Mo-e-Muqaddas movement, the hero opted for discretion, and many thousands of miles of distance between him and Delhi. In
August 1964 he left for London; in his own words, he thought, "Let us
get out before anything happens". He returned only in 1975. But heirs
have a special licence for upward mobility. On 21 August 1981, he was
coronated; on 7 September 1982 that famous crown of thorns physically
reached his head. Within nine days those thorns began pricking, making
Farooq Abdullah bleed just enough to tell him that life without father was
not going to be easy.

Among the legacies that Farooq Abdullah had inherited was the Jammu
and Kashmir Grant of Permit for Resettlement in (or Permanent Return
to) the State Bill, abbreviated, thankfully, to the Resettlement Bill. The
shorter term, in fact, was accurate enough. One of the last bits of
legislation passed by the Sheikh government, it had not yet reached the
headlines because Delhi was wary of entering into any confrontation with
the Sheikh, particularly when he was ill. The legislation gave any Kashmiri
who was a State subject before 14 May 1954, or a descendant (wife or
widow) of the subject, the right to return to Kashmir provided the person
swore allegiance to the Constitution of India and the Constitution of Jammu
and Kashmir. On the face of it, this seemed consistent enough with India's

non-recognition of Pak-Occupied Kashmir as a separate entity. But it was a can of worms. For instance, the law could facilitate the influx of anti-Indian elements deliberately sent across the border, more so since there were no restrictive qualifications regarding those who had joined the Pakistan armed and civil services. Moreover, in Jammu those Hindus who had been able to get evacuee property after the population exchange of 1947 faced the realistic threat that their homes could be reclaimed by returning Kashmiris. However, the bill, though passed, had not become law since the necessary assent of the Governor of the State had not yet come. Farooq would have been content if the status quo remained in perpetuity. The bill could gather dust on the governor's desk for as long as the latter wanted. But a mere nine days after Farooq Abdullah took over, the Governor returned the Resettlement Bill, bringing the dispute into frontpage headlines. Farooq was convinced that this was a trap, a deliberate test to probe his responses, as the bill could easily have been left in barren neglect. Be that as it may, Delhi had a relevant set of questions about this bill—as well as a political signal to send. Farooq's problem was that there was no way he could retreat without indicating that he was betraying the trust that his father had reposed in him. Farooq has written that a rising new influence in Delhi's charmed ruling circle, Makhan Lal Fotedar, was instrumental in provoking this confrontation, but Fotedar denies it.

The Centre had perforce to consider the sentiments of Jammu; it had no other choice. And so, on 23 September the Governor B.K. Nehru sent a lengthy message to the Jammu and Kashmir Assembly asking it to amend the bill to guard against "unintended consequences", and adding two further points: the State's competence to legislate on issues of Indian citizenship was doubtful, and that further study might even make fresh legislation unnecessary. Farooq had to stand by his bill; among other things, this was still his father's legislature, the MLAs who had passed the bill were still in the House. On 25 September, Farooq's Law Minister Pyare Lal Handoo moved the bill again, noting that it should go through in its "original shape". (The man who had originally moved the bill in Sheikh's time, A.R. Rather, was now Speaker.) By the end of the day, however, a classic Kashmir–Delhi crisis was prevented by an appeal from the Congress MLA Mangat Ram to provide time for a "cool and dispassionate" consideration before a final decision was taken by the House. Farooq agreed; and proposed the House pause till 4 October. Id came on 28 September, and Farooq told the Id congregation that unless the six million people of Kashmir had good relations with the seventy million people of India "we cannot march ahead". He did not want confrontation. The Governor left for Delhi on the afternoon of Id; Farooq followed the next day. Farooq had spoken to Indira Gandhi on the telephone on 27 September—and, among other things, already suggested fresh elections. The "cool and dispassionate" discussions began on 29 September. Farooq met Indira Gandhi at her home for about forty-five minutes after 7 in the evening. A compromise was reached. On 3 October, Indira Gandhi told the Congress (I) Parliamentary Party meeting on the eve of the winter session that she had doubts about the legality of the bill; on 4 October, Farooq went ahead and passed it. Then came the agreed compromise: Farooq Abdullah announced that the bill would not be implemented unless the Supreme Court pronounced it valid. The first round of tension had ended in a truce, but it was evident that a battle had begun.

And Farooq, young and naturally ebullient, seemed a trifle too eager to take on all comers, preferring applause to adjustment. You could not fault his crusade against the corruption which had besmirched his father's administration, but was it totally wise to drop all the "stalwarts" of his father's ministry after publicly calling them corrupt? Neither G.M. Shah nor D.D. Thakur found a place in Farooq's Cabinet, with the result that these two longtime antagonists made common cause against the Young Pretender. These were men who had spent their lives specializing in intrigue, and analysing which part of whose back was most vulnerable to a stab. Farooq, still immature, and quite ignorant about the complexities of power, was convinced that he would be victorious merely because he was right. He put the squeeze on his party seniors: witness the Kotwal Commission to investigate fraud in an Anantnag residential colony meant for the poor but being pillaged by the rich. D.D. Thakur had to obtain a stay from the Supreme Court on the plea that the judge was personally biased against him. G.M. Shah and Thakur took the low road of silence, while Farooq stomped along the high one, seeking to correct forty years of problems in about forty days.

Farooq made little secret of his contempt for his brother-in-law, G.M. Shah, but there was more to it than rivalry for the chief ministership. What Farooq resented was the manner in which Shah had usurped and misused power in the name of his father. Shah was in love with authority, both the form and the content of it. He was the only minister who flaunted a police pilot car ahead of his vehicle. As for his behaviour with the people, one incident at least became a major scandal. His car was stuck in a traffic jam once. In a fit of anger Shah got out and beat up the traffic policeman on duty! Sheikh Abdullah eventually pacified the force by calling their representatives to his office, turning his cheek towards them and asking them to give vent to their anger on him. All this endeared the Sheikh to the people, but it did not make Shah any less hated. And so there was great satisfaction when Shah did not find a place in Farooq's first Cabinet. Farooq was confident that he could squash the whole dissident group by the simple expedient of denying them tickets in the next elections. That was one important reason why he wanted Assembly elections quickly.

Mrs Gandhi advised a little restraint. A minimum notice of forty-five days was in any case required by the Election Commission, she pointed out, which would take them into winter—hardly the right time for a Kashmir poll. It was March before Farooq went back to Delhi to pick up the election thread. He found a knot in it. Mrs Gandhi wanted a National Conference–Congress alliance in the Assembly polls along the axis which had almost materialized in 1975. A little surprised, Farooq hesitated. He could not respond without consulting his colleagues, he said. The reaction was uniformly negative: an alliance would be serious encroachment on the National Conference's independent identity. Farooq himself was not keen on the idea. Mrs Gandhi had asked for four seats in the Valley, and Farooq was willing to go so far as to put up weak candidates in those constituencies, but no more. He told the Congress: "An alliance is merely going to create trouble for us. You fight your way, we'll fight our way; later we can reach an understanding".

It was a little unreasonable to expect Farooq to comply. It would have been impossible for him to sell such an alliance to the people of Kashmir. He could be friendly with Indira Gandhi on many levels, from his genuine personal affection for her (he called her 'Mummy') and Rajiv Gandhi, to open political cooperation—as when, on his father's instructions, he had campaigned intensely for Indira Gandhi in the 1980 elections which brought her back to power. But he could not dilute that special meaning the National Conference held for Kashmiris. As Farooq wrote in *My Dismissal* (Vikas, New Delhi, 1985):

> The decision that was made by our party was consistent with the views of Sheikh Abdullah who had always wanted that the National Conference should stand on its own and retain its identity. This would have been seriously jeopardised if we had gone in for an electoral alliance on the lines suggested by the Congress.

But Mrs Gandhi differed with *her* father's Kashmir policy to this extent that she would not abandon the right of the Congress to play a role in defence of nationalism in Kashmir. Jawaharlal had never allowed the Congress to exist in Jammu and Kashmir as long as he was alive; even when he became disillusioned with Abdullah, he still worked only through a wing of the Conference. Mrs Gandhi was convinced that her party had a legitimate role to play, and those who sought to make it a pariah were indulging in an arrogance which she would never tolerate. As she wrote to Mir Qasim in June 1983 when he complained against her policies:

> For me the (1975) accord was, and remains, a method of fruitful cooperation among all the secular and patriotic forces in the state. It certainly did not mean that the Congress should fade into oblivion. I did not and cannot accept this interpretation of the accord. But this seems to be your view. What was worse was that you succeeded in persuading Sheikh Sahib and later Dr Farooq Abdullah to accept your version. This is what lay behind the National Conference's arrogance of power.

It is not too difficult to discern the deep respect for 'Sheikh Sahib' and the frost in the very formal 'Dr Farooq Abdullah'. Indira Gandhi had been scorned, and she was furious. Her offer of an alliance, which she had made in good faith, as insurance for Kashmir's future, had been spurned.Her bitterness against Syed Mir Qasim, who she obviously blamed for sabotaging a Conference–Congress alliance in Sheikh's time, is also all too visible.

The elections were bitter. The National Conference contested all seventy-six seats; the Congress left four seats for smaller allies; the BJP put up twenty-eight candidates in its Jammu stronghold; the People's Conference exaggerated its importance with thirty-eight candidates; and the Jamaat-e-Islami once again tested the waters with twenty-five. Polling was scheduled for 5 June 1983. Mrs Gandhi gave no quarter; she campaigned for ten full days, the majority of the time in the Valley. There was even a feeling among her more optimistic supporters that the Congress just might pull off a surprise. The stand it had taken on the Resettlement Bill would ensure a virtual sweep in the thirty-two Jammu seats—as indeed it did—and if Indira Gandhi, as the daughter of Kashmir, could pick up even eight or ten seats in the Valley, there just might... It was not to be, of course; and in fact it was Farooq who improved on his father's tally of seven seats in Jammu by winning eight. The BJP was wiped out. But the twenty-four seats from Jammu gave the Congress a solid presence in the legislature which would be vitally important in the summer of 1984. That campaign was blotted by personal viciousness that left a lasting bitterness on both sides. Stories were cooked up and planted in the national media against Farooq; and lumpens of the Conference insulted Mrs Gandhi herself by stripping while she was addressing a meeting in Srinagar. The Congress office in Srinagar was torched. Farooq maintained that all this was the product of a dirty-tricks department in the Congress headquarters, but Mrs Gandhi was sceptical of his explanations. "This was another bitter blow to our relationship", says Farooq. The politics of the campaign did neither side proud, nor the country any good. In his overwhelming desire to smash the Congress, Farooq Abdullah dissolved five decades of ideological animosity with Mir Waiz Maulvi Farooq, scion of the family which had feuded with the Abdullah since 1932. The pro-Pakistani *bakra* lay with the Abdullah lion, arousing suspicions in Delhi. Horrible riots had broken out that year in Assam, and Mrs Gandhi faced placards calling Congress a killer of Muslims. Farooq equated the Congress with Hari Singh, accusing both of trying to enslave Kashmiris: the anti-Jammu tinge had communal undertones which a deaf man might hear at fifty paces. The deaf had a great time in Jammu too, where Mrs Gandhi made the Resettlement Bill into a compulsive vote-getter. There was a total polarization of the vote, and both the Conference and the Congress were guilty. Both might have done well to recall Sheikh Abdullah's wise words to *The Indian Express* in April 1981, when Mrs Gandhi suggested that the Hindus of Jammu might be suffering from a feeling of insecurity:

> The war among parties should not harm our national interests... My ancestors were Hindus. In Kashmir we have the same blood, all are brothers and continue to have the same culture. Such remarks, therefore, surprise us all and if the Prime Minister of the country makes such a charge, people outside the state will take it seriously.

But at least one byproduct of the polarization was welcome: the Jana Sangh was wiped out in Jammu and the Jamaat erased from the electoral map of the Valley.

That election of 1983 was a tragedy. It started with Mrs Gandhi refusing to surrender sole-agency rights over Kashmiri secularism to the National Conference. It ended in a bitter gulf that poisoned the peace of the Valley. Perhaps a reconciliation might yet have been possible after victory and defeat, but a slightly brash Farooq, heady with success, decided that the defeat of the Congress in Kashmir was only the beginning of the defeat of the Congress in the rest of the country. As he told his audience at Jama

Masjid in Srinagar after the elections:

> I will fight them (Congress) in the streets and every corner
> of the country. My test is over. But they have to face the
> electorate in the rest of India soon and let us see how they
> fare.

That statement dripped with naïveté. His test was far from over. And as for the Congress and the electorate, Mrs Gandhi had a few things left to do before the next general elections. But Farooq went tearing across the nation, doing the one thing Mrs Gandhi could not afford to ignore even if she was in any mood to indulge him: he had joined a growing coalition which was preparing a common programme as the first step towards a coalition which could defeat the Congress in the 1984 general elections.

The winter of 1982–83 had proved unusually cold for a Congress still basking in the glow of the 1980 elections: in a completely unexpected reverse it was swept out of its southern fortresses of Karnataka and Andhra Pradesh by two leaders articulating regional pride, Rama Krishna Hegde and N.T. Rama Rao. A strange character, and character-actor, Rama Rao was a superstar who had specialized in mythologicals to a point where the people began to attribute a few mythical qualities to him too. Fascinated by the world of real power, all Rama Rao had wanted from the Congress was a Rajya Sabha seat. Rejected, he launched a regional party, the Telugu Desam, which ended three decades of Congress monopoly in Andhra Pradesh. For the want of a Rajya Sabha seat, the Congress lost a state. And its composure. Rama Rao had no shortage of ambition to begin with; having conquered Andhra he was convinced he was destined for higher things. At his initiative, fourteen top non-Congress leaders gathered in the historic city of Vijayawada on 28 May 1983. Among them was Farooq Abdullah, who even interrupted his crucial election campaign to display solidarity with the budding anti-Indira alliance. Mrs Gandhi said publicly she was shocked that Farooq had joined hands with her enemies. There was some reason for the shock, because this amounted to reversal of a well-established National Conference policy. No leader of the freedom struggle could ever have had as much reason for anger and even bitterness against Jawaharlal than Sheikh Abdullah and yet he never opposed the Congress outside Kashmir. He always maintained that the Congress was as necessary for the rest of India as the National Conference was for Kashmir. Abdullah stood by Indira Gandhi through the Emergency, and—as we have seen—sent Farooq to campaign for her return in 1980 although his relations with the Morarji government were very good, and his personal relations with some Janata ministers—like George Fernandes—excellent. Farooq's argument was of course that the change in the equation could not be one-sided; if Mrs Gandhi now felt that the Congress had a legitimate claim in Kashmir then the Conference also could lay claim to an anti-Congress role in the rest of the country.

Mrs Gandhi made every effort to spike this gathering unity, and at least one chief minister, M.G. Ramachandran of Tamil Nadu, returned to his cosy partnership with the Congress by which he kept Madras and Congress took Delhi. Mrs Gandhi expected Farooq to similarly distance himself after Vijayawada, but Farooq would not break ranks with his new-found brothers.

On 5, 6 and 7 October 1983 he even organized an impressive conclave of fifty-nine leaders in Srinagar representing seventeen non-Congress parties, on the sensitive issue of Centre-State relations. Mrs Gandhi treated this as dangerously provocative, more so since the demand for a weaker Delhi had emanated from Srinagar. Beset by rising secessionism in Punjab, led by the young and obviously determined Jarnail Singh Bhindranwale seated inside the Golden Temple, and by rising regionalism in Assam controlled by a handful of equally convinced students operating out of the university campus, Mrs Gandhi's answer was to reaffirm that India's unity could only be protected by a reinforced Centre. She was deeply suspicious of demands for more powers for the States. She publicly doubted the *bona fides* of Rama Rao, the very name of whose party implied a separate Telugu country. It was this anger and suspicion which tilted the scales decisively against Farooq in Indira Gandhi's judgement, and she gave clearance for the plan to topple Farooq by the simple expedient of scissoring his majority in the Assembly, a plan—if Farooq is to be believed—codenamed Operation New Star. (There is no other evidence for such a colourful name. There was Operation Bluestar of course in Punjab, but New Star seems only to be political hype.) Delhi did not have to look very far to find its agents. They were ready, eager and waiting. Their names of course were G.M. Shah and Devi Das Thakur. However, they would not have been successful but for one very serious mistake made by Farooq Abdullah in April.

The day was 29 April 1983 and yet another mammoth crowd had collected at the park named after that great Kashmiri philosopher, essayist and poet Sir Muhammad Iqbal. Farooq Abdullah was launching his campaign that day with an announcement of the list of party candidates. When they heard the names, a section of the audience threw slippers at Farooq Abdullah. They were incensed that after all the dramatic pronouncements by Farooq Abdullah on corruption, the list of candidates had more than half a dozen Shah loyalists with unsavoury reputations. Farooq it appeared had simply caved in to family and cabal pressure, including that of his sister Khalida and his mother Begum Abdullah. Farooq had nothing but extremely lame excuses to offer for the compromise. However, the Farooq wave was strong enough to sweep everyone ashore, ship and flotsam alike. But these MLAs became the source of potential instability because their loyalty was to Shah. What Farooq should have realized, even if no one had told him, was that the balance between the Valley and Jammu being what it was, the defection of a dozen or so MLAs would always be sufficient to bring down a National Conference government. And let this much be said for G.M. Shah: that Trojan never came inside any horse; he flaunted his desire to oust Farooq whenever he had any opportunity to do so. Even during the election campaign he confabulated openly with Congress leaders, and refused to canvass for his own party.

But an extremely naïve Farooq Abdullah thought he had settled the Shah problem by expelling his brother-in-law from the National Conference on 4 October 1983—on the eve of his high-profile conclave. He was, of course, also deliberately snubbing Delhi that day. Shah announced the formation of what he called the Real (Asli) National Conference, made his wife Khalida president, and bided his time. Delhi, on its part, had already achieved the one thing it could not manage in 1953—the division of the Abdullah family. Even Farooq's younger brother, the mercurial and rather unreliable Tariq, joined Khalida and Shah. It was now a question of waiting for opportunities. Any would do. Even a cricket match. And one between an Indian Eleven and the touring West Indies side was scheduled for 13 October, less than a week after the assembly of national leaders of all hues, barring the Congress and the BJP, had left for Delhi after their conference. Ironically, this friendly match had been slotted at Srinagar precisely to indicate to the nation that Kashmir was as untroubled as the rest of India.

The first international cricket match in Kashmir was a three-day game in September 1978 between Australia and India. The Jamaat-e-Islami from Srinagar and the Kashmir Liberation Front from London had threatened violence if the match was played, and the Australians nearly buckled under. But Sheikh Abdullah was Chief Minister and Farooq was president of the Jammu and Kashmir Cricket Association, and they sought—and got—the intervention of the President of India Sanjeeva Reddy to ensure that the match went through. Nothing happened, apart from a reasonable cricket game. Again in 1983 the Jamaat tried blackmail to stop the cricket but Farooq would not be bullied. The one-dayer began in cold, cloudy conditions, and soon became as dull as the weather. That led to the first spot of spectator trouble: booing. But a pattern began to emerge in two small sections of the crowd, one in the eastern stands, and the other in the western: its reactions were partisan—and in favour of the West Indies. Soon the Jamaat flags (green with a star and a crescent) could be seen waving. The problem was that it was very similar to the Pakistani flag, which made it a great story for a Press box full of cricket writers, most of whom had never seen a Jamaat flag in their careers but were certainly familiar with a Pakistani one. For Delhi, this was heaven-sent material for propaganda. The Pakistani flag was fluttering freely in Farooq's reign! Doordarshan and radio repeatedly broadcast highly flavoured news items implying a breakdown of law and order. On 15 October, Mrs Gandhi, at a press conference, even alleged that Farooq had not even condemned these incidents, which was not quite accurate because Farooq had done so, specifically enough, at a meeting in the Kashmir University, in the presence of Governor B.K. Nehru, just the previous day. Farooq, in fact, counter-charged the guilty spectators with being Jamaat and Congress agents working in collusion to discredit him.

Mrs Gandhi's allegation was not a good one to make against Farooq, for if there was one thing about which there has never been any doubt it is his commitment to India and to secularism. And he did not even indulge in the conscious duplicity which his father had often used to keep different segments of the population in the Conference fold. Farooq had other weaknesses, which could be exploited with more credibility—and they were. Naïveté was one. Far more colourful was a streak of happy irresponsibility which was the despair of friends and the delight of foes. But even the overconfident Farooq Abdullah realized by 24 January 1984, during a Delhi trip, that the Union Government was determined to dislodge his government. The interesting thing is that he did not do very much about it. He took a surprise vote of confidence on the opening day of the Budget session in February and thought he had solved his problems. One really should place an exclamation mark after a sentence like that. The process of "wooing" MLAs, as bribery in defection-politics is called, had begun much before this vote and did not cease because of it. Farooq Abdullah, in a discussion with the author, accused Congress MP Tirath Ram Amla of being the chief moneybag of the operation, and D.D. Thakur of targeting the MLAs ready to drink from the cashpool. Naturally such accusations always get denied. However, what cannot be denied is that the toppling game would have been over much sooner were it not for the fact that one key figure, the Governor, B.K. Nehru, refused to cooperate. He told the Centre that the removal of Farooq would initiate a process which Delhi would not be able to control. But Delhi's mind was made up. B.K. Nehru was transferred to Gujarat, and the ever-obliging Jagmohan was sent to take residence in the beautiful palace overlooking Dal Lake.

There has been no year more tense in the life of free India than 1984: Operation Bluestar in the Punjab in the first week of June, the assassination of Mrs Gandhi on 31 October and the general elections in the last week of December. And the unceasing war of attrition between Delhi and the non-Congress governments in which decency and democracy were the prime victims. The hook-or-crook methods used to try and break the governments of Karnataka, Andhra and Kashmir were a blot on the very concept of a federation. Farooq Abdullah, for his sins, was at the very top of the hit list.

In June the Punjab crisis exploded into Army action; by the seventh, Bhindranwale was dead, killed in the battle that raged on the premises of the Golden Temple, leaving the Akal Takht in smithereens and the Sikh community in India feeling suddenly vulnerable, suddenly a minority. The upsurge of Sikh anger extended even to units of the Army, but there was great popular support for Operation Bluestar among the non-Sikh masses. Perhaps buoyed by this, within days, senior Congress ministers and leaders began charging the Farooq government with secret support for the Sikh extremists, of collaboration with Bhindranwale, of allowing training camps on Kashmiri soil and so on. The Centre formally complained that the Farooq government had refused to arrest Sikh extremists in Jammu and Kashmir even though the Union Home Ministry had sent it a specific list. An ill-advised, and much-reported fifteen-minute meeting between Farooq and Bhindranwale earlier that year, during a visit to Amritsar, was played up. Farooq claimed that the meeting was spontaneous rather than conspiratorial, but he was being silly if he thought that it would be interpreted by the rest of the country as in the national interest. Bhindranwale obviously used it to suggest that Kashmir's sympathies lay with his secessionist movement. Farooq's immaturity had again provided ammunition to his enemies. On 15 June 1984 Mohammad Shafi, the information minister of Kashmir, denied at a press conference that Sikh terrorists had ever received training in "fortification and use of arms". He reminded the media that Home Minister P.C. Sethi had told the Lok Sabha on 16 November 1983 that no arms training had been given in the *gurmat* camps held in the state. He pointed out that the disturbances following Bluestar had been controlled effectively; nine people had died in police firing, 313 people were arrested. He did add at the end that though his government had clarified all this in a letter

> Once again we could hardly do anything more than present our case to the people of this country who, in a democratic set-up, are the ultimate arbiters.

But the attack from the Congress only grew louder. On 21 June, the Congress Working Committee took "a serious view" of the situation in Kashmir; the Parliamentary Board followed this up with an expression of grave concern. On 23 June, the PCC Chief Mufti Mohammad Sayeed was summoned to Delhi; on the 26th, inadvertently or otherwise, he hinted that the Farooq government would not last much longer. On 27 June, Jagmohan—also called to Delhi—met the Home Secretary, M.M.K. Wali, and then discussed the plan of action with Home Minister Sethi, before going back to Srinagar. A letter dated 28 June 1984, signed by thirteen MLAs, twelve from the National Conference and one Independent, was sent to the Governor, saying that they had withdrawn support to the government of Farooq Abdullah.

Two reasons prevented immediate action. One: the long month of a summer Ramzan was drawing to a close; it would clearly have been unwise to do anything on the eve of Id. Two: the security arrangements needed beefing up. But the news of these defections was in every political ear—bar one. The only person who had no idea that his majority had fallen apart was Farooq Abdullah. Even when he called on Jagmohan on 1 July and spoke to him for over an hour, he had no clue. Jagmohan, at one point, gently introduced the subject of defections. Farooq recalls his reply: "Sir, they have tried a number of times, and they may continue to try. If there are interested persons at the Centre who want to feed them, then I can't do very much. But if they don't get support from the Centre, they will not be able to do anything."

Question: What was Farooq Abdullah doing on the day they broke his party?

Answer: Chasing timber thieves in Shopian on a motorcycle.

This happens to be perfectly true. Farooq's motorcycle and scooter rides had become nationally famous when he took the film actress Shabana Azmi on his pillion right up to Gulmarg a little earlier. Rather than getting subdued by the reaction, Farooq became even more cavalier. It is not a great secret that Sheikh Abdullah himself was often worried about this streak in his son, and would ask trusted friends to keep an eye on Farooq after he was gone. The father even mentioned this to Mrs

Gandhi and in fact it was she who calmed the Sheikh's doubts by stressing that Farooq's assets—which are many and splendid—more than compensated for any fault. It was Mrs Gandhi who personally ensured that Farooq succeeded his father. There was also the consideration of her own son, Rajiv Gandhi, and she felt that since the two young men were friends their cooperation would be good for Kashmir and India. Moreover—and very rightly too—Mrs Gandhi did not trust G.M. Shah, whereas she knew that even if Farooq erred elsewhere his basic commitment to India would never waver. It was all this, plus her personal affection for Farooq, that had made her optimistic about an alliance with the National Conference in 1983. And, as we've seen, a principal reason for her anger with Mir Qasim was her feeling that Qasim had prevented a Conference–Congress coalition government in 1975, which the Sheikh was in a mood to accept before Beg and Qasim, from their respective perspectives, quietly buried the idea. If. . . there are so many ifs. Of course if anyone could have made a Conference–Congress alliance acceptable to Kashmir it was only the Sheikh; by the time Farooq and Rajiv Gandhi attempted the experiment, the world had been stained by mistrust, betrayal, and a critical change in the environment of the north-west of India. And so much of that pollution originated in the events of 1983 and 1984.

*

At 11.30 on the morning of 1 July 1984 the defectors telephoned Jagmohan asking if he was ready; they were told to reach the Raj Bhavan very early the next morning. Working through pliant bureaucrats, including Director-General of Police Pir Ghulam Hassan Shah (who had been given a special two-year extension by Farooq only on 30 June: it seemed a curious way to reward a benefactor), Jagmohan made arrangements for extra forces to be brought to the Valley. Farooq, although in charge of the Home portfolio, was kept totally oblivious of this order.

It was still dark, more than two hours before dawn on 2 July, when Maulvi Iftekhar Hussain Ansari led the group of thirteen MLAs in a convoy of four cars towards Raj Bhavan. At 6.45 in the morning, a Boeing 737 touched down at Srinagar airport, unloading a detachment of the Madhya Pradesh Special Armed Police which had been secretly summoned by Jagmohan to take care of the expected mass reaction. Fifteen minutes later Farooq Abdullah finally discovered what was happening, thanks to the chairman of the Peoples' Conference Abdul Ghani Lone. Farooq, in fact, was up early not because he thought he would not be Chief

Minister by sunset, but because he was planning to leave for an official tour of nearby districts. Hardly had he put the phone down, when it shrilled again. Jagmohan was on the line. Could Farooq see him immediately? It was urgent. By 7.30 Farooq was at Raj Bhavan. Jagmohan showed Farooq the letters signed by the thirteen MLAs: Hissam Din Bandey (elected from the Sheikh's own Hazratbal); Munshi Habibullah (Kargil); Talib Hussain (Rajouri); Dr Mehboob Beg (son of Mirza Afzal Beg, to Farooq's shock, from Sarnal, Anantnag); Sheikh Abdul Jabbar (Lar); Sona Ullah Dar (Pulwana); Ghulam Hassan Mir (Gulmarg); Mohammad Khalil Jowhar (Bandipora); Hakim Mohammad Yasin (Khan Sahib); Mohammad Dilawar Mir (Rafiabad); and the two nominated women MLAs Khem Lalla Wakhloo and Gurbachan Kumar Rana. Farooq's strength had been reduced from forty-six to thirty-four MLAs, four short of a majority in a House with an existing strength of seventy-seven. As Jagmohan wrote in his formal letter to Farooq, signed at seven on the morning of 2 July 1984:

> They (the MLAs) told me and have given in writing that they have withdrawn their support to your government and pledged their support to Shri Gh. Mohammad Shah, MLC. Simultaneously, Moulvi Iftikhar Hussain Ansari, MLA, and leader of the Congress-I legislature party, J and K, has informed me in writing and in person that the Congress-I legislature party having strength of 26 MLAs, had decided to support Shri Gh. Mohammad Shah...In these circumstances, I advice you to submit your resignation as Chief Minister forthwith.

There was an interesting postscript to this letter obviously added after Farooq left:

> P.S. We have since met and discussed the matter. You advised me to impose Governor's rule under Section 92 of the Jammu and Kashmir Constitution and keep the Legislative Assembly in suspended animation. I shall be grateful if you could kindly send me your confirmation in this regard in writing immediately.

Farooq Abdullah was clearly flustered at his meeting with Jagmohan. Instead of challenging the Governor's right to accept the legitimacy of the defections without waiting for the Speaker's adjudication, as he should have done, or stating clearly that under Kashmir law he had the right to recommend the dissolution of the House and ask for fresh elections as his father had done in 1977, Farooq suggested Jagmohan should take over under Section 92! He was clearly unprepared, either intellectually or psychologically, for the defection. It was all quite amazing, and only a person as essentially careless as Farooq could have remained so ignorant. Jagmohan's letter reached Farooq at nine. He summoned an urgent Cabinet meeting and sent a reply—the grammar was even worse than Jagmohan's, which is saying a good deal—by 10.30. Only now did he ask for fresh elections. Jagmohan, tempted by the prospect of taking over himself, explored various options with Delhi. Farooq could have, if he wanted, spoken to Indira Gandhi and Rajiv Gandhi at that point, but he refused to get in touch. He was once again being led by his emotions. By two in the afternoon word had spread through Srinagar that it was the Governor who was taking over, and there was panic in the defectors' camp. Delhi quickly aborted Jagmohan's ambitions. At 5.30 in the evening he dismissed the Farooq government. G.M. Shah was sworn in. To everyone's astonishment he named all the thirteen defectors Cabinet Ministers! This rather silly move on the part of G.M. Shah effectively prevented any further serious erosion from National Conference ranks; Shah had made himself ridiculous by his very first decision.

There was more black comedy in store on 31 July, the day G.M. Shah had to prove his majority in the House. Vociferous non-Congress MLAs like Lone and Bhim Singh were arbitrarily picked up by the police to prevent them from coming to the House. When the Speaker ruled against the defectors, Shah's supporters simply lifted him bodily and threw him out of his chair. The people of Kashmir were however in no mood to laugh. All the sins of Farooq were forgotten; he had stood by Kashmir, they would stand by him. His mother Begum Abdullah articulated the mood very effectively in an interview to *The Telegraph* on 3 July: "I have been in politics for decades and I know how to fight". Nine years of effort at integration came to a halt; and once again the trend reversed towards sullen suspicion of Delhi, towards the conviction that the Kashmiri Muslim was never really going to be trusted. Events in Delhi, in the meanwhile, evolved towards an unprecedented tragedy. Operation Bluestar won Mrs Gandhi back her country, at the price of her life. On 31 October 1984 Mrs Gandhi was cruelly martyred by her own Sikh bodyguards after she had contemptuously rejected the advice of her security people that they be removed purely because they were Sikhs. The deep shock and anger in the country converted into a deluge in favour of Rajiv Gandhi in the winter general elections. Only three parties were able to survive: the CPM-led Left Front, to a partial extent in West Bengal;

and the two Chief Ministers who had been victims of Delhi that year, Rama Rao and Farooq Abdullah.

The young and confident Rajiv Gandhi began his post-election phase by signalling change in all directions: the economy, the polity, foreign affairs. Where the theme of Mrs Gandhi's last years had been confrontation in defence of India's unity, Rajiv Gandhi clearly felt that the nation's unity was better served by accommodation and absorption of regional forces into the power structure: 1985 became the year of accords, in Punjab first and Assam later. But the accord which could have been easiest took the longest. Even after a few months, it was obvious that the G.M. Shah decision had boomeranged. Rajiv Gandhi's first meeting with Farooq as Prime Minister took place in January 1985; the vibes were warm again, according to Farooq. He was nominated leader of the official delegation to the Haj sent each year by the Government of India; the entente picked up speed from there. Farooq Abdullah had become a touchable again for Delhi. But the problem was not Rajiv Gandhi so much as the Kashmir Coterie, though the former can hardly escape responsibility for giving this group such a long rope. In addition, there was Mufti's ambition to take into account. Mufti, now a Cabinet Minister, agreed that Shah was a disaster, but he saw no reason why he himself should not replace Shah. G.M. Shah was finally dismissed in early 1986. Rajiv Gandhi was on a tour of Arunachal Pradesh that day; a telephone call from M.L. Fotedar informed him the deed was done. For a change, a Delhi decision caused some joy in the Valley. But Farooq Abdullah was not inducted simultaneously into office. The "vacuum" that Nehru never allowed in August 1953 or Mrs Gandhi in September 1982 or even July 1983 was now permitted; for the first time since the days of Hari Singh, Srinagar was ruled by a non-Kashmiri. Jagmohan's old dream was finally fulfilled. Kashmir came under Governor's Rule.

It was meant to be a temporary arrangement; it went on for more than six months while Farooq Abdullah and Rajiv Gandhi squabbled over their terms of endearment. Farooq wanted fresh elections and a new legislature. Rajiv Gandhi, having stopped Mufti from replacing Shah, was not going to allow his generosity to go beyond a point. One chance had been missed in 1975; in 1983, Farooq had sabotaged the move. In 1986 Rajiv Gandhi insisted on a Conference–Congress coalition as the *quid pro quo* for Farooq's return. And in the electoral adjustments, Congress demanded its familiar four seats in the Valley. Farooq Abdullah held out for as long as he could. Then he succumbed. Hindsight is an unfair judge. But at least both Farooq Abdullah and Rajiv Gandhi agree in retrospect that their electoral alliance and the ensuing coalition government were very serious mistakes which led indirectly to the rise of the violent secessionist movement of 1990.

It is important to get the cause and consequence right. Farooq Abdullah and Rajiv Gandhi did not ever encourage any secessionist force, or even flirt with them for electoral gain. In fact, it must be said and reiterated that every fault of Farooq Abdullah pales before his passionate commitment to the unity of India, and to his uncompromising attack on fundamentalists. His speeches in the elections of 1987, when the Conference–Congress alliance was pitted against a self-proclaimed extremist Muslim United Front which wanted an "Islamic" Kashmir separated from "Hindu" India, which campaigned with the *Holy Quran* in one hand and the Kashmiri flag in the other, were a remarkable display of faith in the face of the severest onslaught faced by secular parties in Kashmir. But it was a tainted alliance. Farooq's compromise with the very people who had manipulated 1984 ravaged Farooq Abdullah's credibility. He was charged with betraying his father's fifty-year legacy of pride. It created a vacuum where the National Conference had existed, and extremists stepped into that vacuum. Kashmiriyat had become vulnerable to the votaries of violence and Muslim hegemony, both injuring Kashmir and perverting Kashmiriyat. Sheikh Mohammad Abdullah had structured the resurrection of his people on Muslim-Hindu harmony, on the traditions of Nuruddin Rishi and Lal Ded, on the philosophy of Sufism, on non-violence and a mutually regenerative creativity. That pride was suddenly handed over to the forces Abdullah had fought against all his life—indeed, the gift surprised even the recipients. Sheikh Abdullah did not keep the Congress of Jawaharlal and the Congress of Indira away from Kashmir because he had anything personal against them; the Congress was always a friend, but still the outsider. It was an equation which had worked. That delicate bridge collapsed under the weight of an embrace.

It is a little pointless going into the details of the sordid politics of Delhi in 1987, 1988 and 1989, when a revolt against Rajiv Gandhi manipulated by Arun Nehru and his friends like Mufti (at least partly motivated by anger at the return of Farooq Abdullah) blossomed into a split in the Congress and the emergence of V.P. Singh as the latest champion of the hate-Congress movement. It is noteworthy, though, that as far as Kashmir was concerned, the very architects of 1984 now stood back and watched Rajiv Gandhi squirm helplessly as the spreading tentacles of that mistake coiled around him. The militants moved rapidly from the fringe to the mainstream, at a pace which neither they nor their mentors in Pakistan expected. In fact the pattern of 1989 was that they used particular points of the calendar to test the level of response, and each time it rose higher than their expectations. If, for instance, you draw a graph from the India-Australia cricket match in 1978, when the Jamaat threat of violence proved an exercise in impotent bravado, then the sectional protest at the India-West Indies match in October 1983, after the dismissal of Farooq, becomes a significant pointer. From there to 7 May 1989 was a journey towards suicide.

*

The rule of the Dogras has long gone, but they still call it the Durbar: on 7 May each year the Durbar moves from the winter capital of Jammu to the summer capital of Srinagar. Chief Minister Farooq Abdullah looked out of the window of his office in Srinagar on 7 May 1989; not a soul moved outside. The capital was totally deserted in response to a call for a *hartal* by the militants to coincide with Durbar day. Farooq Abdullah turned to one of his seniormost bureaucrats, as well as a personal friend, Ashok Jaitley, and said: "This is my government!" Unable to contain his frustration he added something unprintable about the militants. The mood of anger had already become an impending storm; it was only a question of when and how it would break. At his Id speech at Hazratbal a few days before, Farooq Abdullah had been—characteristically—blunt. He warned the people very candidly that they would have to pay a very heavy price in blood if they flirted with the kind of armed insurrection that was causing havoc in the Punjab. (The most endearing aspect of Farooq Abdullah is that he is straightforward. It does not always make for good politics; but it is the sign of a good man.) The storm did not break that summer of 1989; the tourist season was splendid, and all seemed fine indeed on the surface in Paradise, though the rigmarole of meetings intensified inside the secretariats of Srinagar and Delhi as the storm signals were picked up and analysed. But even the pessimists were not fully prepared for the massive endorsement of the militants in the general elections of November 1989. Only five per cent of the electorate voted after a boycott call. The stage was clearly set for a decisive act in the drama.

Questions bubble up. If there had been no 1975, the violence of 1990 might have been more explicable. But after the brilliance of 1975, 1984 seems all the more unforgiveable. What is it in us which makes us so ahistorical? Indians know history: how many civilizations can boast a longer continuous stream of chronicles? Then why do we never seem to use the past as a working guide for the present? Why does compromise always prevail over conviction when the record shows over and over again that compromise is a mistress of doubtful fidelity? Why does greed take precedence over investment? Why are the guardians of power trapped by illusion so easily? Why is today's petty reward so much more important than the stability of the next ten years? Why is policy in our country so often handcuffed to personal hatred? A little maybe; after all, we are talking of human beings; but so much? The Kashmiri nose is a long one, but is there no one who can look beyond it? If one had to single out the one fact that did the most damage in the management of Kashmir, then there would probably be no reason to go further than the sheer pettiness of the cabals in both Delhi and Srinagar that placed their separate collective interests over the national need. An insular horizon can be a dangerous limitation.

And when in December 1989 V.P. Singh got an opportunity to prove that the solutions that had evaded Rajiv Gandhi were within his reach, he placed a Kashmiri in charge of the nation's domestic welfare—none other than Mufti Mohammad Sayeed, minister under G.M. Sadiq, claimant for office in 1975, chief of the Congress in 1977, a gadfly for Sheikh Abdullah, a tormentor of Farooq Abdullah, Union Cabinet Minister for Tourism under Prime Minister Rajiv Gandhi, fellow-dissident in the company of Arun Nehru by 1987, leading rebel after his resignation from the Cabinet, ostensibly over the anti-Muslim outrage at Meerut, handsome victor from Muzaffarnagar in 1989, and now at the pinnacle of his life, Home Minister of India, occupant of the chair once held by Sardar Vallabhbhai Patel. The militants decided to test the nerve of the most powerful Kashmiri Muslim ever in Delhi's history.

Chief Minister Farooq Abdullah was on a holiday in London when he received a telephone call on 8 December 1989 from Ashok Jaitley, then the presiding bureaucrat in Jammu and Kashmir in the absence of the Chief Secretary, Moosa Raza, who was in Delhi that day on work. Jaitley had some bad news to give. At four in the afternoon that day, Dr Rubaiya Sayeed the unmarried third daughter of the Union Home Minister, had been kidnapped about 500 metres from her home at Nowgam, when she was returning from the Lal Ded Memorial Women's Hospital in a Matador van. Four militants had stopped the vehicle, taken Rubaiya off it at gunpoint and disappeared in a Maruti car. At about five-thirty a phone call came to the Srinagar bureau of the *Kashmir Times* from someone claiming to represent the Jammu and Kashmir Liberation Front. He said that his group's "mujahideen" had kidnapped Dr Rubaiya Sayeed, and she would remain their hostage until the government released Sheikh Abdul Hameed, a JKLF "area commander" hospitalized at the Sher-i-Kashmir Institute of Medical Sciences after being wounded and arrested in an encounter; Ghulam Nabi Butt, younger brother of the late Maqbool Butt; Noor Muhammad Kalwal; Muhammed Altaf; and Javed Ahmed Zangar. The editor of the *Srinagar Times*, Muhammad Sofi, phoned both the Home Minister and the government to pass on the news. The first reaction of the Kashmir Cabinet, sitting in the absence of Farooq, was to meet the demands of the militants and free Dr Rubaiya Sayeed, if Delhi approved. Everyone suggested a little patience. Farooq caught the earliest plane out to Delhi. Senior IB and police officials, including Ved Marwah, Director General of the National Security Guards, reached Srinagar before dawn the next day.

It did not prove very difficult to establish contact with the militants. In fact journalists were the best conduits and negotiations opened through Zaffar Meraj of the *Kashmir Times*, while Shabnam Lone, daughter of A.B. Ghani Lone and Maulvi Abbas Ansari of the Muslim United Front were tapped as possible channels. On the 10th, word came from the JKLF that Sheikh Hamid and Nabi Butt be sent to Pakistan. The demand was rejected. Then Delhi showed its first weakness; it said it was willing to send the prisoners to Iran or Dubai, which do not have an extradition treaty with India. On this day the militants changed one of the names on their list, substituting Abdul Ahad Waza for Zangar.

By now something interesting had happened: the kidnapping of a young, unmarried woman had aroused great anger in Kashmir. The action was against Islam and against the culture and spirit of Kashmir. The father of an absconder named Ashfaq, Abdul Majid Wani told the government on the 10th that the militants had realized that they had blundered—and that his information was that Rubaiya would be freed because of public sentiment even if not a single prisoner was released. Farooq reached Delhi and met the Prime Minister and the Home Minister before leaving for Srinagar. Suddenly, a little out of the blue, a judge of the Allahabad High Court, Moti Lal Bhat, entered the picture. A friend of Mufti, he began negotiating directly with the militants on behalf of the Home Minister. Bhat worked through Mir Mustafa, an Independent MLA, Mian Abdul Qayoom, an activist-lawyer of the Jamaat-e-Islami and Dr Abdul Ahad Guru, the physician who was treating Sheikh Hamid. The modalities of the exchange were being discussed, without any final decision being taken, when at 2.30 a.m. on the 13th Moosa Raza informed Farooq that the Cabinet Secretary desires the State Government to note that it is their undiluted responsibility to ensure the safe release of the hostage without injury to her and we expect that all actions you take will be consistent with these requirements.

At 3.30 in the early morning, two Union Cabinet Ministers, Inder Gujral and Arif Mohammad Khan, personally flew into Srinagar—in the belief that Farooq was coming in the way of a deal. They had some reason for this view, because Farooq held the position that abject surrender to the terrorists' demands would have the gravest consequences. As Farooq wrote in his confidential letter (extracts of which were published in *The Telegraph*, Calcutta) to the then Governor of Jammu and Kashmir, General K.V. Krishnarao:

I also informed them (the Ministers) that the consequences of the exchange of five militants for Dr Syed (sic) was a heavy price to pay for the nation as it would open the floodgates for the future and provide a boost to anti-national activities of trying to separate Kashmir from India. This was a game of nerves and if we had persisted with the first negotiator, Mr Wani, the girl would have been released without exchange of militants. Both Ministers were in full agreement with this assessment.

But the government of V.P. Singh did not have the nerve to hold out. At 7 p.m. on 13 December 1989 Dr Rubaiya Sayeed was set free, two hours after the government released the five militants. Thousands of young men gathered at Rajouri Kadal to take the militants out in a triumphant procession, but they quickly disappeared to their hideouts—and from there to Pakistan-Occupied Kashmir. In April the government claimed to have cracked the case, after Ali Mohammad Mir, a senior government officer, was arrested and confessed during interrogation that the conspiracy was organized at the home of Mushtaq Ahmad Lone, in Chanpora; others allegedly involved included Yasin Malik, Ashfaq Majid Wani, Iqbal Gangroo and Salim Mir. Mir had driven Rubaiya to Sopore where she was kept at the official residence of another government officer, Javed Iqbal Mir. After three days she was shifted to the home of Mohammad Yaqoob, owner of a plastic factory at Sopore. But by April too many tragedies had taken place. It was not just that militants of the Hizb-ul Mujahideen punished one of the negotiators, the Independent MLA Mir Mustafa, with death by hanging at Batamalloo on 25 March 1990; Kashmir itself was awash in blood by then.

After the kidnapping incident, Delhi decided to get "tough". With the 1984 clique now in control of the Home Ministry, tough meant sending Jagmohan back. Farooq, whose return to office had coincided with Jagmohan's departure, resigned and simply took leave of his state for a while. His attitude was: he was being blamed for everything; very well, he was going to step aside and let everyone else experiment with their solutions. He told the people that they were welcome to test out how far their battle for "*Aazaadi*" (freedom) would take them. Since he himself was not in favour of *Aazaadi* he was going to go a few thousand miles away, right up to London, to play a little golf. There was some method in this apparent madness. Farooq knew that there was absolutely nothing he could do in the imminent violent test of nerves between the people and the government: he could only be relevant once again when passions on both sides had been cooled by a reawakening of reality—when the people eventually understood that it was not possible to break the unity of the Indian state even by terror and the Indian state realized that it was not easy to break the will of the people, even by savage repression. As long as terror and repression sustained each other, Farooq really had no place in the equation. Someone told him after he resigned that the people of Kashmir were unhappy with him. "Well, " he replied, "I am unhappy with them too". The situation in 1990, however, quickly went out of the realm of mere accusations. The confrontation burst into the open on 19 January.

Jagmohan had just taken over, and, although he maintained he had nothing to do with this particular decision, on the night of 18 January paramilitary forces began the most intense house-to-house combing ever seen in Srinagar. Such operations are never pleasant; but the Home Ministry's orders were clearly to put the fear of Almighty Delhi into the heart of every Kashmiri. The militants, in high spirits after bringing the Union Government to its knees in the Rubaiya episode, were itching to convert their movement into a mass uprising. The government of V.P. Singh, Mufti Mohammad Sayeed and Arun Nehru, embarrassed and stung by the nationwide outrage at the surrender to terrorism, were equally determined to retake the initiative. Till 19 January 1990 mass support for *Aazaadi* was implicit, not explicit. That changed with the arrival of Jagmohan. First frightened, and then discovering the courage of desperation, the people began pouring out into the streets that day. The most startling presence was that of the women, old, middle-aged, young. The administration got completely unnerved, and gave orders to fire. The number is disputed, but there is no doubt that paramilitary bullets left more than fifty dead in the cold at Gowkadal that day. It was a mood with a memory, of course; 19 January became the catalyst which propelled it into a mass upsurge. Young men from hundreds of homes crossed over into Pakistan-Occupied Kashmir to receive arms and training in insurrection. Benazir Bhutto, her support base wiped out by malfeasance and misrule, desperate to save herself, whipped out the Kashmir card, always the least expensive route to popularity in Pakistan. (It didn't help.) Pakistan came out in open support of secession, and for the first time did not need to involve its regular troops in the confrontation. In Srinagar, each mosque became a citadel of fervour; the *khutba* became a sermon in secession, the loudspeakers played tapes that echoed against each other from the minarets, or picked up a dying chant and threw it further: "*Hum kya chahte hain? Aazaadi. . . Aazaadi. . . Allah-O-Akbar!*" In Delhi, Doordarshan, still excited about its pyrrhic post-Congress flexibility, went overboard with live coverage of the mass movements against authoritarianism in East Europe and Central Asia, inanely oblivious of the tremendous impact each visual of a woman kissing the *Quran* and taunting a soldier was having on Kashmir. It was all quite extraordinary. The air of Srinagar was taut with the sheer strength of the popular cry for freedom, as the conviction took hold that what was happening in East Europe could be repeated in Kashmir. Jagmohan's response was to combine a programme of pure terror with the politics of pure manipulation. On the one hand, he encouraged the growing Hindu-Muslim divide, and persuaded the already frightened Hindus in the Valley to migrate, convinced that their refugee status would generate support for the whiphand-tactics which appealed to his temperament. Simultaneously, he felt that this was the moment to finish both the National Conference and the Congress from the Valley. And he proposed to fill the political vacuum with the militants! He was quite ready to offer them power in Kashmir as the *quid pro quo* for technical acceptance of India's geographical boundaries. It did not work: first, because neither the Congress nor the National Conference were ready to accept burial before death; and second, because Jagmohan overreached himself to a point where even the funeral procession of Maulvi Farooq, who too was gunned by a militant group to the extreme of the extremists, was not spared paramilitary bullets. Two bullets pierced the coffin. And another opportunity to turn public resentment against the excesses of militants was lost. Maulvi Farooq's sixteen-year-old son and successor, Umar Farooq, told the four hundred thousand people gathered for special prayers in his father's memory on May 31,

1990:

> I appeal to President Mikhail Gorbachev, President George
> Bush, and the leaders of Islamic nations to use their good
> offices with the government of India and help Kashmiris
> win the right to self-determination.

The year was littered with martyrs, of one cause or another. The nation shuddered in shock at the execution of Professor Musheerul Haque, Vice Chancellor of Kashmir University; Mir Mustafa; H.L. Khera, General Manager of HMT; Lasa Koul, the director of the Srinagar Doordarshan Kendra and the revered Maulana Masoodi, one of the heroes of the National Conference movement, the chief of the Action Committee during the Mo-e-Muqaddas crisis, and now spending the last days of an ageing life in solitude and silence.

A small ray of political hope appeared when George Fernandes, Union Railway Minister, was given additional charge of Kashmir in March, but his positive beginning was sabotaged when V.P. Singh succumbed to BJP-Jagmohan pressure. Politics, not policy, was the sole motivation of the eleven months of V.P. Singh's prime ministership, and blood stained more than one corner of India, as each of his "moves" evoked an opposite if not always equal reaction. Kashmir, tragically, was emptied of its Hindus by this awful violence—so that for the first time since Bud Shah brought them back Kashmir's Pandits were forced to leave their homeland. That was the saddest wound on Kashmiriyat.

Ever since 19 January it had been one long sequence of protest, violence, repression and curfew. February was particularly bad: one stretch saw nearly a fortnight of imposed stillness.

When it was lifted on 24 February a fascinating procession began to evolve with a life of its own, and more than a hundred thousand people began a journey—to the shrine of their saint and symbol, the child of Lal Ded, Sheikh Nuruddin Rishi, to the shrine built by Sultan Zainul Abidin, the Bud Shah whose kingdom blossomed in the harmony of the Pandit and the Sheikh.

Sultan Ali Shah Chak added a veranda and wooden pillars to Bud Shah's structure; the Afghan Atta Mohammad Khan began reconstruction but was defeated and deposed before he could finish the work. It was left to Sheikh Mohammad Abdullah and Bakshi Ghulam Mohammad, Prime Minister and Deputy Prime Minister of Kashmir to complete this reconstruction of Charari Sharif in 1951. In 1964, on his release from prison, Sheikh Abdullah took over as president of the Auqaf Trust which manages the shrine. Each day thousands come, and each year on Urs (the death anniversary) the number multiplies as Kashmir bows its head to the child of Lal Ded. In that sorrow of February 1990 Kashmir once again turned towards Nuruddin. And there too, beside the despair, lay a slice of hope: for the Kashmiri would only turn to Charari Sharif to seek protection, never to seek vengeance. In the difference lay the hope. The Kashmiri had turned in his anguish to that history which lived in song. And in song lived the memory of Nuruddin's birth.

His father was the scion of a Hindu Thakur clan which had been banished from its estate in Kishtwar in Doda. His name was Salar Sanz and he led a life of wandering until he found Yasman Rishi; Salar became a disciple of this saint and converted to Islam, taking the name of Salar ud Din. It was Yasman Rishi who arranged his marriage to Sadra, a girl of the same Thakur clan who had been the only survivor of a battle at Duderkot and been brought up by a chowkidar. When the chowkidar died Sadra came to seek the blessings and protection of Yasman Rishi, and he made her the bride of his young disciple Salar; they settled in the village of Khai Jogipora.

One full moon night when Salar was doing his rounds as watchman he overheard a conversation taking place in a sadhu's hut. The sadhu, who studied the stars, was telling his wife that a bouquet of roses would appear in the spring of Khai Jogipora just before dawn; any woman fortunate enough to inhale the fragrance of those flowers would give birth to a great preordained saint. Salar rushed home and took Sadra to the spring. They found the roses on the pure water of the spring and Sadra breathed in the divine fragrance. Nine months later, on the tenth of Zill Haj, the day of the Qurbani, in 1377, Nuruddin was born. But for three days this infant did not drink milk from Sadra's breast, to the great anxiety of his parents. And then in the evening of the third day the Yogini Lal Ded entered their house, took the child in her lap and whispered: "You have not felt shy of being born; then why do you feel shy of tasting the pleasures of this world?" Then she placed the child's mouth to her own breast, and gave him his first drop of food. As she left Lal Ded told Sadra: "Take great care of my spiritual heir". Salar and Sadra named their child 'Nund' or the pious one. The name Nuruddin, or the light of the faith, was given to the child by the divine, Syed Hussain Simnani.

The last journey Nuruddin undertook before he died at Charar, in an orchard gifted to him by Sangram Dar, where he had built his abode in the middle of a dense forest, was to visit every one of the thirty-six parganas of his beloved Kashmir. When he was no longer able to walk, his friend and disciple Baba Nassar carried the Sheikh on his shoulders in a basket of willow twigs. All his life he wore nothing but a coarse *pheran* still preserved as a relic. He died on the 26th of Jami-du-Sani in 1438. Within two days nine hundred thousand people had gathered at Charar from every part of Kashmir, including Sultan Zainul Abidin himself. The Sultan wanted to take the body to Srinagar for burial, but the people would not allow a mere king to take their saint from them. Every Kashmiri wanted to take Nuruddin's body away with him, to bury it in his own village. It seemed an intractable dilemma. Then Baba Nassar went towards the coffin. When he returned he announced that the body would choose its own place for burial. The body was bathed, and funeral prayers were offered on a hilltop. And then the people saw the coffin soar towards the heavens, and each person began to believe that the coffin was flying towards its own home. Satisfied, the people dispersed. Baba Nassar then declared that the body had returned from the heavens to a point near a rose-bush in Charar. The shrine begun by Sultan Zainul Abidin and completed by Sheikh Abdullah surrounds that point. Sheikh Nuruddin summed up his life in a beautiful song, translated by the Sahitya Akademi award winner G.N. Gauhar for his book, *Sheikh Nuruddin Wali*, published by the Akademi in 1988:

> On my birth the cradles were decorated,
> In the third year my hands were tied,
> In the twelfth year my vision became clearer,
> In the fifteenth I got engaged,
> And in the sixteenth year the stream of my conscience was
> overflooded,
> In the eighteenth I fell in the lap of eternal love,
> In the twentieth year of my life the fire within me was burnt
> by the fire of love,
> In the twenty fifth year I became the target of accusation,
> And in the thirtieth year my youth decayed,
> In the fifth decade of my life I was made to wander around
> the world,
> During the sixties I shall be taken to my grave.

Charari Sharif and Hazratbal were the two symbols of Sheikh Mohammad Abdullah's philosophy and commitment. It was this message of unity across the religious divide which made him lead the Muslim Conference into the National Conference and then the Riyasat of Jammu and Kashmir into the federation of secular India. In Charari Sharif and Hazratbal lay the logic of accession, for religion could not be the basis of Kashmir's political definition to a disciple of Sheikh Nuruddin. Sheikh Abdullah's last great speech, at Iqbal Park on 21 August, the day he anointed Farooq, ended with his favourite couplet:

> *Auron ka hai payam aur, mera payam aur hai*
> *Ishq ke dardamand ka tarz-e kalam aur hai*

> (Others have their message, he said; I have another message—for those who have suffered from love speak another language.)

The best epitaph of Sheikh Mohammad Abdullah could only be this: This man was much more important than his mistakes.

Sheikh Mohammad Abdullah's final resting place lies adjacent to Hazratbal, across the road from the spectacular *Chinar* trees of Naseem Bagh, each several hundred years old, each leaf a magic photograph of the enchantment of Kashmir, the silhouette of the distant Zattawan mountains drawing a boundary for the eye, the tranquil Dal Lake beside the *mazar* a central image of the peace and majesty of a Valley which even the gods could not leave. The grave itself is an unassuming marble structure.

Around this *mazar* of simple dignity today sit men with guns. Policemen brandishing an army's arsenal. So much of the Sheikh's life was spent under the eyes of policemen; even in death they still surround him. How enemies change. . . . But this much is certain. Kashmir will never be at peace with itself as long as the *mazar* of Sheikh Mohammad Abdullah needs to be protected with guns.

Select Bibliography

Abdullah, Dr Farooq, *My Dismissal*, Delhi: Vikas, 1985.

Abdullah, Sheikh Mohammad, *Aatish-e-Chinar*, Srinagar: Ali Mohammad and Sons.

Afzal, Mirza Mohammad, *On the Way to Golden Harvests: Agricultural Reforms in Kashmir*, Jammu: Jammu and Kashmir National Conference, 1950

Anand, A.S., *Development of the Constitution of Jammu & Kashmir*, Delhi: Light and Life Publishers, 1980.

Anderson, Walter K. and Damle, Shridhar D., *The Brotherhood of Saffron*, Delhi: Vistaar, 1987.

Bamzai, Prithvi Nath Kaul, *History of Kashmir*, Delhi: Metropolitan Book Company, 1962, 1973.

Barton, Sir William, *The Princes of India*, London: Nisbet & Company, 1934.

Bhutto, Zulfiqar Ali, *The Myth of Independence*, Karachi: Oxford University Press, 1967.

Birdwood, Lord Christopher and Broomhead, *Two Nations and Kashmir*, London: Robert Hale Ltd., 1956.

Bourke-White, Margaret, *Halfway to Freedom*, New York: Simon & Schuster, 1949.

Brecher, Michael, *The Struggle for Kashmir*, New York: Oxford University Press, 1953.

Campbell-Johnson, Alan, *Mission with Mountbatten*, London: Robert Hale Ltd., 1951.

Chandra, Bipan, *Communalism in Modern India*, Delhi: Vikas, 1984.

Chatterjee, Bhola, *Conflict in JP's Politics*, Delhi: Ankur.

Doughty, Marion, *Afoot Through the Kashmir Valley*, Delhi: Sagar Publications [reprinted], 1971.

Fazl, Abul, *Ain-i-Akbari*, Delhi: [reprinted] Oriental Books Reprint Corporation, 1977.

Francke, A. H., *A History of Ladakh*, Delhi: Sterling Publishers, 1977.

Frykenberg, R.E.(ed.), *Delhi Through the Ages: Essays in Urban History, Culture and Society*, Delhi: Oxford University Press, 1986.

Gandhi, Indira, *My Truth*, New York: Grove Press, 1980; [reprinted] New Delhi: Vision Books, 1981.

Gauhar, G.N., *Sheikh Nuruddin Wali*, Delhi: Sahitya Akademi, 1988.

Gopal, S., *A Biography of Jawaharlal Nehru*, New Delhi: Oxford University Press, 1974.

Gundevia, Y.D., *Outside the Archives*, Hyderabad: Orient Lor.gman, 1984.

Hasrat, Bikramji, *Dara Shikoh: Life and Works*, Delhi: Munshiram Manoharlal, 1982.

Hassan, Mahibul, *Kashmir Under the Sultans*, Calcutta: Iran Society, 1969.

Hodson, H.V., *The Great Divide: Britain, India, Pakistan*, London: Hutchinson, 1969.

Hughes, Thomas Patrick, *Dictionary of Islam*, Delhi: Rupa [reprinted], 1988.

Hussain, Syed T., *Reflections on Kashmir Politics*, Delhi: Rima Publishing House, 1987.

Jetley, Nancy, *India-China Relations 1947-1977*, Delhi: Radiant, 1979.

Kapur, M.L., *Kingdom of Kashmir*, Jammu: Jammu & Kashmir History Publications, 1983.

Kaul, Santosh, Bhatt, Ram Krishen Kaul and Teng, Mohan Krishen, *Kashmir: Constitutional History and Documents*, Delhi: Light and Life Publishers, 1977.

Lawrence, Sir Walter, *The Valley of Kashmir*, London: Oxford University Press, 1895.

Mansergh, Nicholas and Moon, Penderel (eds.), *The Transfer of Power*, London: HMSO, 1981.

Menon, V.P., *Story of the Integration of the Indian States*, Calcutta: Orient Longman, 1956.

Moon, Penderel, *The British Conquest and Dominion of India*, London: Duckworth, 1988.

Mullik, B.N., *My Years With Nehru*, Agra: Deep Publications, 1971.

Musa, General Mohammad , *My Version*, Delhi: ABC, 1983.

Nehru, Jawaharlal, *The Unity of India: Collected Writings 1934-1940*, London: Lindsay Drummond, 1948.

Nehru, Jawaharlal, *A Bunch of Old Letters*, Bombay: Asia Publishing House, 1958.

Nicholson, A.P., *Scraps of Paper*, London: Ernest Benn, 1930.

Pandit, R.S., *River of Kings*, Delhi: Sahitya Akademi, 1963.

Pannikar, K.M., *A Study of Kashmir and Jammu*: Oxford University Press, 1948.

Pannikar, K.M., *Gulab Singh: The Founder of the Kashmir State*, London: Allen & Unwin, 1953.

Peissel, Michael, *Zanskar: The Hidden Kingdom*, London: Collins and Harvill Press, 1979.

Sahni, Sati, (ed.), *Centre-State Relations*, Delhi: Vikas, 1984.

Sen, Dr Amartya and Derze, Jean, *Hunger and Public Action*, London: Clarendon Press, 1990.

Sheikh Mohammad Abdullah, Srinagar: University of Kashmir, Commemoration Volume, 1983.

Singh, Dr Karan, *Autobiography (1931-1967)*, Delhi: Oxford University Press, 1981.

Singh, Khushwant, *A History of the Sikhs*, Princeton: Princeton University Press, 1963.

Thorpe, Robert, *Cashmeer Misgovernment*, London: Longman Green & Company, 1870.

Vashisth, Satish, *Sheikh Abdullah Then and Now*, Delhi: Maulik Sahitya Prakashan, 1968.

Younghusband, Francis, *Kashmir*, London: Adam & Charles Black, 1909.

Official Publications

Constituent Assembly Debates: Government of India, 1950.

Pakistan's War Propaganda Against India: Government of India, 1951.

Parliament Debates: Government of India, 1975.

Simla Agreement: Pakistan's Interpretation: Government of Pakistan, 1990.

Twelve Months of War in Kashmir: Government of India, 1948.

White Paper on Indian States: Government of India, 1950.

White Paper on Jammu and Kashmir: Government of India, 1948.

White Paper on the Jammu and Kashmir Dispute: Ministry of Foreign Affairs, Government of Pakistan, 1990.

White Paper on Kashmir: Government of India, 1947-1956.

Index

Abbas, Ghulam, 74, 83

Abdali, Ahmad Shah, 47–48, 50, 56

Abdullah, Dr Farooq, 165, 190, 192, 215;as member of the Mo-e-Muqqadas Action Committee, 160, 166; visits Pakistan-Occupied Kashmir, 186; learns about Sheikh Abdullah's death, 193; becomes Health Minister, 194; becomes Chief Minister, 194; becomes President of the National Conference, 196, 223; visits London, 197; supports the Resettlement Bill, 198–99; as a secular leader, 199, 206, 209, 213; excludes G.M. Shah from his Cabinet, 199; refuses a Congress–Conference coalition, 200, 204; wins elections, 201; campaign against the Congress, 202, 206; campaign against Mrs Gandhi, 203; organizes a conclave on the Centre–State issue, 205; expels G.M. Shah from the National Conference, 206; meets Jarnail Singh Bhindranwale, 207; support withdrawn in favour of, 208; the dismissal of, 209–11; recommends the dissolution of the House and fresh elections, 210; meets Rajiv Gandhi, 212; nominated leader of the official delegation to the Haj, 212; campaign against the militants, 214, 217–18; returns to Delhi after the abduction of Dr Rubaiya Sayeed, 216

Abdullah, Sheikh Mohammad, 40, 60, 100–01, 109, 113, 122, 157, 161–62, 165, 194–95, 197, 200, 205, 209, 215; born, 72; early and higher education, 72–73; member of the Reading Room Party, 72–73; President of the Muslim Conference, 73; arrests of, 73, 90, 152–53 (under the Kashmir Conspiracy Case), 158, 169, 182;as a secular leader, 74, 76, 79, 82, 84–86, 102, 141–42, 167, 185, 188–89, 192, 202, 213, 222–23; launches civil disobedience movement, 74; wins Praja Sabha elections,75; intensifies demand for a Responsible Government, 75, 81–82; launches the National Conference, 76; campaign against the Muslim League, 77; friendship with Nehru, 78, 80, 105, 138, 166; friendship with Gandhi, 80, 105, 138; merges the National Conference with the All-India States' Peoples' Conference, 82; supports the Indian National Congress,

83–84; launches the New Kashmir Plan, 84; egalitarian concepts of, 84, 138–39; as a champion of equal rights to women, 84; campaign against Jinnah, 85–86, 119; Nehru's support to, 87, 96–97, 104; accident suffered by, 88; launches the Quit Kashmir movement, 88–89; Nehru's support for the release of, 91–92; drafts a statement for his own release, 92–93; V.K. Krishna Menon recommends the release of, 94; campaign against Pakistan, 105, 119, 141; visits Delhi, 105, 166; functions as Head of the Administration in the Interim Government, 120; accused by Pakistan of being a "quisling", 123–24; sets course for a new Constituent Assembly, 135–36; becomes the Prime Minister of the Jammu and Kashmir state, 137; campaign against the two–nation theory, 137–38; appoints a Land Reform Committee, 139; floats option of an Eastern Switzerland, 140–41; stresses on the independence of Kashmir from both India and Pakistan, 141-42, 147, 151, 169; campaign against the Indian National Congress, 144, 169; discontentment with Nehru, 145–49; accused by Patel, 146; arrests Shyama Prasad Mookerjee, 150; release of, 155, 166, 185; demands for a plebiscite, 159, 168; floats the idea of a Confederation, 167; visits Pakistan, 167; proposes an Ayub-Nehru summit, 168; meets Bhutto, 169; launches the Khudai Khidmatgars, 183; recommends peaceful negotiation in the Shimla spirit, 185; accepts ratification of the accession, 187; agrees to a Congress–Conference coalition, 189; becomes the Chief Minister, 190; helps Mrs Gandhi in 1977 elections, 191; recommends to dissolve the House and fresh elections, 191; suffers a heart attack, 192–93; death of, 193; makes Dr Farooq Abdullah President of the National Conference, 196; supports the Emergency, 203

Abdullah, Syed, 156

Abidin, Zainul (also called Shahi Khan or Bud Shah), 6–7, 25–30, 32–33, 220–21

Achala, 22

Ahmed, Aziz, 176

G
Aug. 2003